EXCITING ICT IN
ENGLISH

Tony Archdeacon

Published by Network Educational Press Ltd
PO Box 635
Stafford
ST16 1BF

First published 2005
© Tony Archdeacon 2005

ISBN 1 85539 193 7

Managing editor: Stephen Thomas
Cover design: Neil Hawkins, NEP
Layout: Neil Hawkins, NEP
Illustrations: Katherine Baxter

Printed in Great Britain by MPG Books Ltd, Bodmin, Cornwall

Contents

Foreword

I have had the great honour and pleasure to travel a lot of the world for over a decade talking, advising and consulting about ICT and learning. It is a personal passion and, being married to a teacher, an issue that concerns me both professionally and personally. When I started I met many enthusiasts who shared a dream that we could use ICT to transform the experience of education and deliver a global aspiration of education for every citizen of the world. Against these lofty ambitions the perennial constraints of budgets, political will and professional inertia were easily visible. There were many fears expressed to me. Most importantly, there was a concern that, somehow, ICT would be used as an excuse to sack teachers and close schools and pump learning into kids' heads through impersonal technology.

Being an optimist, my experience over the last decade has kept those lofty aspirations alive. It has also made the fundamental truths about both education and learning clear to me. First, learning is at its heart a social and a socializing experience. ICTs are very powerful tools, but smart technologies need smart people, they don't replace them. In a world where technology is increasingly pervasive, teachers become more not less important.

Second, as the world becomes increasingly connected, as technology and science develop at an ever-increasing pace, the economic and social future of any country is increasingly tied to its commitment to education and training, not just for the elite but for every citizen and community.

Third, the goal is not just raising standards but changing culture. I describe this using the analogy of the driving test, a rite of passage for many young people. The emerging global information society requires us to create a new generation who, when they leave school, put on their L-plates and think 'I am a learner', rather than take them off and say 'I have passed'.

We can only make this happen on the scale needed if we value and invest in our teachers as lifelong learners themselves, not just in their 'subject skills'. To do this we need to marry the big picture of a transformed experience of learning to ICT practice, but also to new theories of learning such as learning styles or multiple intelligences. For teachers to be seen as learners themselves we need to build bridges between different areas of research – in education, learning theories, ICT and management, to name but a few.

Reading the first few titles in this series, it is wonderful to see words like creativity, personalization and exciting being based on actual evidence, not just lofty aspiration. The rate of change of technology in the next decade will at least match the progress in the last. The materials available to enrich good teaching and learning practice will grow exponentially. None of this will have the profound change that many aspire to if we cannot build the bridge between theory and what happens in individual lessons, be they in art, maths, music, history, modern languages or any other area of the curriculum.

The notion of ICT as a tool across the curriculum was greeted sceptically a decade ago. Many professionals told me that ICT may be important in maths or science, but irrelevant in the arts and humanities. My own experience is that the most exciting innovations have actually been in arts and humanities, while the notion of maths as a visual discipline seemed alien a few years ago. It has not been ICT but innovative teachers, researchers and indeed publishers who have pushed the art of the possible.

In a lot of my work, I have encouraged the notion that we should see the era we live in as a New Renaissance, rather than a new Industrial Revolution. While the industrial revolutions were about simplification and analysis, the era we live in is about synthesis and connection. We need our learners to embrace both depth and breadth to meet their needs to learn for life and living.

To the authors of this series, I offer my congratulations and sincere thanks. In bringing together the evidence of what works, the digital resources available and the new theories of learning, along with the new capabilities of ICT, they bring the focus onto the most important element of the transformation of learning, which to me is the learning needs of the teaching profession.

To the readers of this series, I make what I believe is my boldest claim. This is the greatest time in human history to be a teacher. Our societies and economies demand education like never before. Our increasing knowledge of how we learn and how the brain works, together with the availability of powerful ICT tools, make this a time when the creativity, professionalism and aspirations for a learning society are at a premium. Teaching is a noble profession. It is after all the profession that creates all the others.

There are many things that we do not yet know, so much to learn. That is what makes this so exciting. I and my colleagues at Microsoft can build the tools, but we believe that it is putting those tools in the hands of innovative, skilled and inspirational teachers that creates the real value.

I hope that after reading any of the books in this series you will feel the excitement that will make learning come alive both for you and the children you teach.

Best wishes.

Chris Yapp
Head of Public Sector Innovation
Microsoft Ltd

Author's acknowledgements

With thanks to all the educational practitioners who have shared with me their ideas, research and enthusiasm, especially those involved with the case studies: Fern Faux, Tim Shortis, Dan Sutch, John McKenzie, Vivi Lachs, Andrew Wilson, Peter Sansom, Ann Sansom, Duncan Grey and Neil Shaw. I am also indebted to John Davitt for introducing me to accelerated learning approaches and for convincing me of the value of multimedia tools in English teaching.

Introduction

Literacy has always been about technology, from using tools to make marks on a slate, to the technological revolution of the word processor. In the sixteenth century, the printing press made access to literature – both ancient and new – easier, and today the internet is providing unprecedented access to both literature and all kinds of media. The 'exciting ICT' of the sixteenth century was the printed book: it redefined the possibilities of text, created new readers, and changed the role of the teacher forever. Where most learning had involved listening to the teacher who had the book and acted as intermediary, now learning could be direct from the book, and the teacher had to adapt and create a new role. The English teacher of today, likewise, needs to adapt to a new technological revolution in the means of communication, and this book is about how we might adapt and how we are already adapting. The book and its accompanying CD-ROM explore how we can use the new technology in our classrooms. It's not only about using ICT to be more efficient or effective at teaching what you already teach, it's also about adding new dimensions to the teaching and learning of English. The book presents a systematic examination of the ways ICT and English might be combined, along with inspiring case studies, suggestions and practical ideas for how you can extend the boundaries of your subject.

Government guidance from 2002 on ICT in English lists the ways ICT can contribute to English teaching 'as a medium and as a tool':

1. Exploring and investigating

2. Responding and interpreting

3. Reflecting and evaluating

4. Composing and transforming

5. Presenting and performing

WEBSITE
6. Communicating and collaborating.[1]

In practice, however, the emphasis has persistently been on the 'tool' function of ICT, playing down the importance of ICT as a medium. If we can start to appreciate ICT as a new medium, or rather as a group of new media, then perhaps we will start to see its proper place in English teaching, and that is one of the shaping ideas of this book.

Terms of reference

The kinds of terms used to describe teaching and learning of English are many and varied these days, but we still seem to have a fondness for groupings of three. We have the three-way division of the English curriculum into Speaking and Listening, Reading and Writing, and latterly we have the tripartite division of English reading and writing into word, sentence and text levels. And now of course, we understand a lot more about the three sensory modalities of visual, auditory and kinesthetic (VAK) learning. In considering English in the context of ICT, however, another distinctive triplet is useful: text, image and sound.

Text

These days, 'writing' has almost become an obsolete term, evoking an old-fashioned skill reserved chiefly for writing greetings cards or postcards. Certainly the word does not adequately describe the process of composition or editing now entailed in new media. Its implication of a written page is also misleading: now the media that receive text are multiform, and so understanding electronic text involves a great deal more than understanding the sequences or arrangements of words. We are a long way off having a grammar of electronic text, but if we ever reach that stage it will be by taking into account both words and medium. In a quite different way, our definition of text has also to include within it the notion of 'data' or information, where the basic unit is the alphanumeric character rather than the letter, and text is something to be organized so that its parts are easily accessible. There is another, superordinate usage of 'text' which would include moving images and any other signifying system. For purposes of clarity I have avoided this wider usage, so 'text' should be understood to mean words written, typed, or in other ways visually conveyed to a reader.

Image

We need to think of text as more than just words on a page, or even words on a screen, and to remember that our students are becoming increasingly visual learners. With ICT the medium itself is part of the message, just as paragraphs are for the word on the page. Likewise we need to think of images and sounds as being conveyors of meaning just as words are. We are already seeing moves towards acknowledging 'visual literacy' as a significant feature of ICT-related English, but what that means in practice is still evolving. In practical terms it will mean learning some specifically image-oriented software, but in time we will also need to develop the language and principles of visual literacy. One area of visual literacy teaching and learning which is perhaps better developed than most is that of the moving image, and progress here has been accelerated in recent years by the rapid development of digital video editing.

Sound

Speaking and Listening as a teaching category is really about oracy, and it ranges from speaking or reading aloud to group discussion, while drama too is sometimes included. Our category of 'sound' has to be a wider one than this. While ICT can of course facilitate both the teaching and the assessment of Speaking and Listening, it also adds new dimensions which can extend the traditional boundaries of English. In these contexts the use of sound is not just about the performance skills of speaking and listening, but about using sound in much more varied ways in the communicative process.

Schematically then, these are the terms I am using when I refer to text, image and sound:

Text:
➡ printed words

➡ initialisms, condensed spellings, and so on

➡ the medium in which words appear/are delivered

➡ information/data.

Image:
➡ symbols (clip art, icon, 'graphic' and so on)

➡ associative imagery

➡ the 'moving image'

➡ interactive images

➡ animations.

Sound:
➡ recorded speech

➡ digital noises

➡ sound effects

➡ music (sound imagery).

The virtual and the kinesthetic

There is another element which is not encompassed by this schema: physicality. We communicate a great deal by our movements, gestures and even touch, in ways that go beyond simple visual image. Traditionally, it has been in drama that this kinesthetic aspect of English has featured most prominently, but new possibilities have been opened up by ICT. A virtual or 'immersive' world is conducive to kinesthetic learning in a way similar to activity in the physical world.

So thinking of ICT as a medium opens up all sorts of new possibilities for English teachers. We can experience text as non-linear (Chapter 1) and as audio-visual (Chapter 5). We can view writing as multimodal (Chapter 4) or in completely new forms such as text message poetry (the g8way project case study) or 'augmented reality' narrative (the Magic Book case study). The young people we teach are already excited by the possibilities of electronic media, and we can harness this best if we engage with ICT both as a medium and as a tool in our English teaching.

NOTE:

Please note that throughout the book all relevant website addresses (URLs) have been placed in the reference sections at the back of the book. These sections can also be found on the CD-ROM, where the hyperlinks are active and can be clicked on to take you directly to the site.

Chapter 1

The excitement of electronic text

Part 1: Visual aids to structured writing

In this section you will:

- consider why mapping software and templates can be useful to English teaching;
- look at some general approaches to the use of mapping software and templates;
- consider practical ways you can apply this technology in your teaching;
- look at examples of good practice and advice in this area.

Part 2: New types of text

In this section you will:

- examine the nature and importance to English of new textual forms resulting from ICT (such as hypertext and email);
- consider how hypertext and other new text types might, and should, be studied in English;
- look at examples of good practice and advice in this area;
- see some practical ways you can apply this technology in your teaching.

Part 1

Visual aids to structured writing

Why do it?

There are obvious ways in which electronic text lends itself very helpfully to all aspects of the editorial process: planning, drafting, proofing and publishing. Whether it is the ability to navigate around your text using a 'document map' or simply the ability to move around 'chunks' of text using 'cut and paste' methods, we seem to have been given greater control over the organization of text than was ever possible before. The whole editing process has always been a kinesthetic experience: one of moving text around and rearranging and trimming; and it's a visual one – the text undergoes re*visions*. In MS Word you can split your screen, compare documents where differences are automatically highlighted, track changes through similar methods, and search for and replace words or phrases. The use of a word processor both accelerates and compresses the editing procedure, thanks to the ability to see different parts of your text in separate windows on a single screen. The value of this is partly the time it saves a writer or editor, and partly the ease with which you can relate parts and whole. There are some specific tools which are designed to assist with the shape and the structure of a text: mapping software and templates. These are worth considering closely because they offer two very different approaches which might prove complementary.

Mapping software

The mapping tools available now are conceptually little different from the flow charts and spider diagrams which have been ubiquitous from the boardroom to the schoolroom since the 1970s.[1] Now that so much presentation in the corporate world and elsewhere goes on via the medium of digital slide shows, the flow-charts methodology has moved from the blackboard and flip chart to the electronic whiteboard, and now there are numerous business-oriented software packages available to facilitate the same process, as well as some aimed at the education market, often in the name of accelerated learning.

Templates

From an early stage in the development of word processing and publishing software applications there has been an appreciation of the way templates can facilitate quality in terms of both presentation and organization of material. They provide short cuts to an end product which conforms to certain formats, whether a letter or a fax, a memo or a report, a menu or a flyer. Similarly, a framework can be a great help to a young learner, especially to a writer low in confidence, and it has been recognized for some time that electronic templates are particularly versatile aids to this methodology.

General approaches and principles

Mapping

There is a very useful chapter in Vivi Lachs' *Making Multimedia in the Classroom* on 'New structures and making maps' which explores some of the new possibilities for text structure made possible by electronic text.[2] One of the types of mapping described is 'brainstorming', which has been a common methodology since Tony Buzan developed the technique of 'mind mapping' in the late 1960s.

The principles of mind mapping are really quite simple, as explained on the Mind Mapping website:

a) The subject of attention is crystallized in a central image.

b) The main themes of the subject radiate from the central image on branches.

c) Branches hold a key image/word printed on the associated line – details radiate out.

WEBSITE

d) The branches form a connected nodal structure.[3]

Add into that the use of tapered lines leading from the centre and the use of different colours for the linking branches or images, and you have a 'mind map'.

Fig 1.1

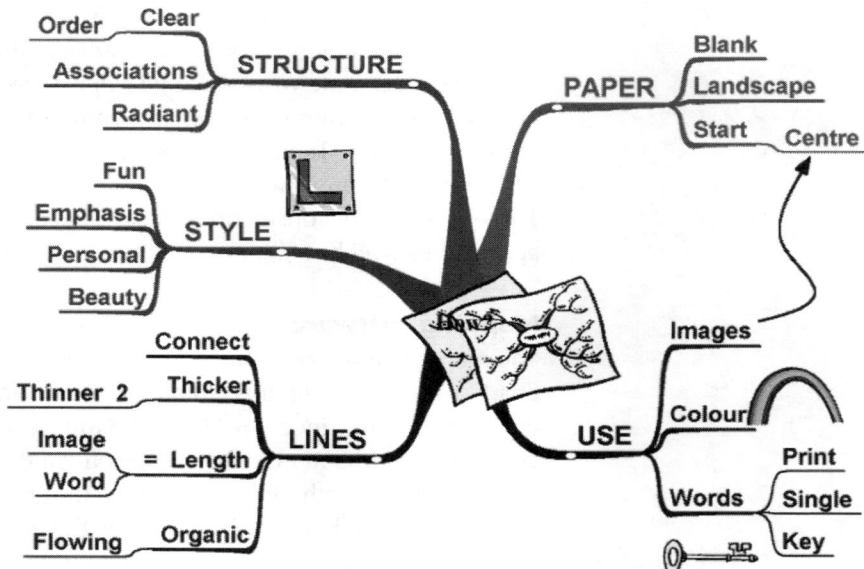

This in particular has been embraced as a method for accelerated learning, and recently also in assisting dyslexic adults and children, so there are now 'graphic organization' tools which sell themselves on the back of the interest in mind mapping business and learning methods.[4] Whether mind-mapping is in itself a learning process is an interesting question, but my interest in it is from the English writing perspective: can it help learners to write? The recent QCA report on Planning for Writing based on a study of classroom practice at Years 6 and 9 indicated a 'dominance of spider plans' as a brainstorming device in preparation for writing.[5] However, these were seen primarily as a way of generating content rather than organizing it, and flow charts which might have a more structured approach were actually less commonly seen. We need to look, therefore, at how the mapping approach can genuinely assist in structuring ideas, thereby improving whole text structure and cohesion.

Beyond templates – enabling not restricting

Obviously, ICT is quite a structured way of communicating, and that structure is to some degree dictated by the medium, be it email, text message, word processor and so on. If we provide just enough structure to make the writer feel at ease, then the writer will find this enabling rather than restricting. If you were a primary school teacher in the UK, working to the national literacy strategy introduced in 2000, you would be familiar enough with the concept of 'writing frames', which provide a learner with a preset shape for their writing, typically broken down to paragraph level. As with the concept of teachers 'modelling' skills that they want pupils to learn, these have been very influential ideas in the quest to 'raise standards' in literacy in recent years. They have had some positive effect, in enabling children to bypass the anxiety often occasioned by a blank page, and to structure their thoughts on set topics. This can of course be useful, for example, in training learners to construct an argumentative essay. One could usefully provide a frame which consists of an introductory paragraph, one paragraph in favour of a motion, one paragraph against and a conclusion. This is effectively teaching the basics of dialectical thinking: thesis, antithesis and synthesis. The danger is that one thinks of this teaching process as being simply a 'drag and drop' operation whereby the learner merely has to take ideas provided by the teacher and put them in the right order.

Jerome Bruner's structuralist principles of knowledge and learning have been very influential on recent approaches to teaching literacy:

1. Instruction must be concerned with the experiences and contexts that make the student willing and able to learn (readiness).
2. Instruction must be structured so that it can be easily grasped by the student (spiral organization).
3. Instruction should be designed to facilitate extrapolation and/or fill in the gaps (going beyond the information given).[6]

These ideas were implicit in the notion of 'scaffolding' through writing frames which has been promoted as an approach to writing in primary education. But the key to active learning is in the third of these rules, where the need is stressed for extrapolation, or going beyond the information given. ICT can be a very useful tool in providing the conceptual scaffolds for writing, but there are of course worries in relation to excessive use of templates. As with the use of clip art, it seems anti-creative. Alternatives are circumscribed; there seems to be a lack of questioning about things like structure; structure is just accepted as a 'given'.[7] There is also a rather simplistic equation of structure with paragraphing, which is less helpful with older pupils. Perhaps what we should do is use the technology to facilitate thinking beyond the template.

Teaching ideas, examples and advice

1. Templates

a) Standard templates

WEBSITE

WEBSITE

Templates, as I have indicated, have been popular with those promoting improvements in literacy in recent years. The usefulness of ICT here has also been widely acknowledged. For example, the ICT subject association NAACE recommends 'using a writing template to develop a newsletter' among its ICT and literacy guide lesson plans.[8] While this document is a valuable point of reference, it is a shame that no illustrative material is available to accompany these lesson plans – what a newsletter template might actually look like is therefore not addressed. It refers to a standard newsletter template from some publishing software, but many templates are available online, even if you don't have the software, as downloadable Word documents from the Microsoft Office Online site.[9] Here you can choose from templates of greetings or invitation cards, brochures and flyers, posters, menus, newsletters and so on; or by using your imagination and these as a model, you can develop your own templates for a range of 'text types' required for English teaching. There is no reason, however, why we should not provide scaffolding for 'multimodal' texts too, as some of our additional examples will show.

WEBSITE

Trevor Millum provides a number of worthwhile ideas for templates for seven-to-eleven year olds in his book *ICT and Literacy*.[10] Using a search website you can also find various electronic templates or frames online, even for literature work: for example, the examining board NEAB has a set of templates for use by lower ability students working on the GCSE anthology of poems.[11] A search for 'story templates' for example will return a great deal of material, of varying quality. A search for 'writing frames' returned such useful material as Kent NGfL's downloadable Word templates for three types of writing, which come with instructions on how to make a template using protected fields:

WEBSITE   **Fig 1.2**[12]

b) Differentiated templates

One way of ensuring that their use is not too heavy-handed is to have differentiated templates, with varying degrees of 'structural support' provided; again, electronic templates make it much quicker and easier to make this sort of provision.

For any set task you could produce a number of templates providing varying degrees of support, and point pupils to the appropriate one. This might seem like multiplication of workload, but it need not be: start with a highly scaffolded template, then save a series of copies with elements gradually removed or modified for the more able pupils.

WEBSITE

It does not seem appropriate to suggest or provide templates here, because there will be as many templates as there are writing tasks (or indeed several times more because of the need for differentiated templates). The effectiveness of these will therefore be dependent on your own imagination and skills as a teacher. There are also various approaches or models that can be used. At one end of the scaffolding spectrum there might be boxes with questions in, or just paragraph headings. Then there might be openings of sentences for a sequence of paragraphs. At the other extreme you can provide a substantial amount of text with gaps to be completed by the pupil. A simple poetry-writing task I devised for Year 2 children might act as an illustration of the principles.[13] The provision of templates, appropriately modified for different levels of ability, acted as a catalyst for a great deal of writing by the children.

The idea was to create a potential chain of verses all following the same structure and with the scope to involve a great deal of observation, reporting and descriptive writing. A suggested first verse was provided in full:

This classroom is <u>full</u>:

Full of desks and chairs

Full of pencils, pens and paper

Full of busy children doing work

Full of colour on the walls

Full of teacher's loud voice

Full of the sound of ticking brains.

This classroom is full: please try somewhere else.

The students then wrote a series of subsequent verses with familiar locations such as the playground and the supermarket.

I think there are two things which were vital to the success of the experiment, and they were as much to do with the excellence of the teaching as the template.

First, the template needed to be understood. They read it aloud chorally in order to emphasize the repetitions which are the essence of the structure. To focus on the content and establish expectations for their own writing, the teacher used a whiteboard and asked for alternatives to some of the highlighted words.

This classroom is full:

Full of desks and chairs

Full of pencils, pens and paper

Full of busy children doing work

Full of colour on the walls

Full of teacher's loud voice

Full of the sound of ticking brains.

This classroom is full: please try somewhere else.

The level of engagement from the children was high, and the results were very impressive as these five-to-six year olds experimented with alternative words to fill the template. They followed this up by sending their poems to a children's poetry website Poetry Zone where they were published alongside those of other children:[14]

WEBSITE

Fig 1.3

Green is like fresh leaves falling
Silver is like a mirror

Our Supermarket Is Full *by Elizabeth and Dimple (aged 6)*

Full of chicken korma and chocolate sweets
Full of yellow sweet corn and orangey carrots
Full of busy people buying interesting food
Full of marvelous fruits
Full of crunchy French sticks
Full of the sounds of lots of people nattering

Natter natter natter
This supermarket is full: please try somewhere else.

Colours *by Daniel Thys*

Pink is a rose silently talking

Our Classroom is Full
by Jack, Isaac, Sean, Sonika and Charmaine

Our classroom is full.
Full of desks, rubbers and excited children
Full of pencils and fantastic pictures
Full of busy children getting ready for P.E
Full of clever children on laptops
Full of the teachers banging voice
Full of the sound of clicking chunks and ticking brains
This classroom is full: please try somewhere else

Our Playground is Full *by Matthew and James*

This playground is full.
Full of happy children and teachers
Full of children big and small
Full of busy children
Full of green swaying trees
Full of noisy children running
Full of the sound of bells ringing
This playground is full: Please try somewhere else

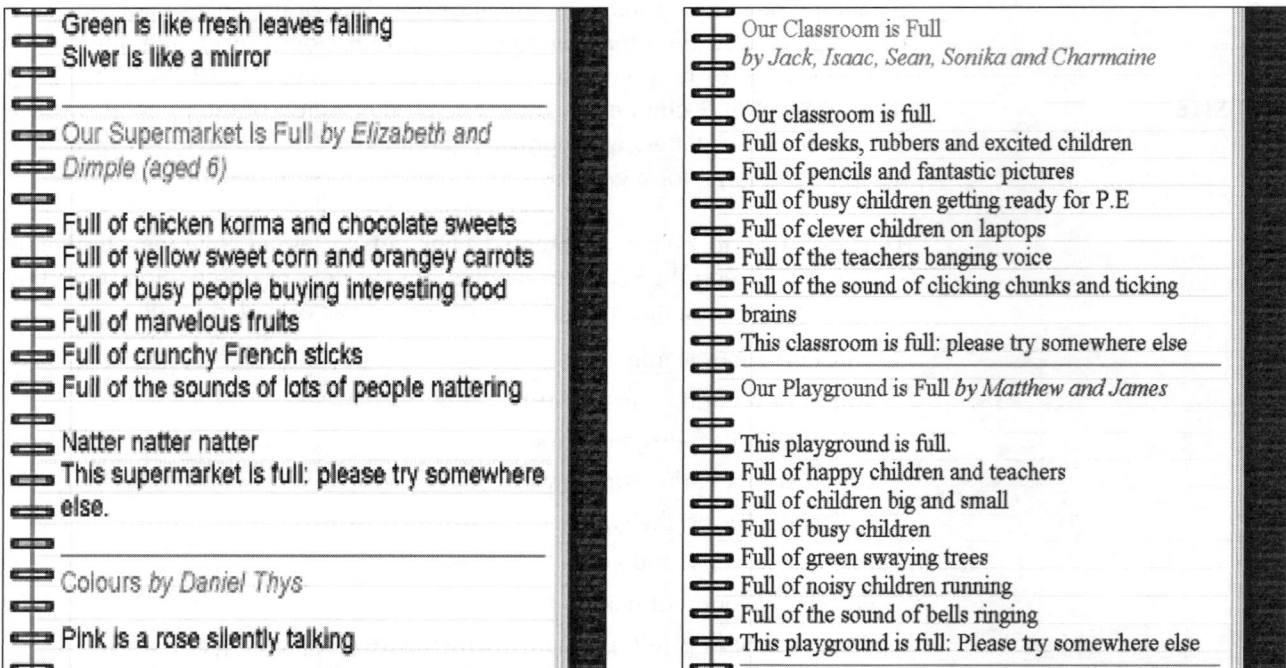

The second factor is the teacher's input in modifying the template appropriately for differentiated need was vital – a reminder of the principle that ICT often needs to be mediated by the teacher when it is being used as a learning tool as opposed to as a medium for study. In some cases the learner's input might be just a single word in a line: only a teacher with experience of the learners can determine the degree of support needed. In doing this yourself, you don't need to start from scratch. Take one of the templates provided by standard word processing and desktop publishing software packages, then modify appropriately, adding different levels of support. The example in figure 1.4 was produced from the 'brochure' template found in MS Word via File > New > Publications.

Fig 1.4

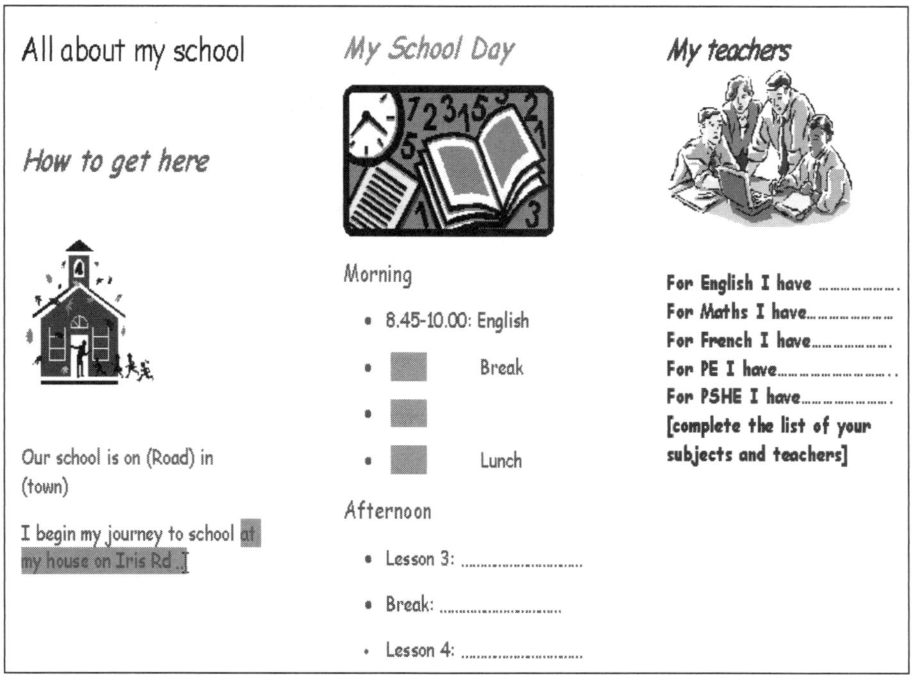

All about my school

My School Day

My teachers

How to get here

Morning

- 8.45-10.00: English
- ▮ Break
- ▮
- ▮ Lunch

Afternoon

- Lesson 3: ....
- Break: ....
- Lesson 4: ....

Our school is on (Road) in (town)

I begin my journey to school at my house on Iris Rd. I

For English I have ....
For Maths I have................
For French I have................
For PE I have........................
For PSHE I have.................
[complete the list of your subjects and teachers]

2. Mapping tools

a) Software

The use of 'mapping' software is becoming common across subjects, but has obvious applications in English for the preparation of extended writing. There are several options for mapping software, such as Mind Mapping which is aimed at business, and Mind Genius which has a schools version.[15] The key question for the English teacher is: if you are writing a story or an essay based on the mind map, where do you go from there? *Inspiration*, and the junior version *Kidspiration*,[16] is a widely used and helpful method of harnessing ICT to aid in the planning process for the composition of extended writing. The UK government's Literacy Time website recommended the use of such software in literacy teaching for the following purposes:

Brainstorming – for example, identifying what is known at the start of a topic.

Outlining – identifying/summarizing key points.

Planning writing – perhaps story outlines or sections of a report.

Organizing ideas and making links between them.[17]

Elementary (primary) school teachers in North Canton City Schools, Ohio, explored ways to integrate visual learning and thinking skills into their curriculum areas during a professional development study group. Using *Kidspiration*, they created lessons and concept maps for their classes, which have been put online as a substantial resource for early learners.[18] The value is in the way any piece of work is seen in terms of its internal links and interconnections. Figure 1.5 shows a simple approach to writing about a poem (aimed at older pupils) from another very useful and imaginative collection of *Kidspiration* ideas from Canby School District.[19]

WEBSITE

WEBSITE

WEBSITE

WEBSITE

WEBSITE

Fig 1.5

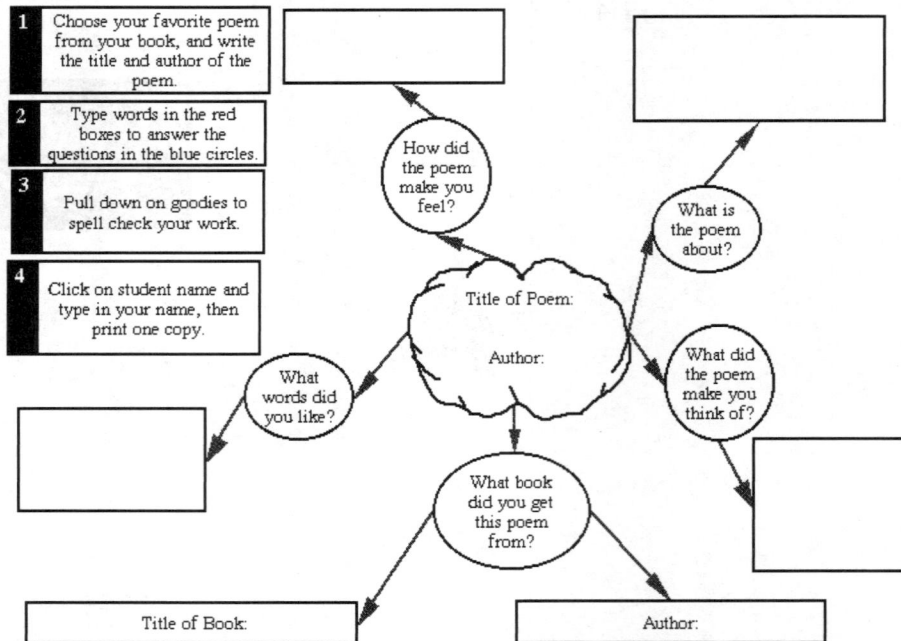

The software provides handy short cuts from the planning stage to the composition stage. You can insert text into shapes on a flow chart, add notes to the shapes on the chart, and then collapse it into numbered paragraphs using the 'Outline' view. So in theory you can switch from a graphically arranged set of ideas with attached text, to a linear sequence of text at the click of a mouse. This seems a marvellous idea at first glance but is only going to work in certain circumstances and it is doing a disservice to teachers and pupils to suggest that the movement from chart to essay can be a one-click process.

b) From planning to text

The planning of a story might involve headings and then notes in several different strands (for simplicity, let us say plot, character and theme) which would be no use at all collapsed into a numerical sequence of paragraphs. Furthermore, when you consider the planning involved in a story with alternative endings, it is clear that a quite complex structure might be required, as Vivi Lachs has shown.[20] Of the three electronic story template examples in figure 1.6 only one of them – the one that simply has boxes for beginning, middle and end – could be envisaged working on the one-click *Inspiration* model.

WEBSITE   **Fig 1.6**[21]

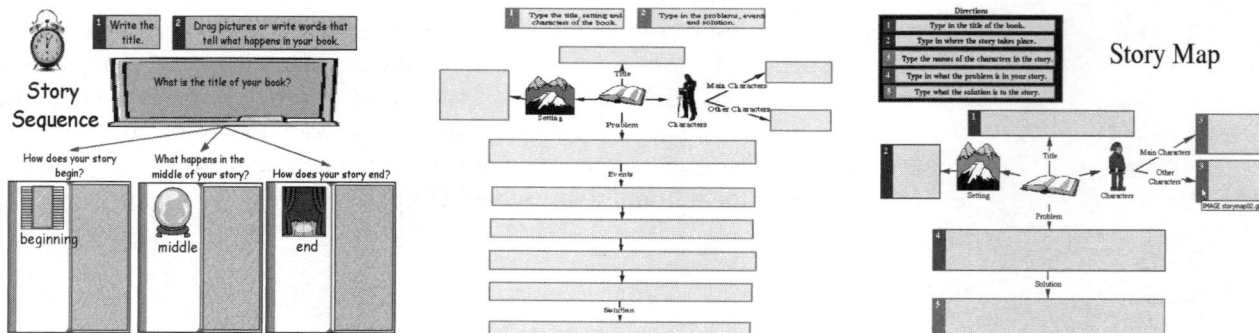

It is clear that if we start with a free-association approach, with multiple lemma branching from a central point, we are not suddenly going to have the material for an essay, no matter how much we develop those branches. We still have to decide several things about the resulting text:

➡ Which of my associated ideas is actually useful or appropriate to the essay?

➡ What is the best order for the different themes branching from my centre?

➡ How am I going to conclude the essay?

If we think about the writing of an essay with the title 'Litter' and imagine a mind map developed from the word 'litter' in the centre, our initial brainstorming might produce this selection of ideas from children:

Fig 1.7

You might also want to ask about balance between different areas, because a brainstorm is likely to prompt associated ideas of varying degrees of importance. This raises a key issue of whether there is some sort of hierarchy to those associated ideas which is not actually described by the mind map: why are crisp packets, bins and street on different levels? If we take one of the actual maps which Vivi Lachs uses as illustration – a brainstorm on the Tudors – we see that in the first iteration of the brainstorm chart, where all the associated ideas are at one remove from the centre, 'maze' has a conceptual status equal to 'Shakespeare', and even in the modified version, Henry VIII is on a level with The Globe.

Fig 1.8

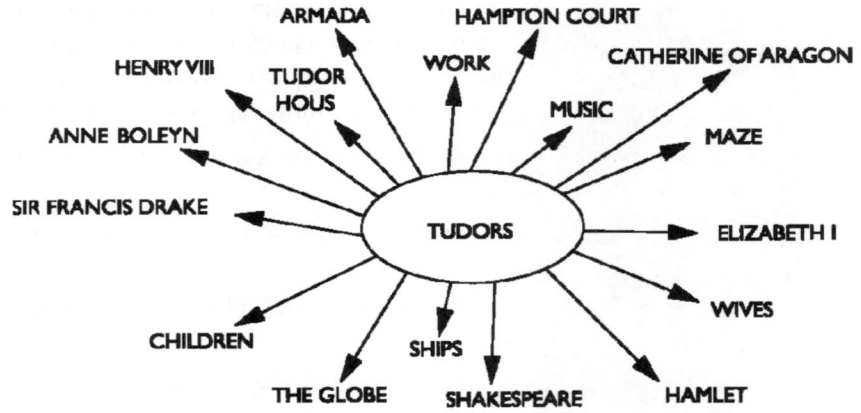

Tudor brainstorm.

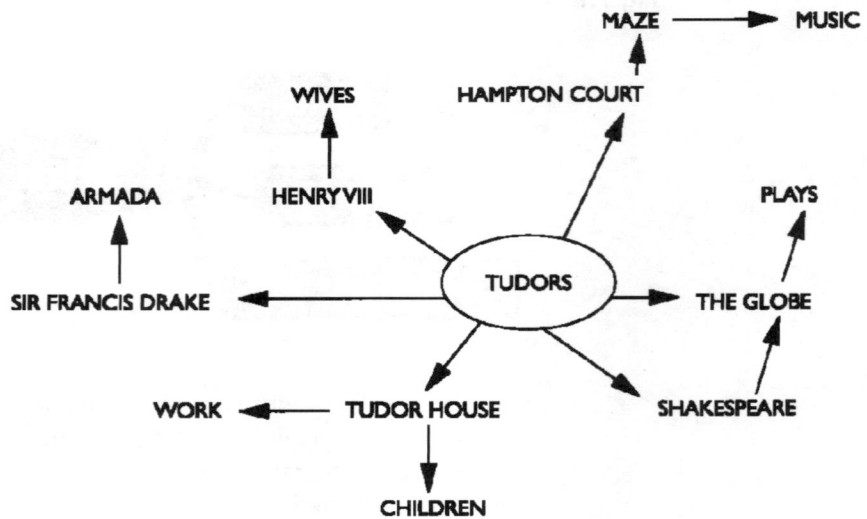

Grouping the brainstorm.

There is clearly a lot of work still to be done by the learner, and plenty of guidance from the teacher, before these ideas can be presented in a balanced and sequential way. As the actual practice of mind-mapping techniques with adults demonstrates, the ability to pick 'main themes' as first level branches is required to start with in order to make a coherent map. In other words effective use of mind mapping actually presupposes hierarchical ordering of ideas. As the Mind Mapping site puts its, 'the main themes, connected to the central image on the main branches, allow their relative importance to be seen. These are the Basic Ordering Ideas (BOIs) and aggregate and focus the rest of the Mind Map.'[22] Perhaps, then, for teaching purposes we need to combine mind mapping approaches with more hierarchical structuring of ideas or information.[23] The Literacy Time guidance on using *Inspiration* showed an appreciation of the structured teacher input needed in order to move towards a piece of extended writing:

WEBSITE

> The example opposite shows a chart for collecting information about a particular character in a story. The first shot shows the web as might be created during a lesson or series of lessons:

Fig 1.9

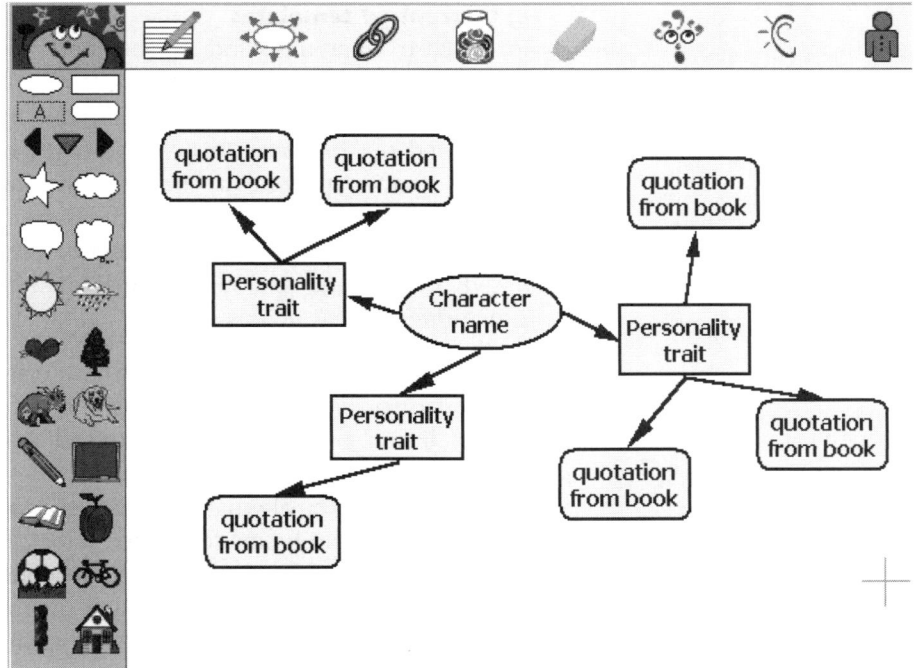

After a few mouse clicks to apply some formatting, the rough diagram can be transformed and presented as the finished product or used as the basis for further writing.[24]

WEBSITE

Fig 1.10

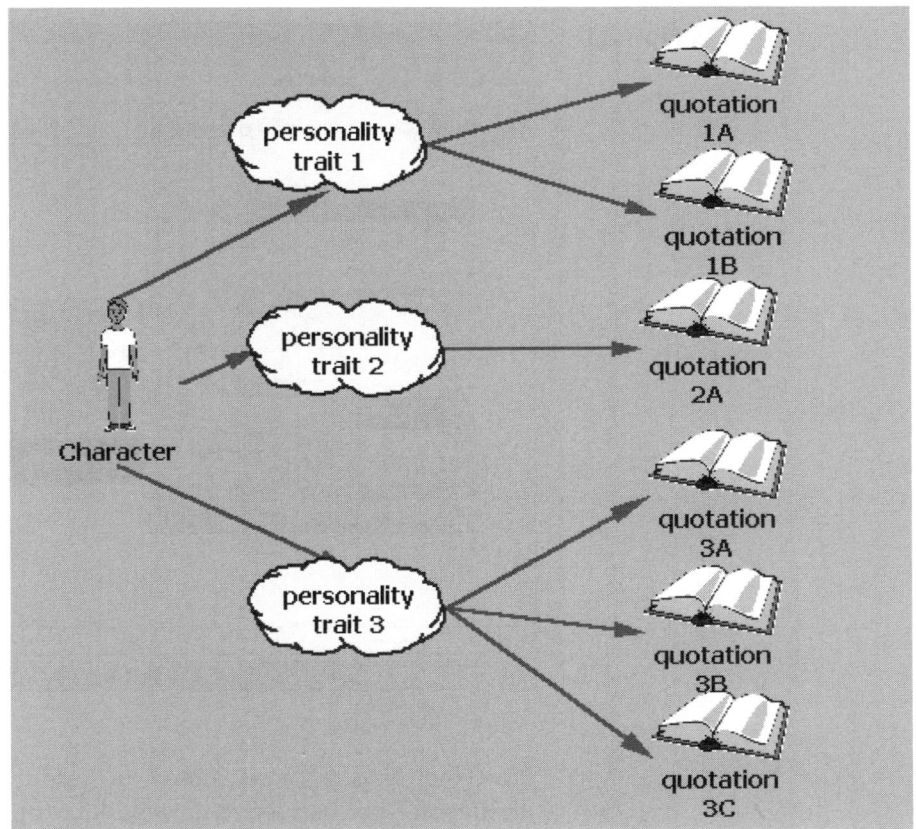

Here, in a very simple example, we have at work that principle of hierarchization of information/material which is the key to moving successfully from planning to actualizing in the writing process.

c) Conceptual templates

In a sense what this kind of software offers, if we are willing to use it imaginatively, is a way of producing 'conceptual templates' for writers, where 'template' need not be understood visually in the simple terms of a skeleton to be fleshed out or boxes to be filled. My poem templates were intended to suggest a pattern rather than enclose with a frame, and some of Trevor Millum's 'frameworks' take a similar approach. There is an interesting and relevant Key Stage 2 lesson plan in the NAACE document for 'Writing a Multimedia Book' based on different versions of the Red Riding Hood story. The preparatory structuring of ideas here is subtle:

> ...the pupils had used a matrix created by the teacher to compare similarities and differences between aspects of the story; opening and conclusion, plot, setting, characters, dialogue... [25]

So by examining the alternative narratives in a structured way via a 'matrix', the template effect can be made implicit rather than obvious and intrusive. Focus on the narrative elements provides the conceptual frame for producing the multimedia versions of the story. That matrix itself might be highly visual of course (though we don't see the teaching materials in this case) highlighting key features of the stories in a schematic way. The stories used included some from the online collections of fairytales at the University of Mississippi, which are used below in a map using Mind Genius.[26] Here the mapping software has been used to highlight visually the differences between versions of the Cinderella story.

WEBSITE

Fig 1.11

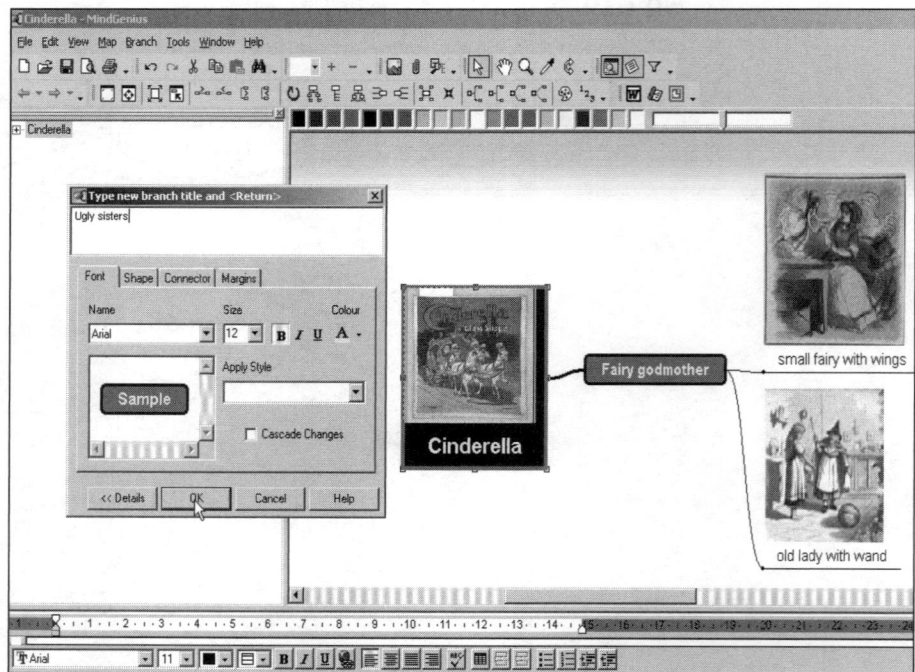

Projected onto a large screen or using an interactive whiteboard the illustrations can be seen in juxtaposition by a group, and can be annotated either by the teacher or by pupils.

▌ Conclusions

With its metaphors of frames, scaffolds or skeletons, the template is, like the mind map, at its heart a visualization of ideas, and yet in some ways these two notions seem to pull in opposite directions. While some people see mind mapping as 'graphic organizing' of ideas, others will emphasize the way it encourages practitioners to create 'associative links' between ideas. These two approaches – one structuralist, the other creative – seem to be at odds with each other when applied to writing. One is about clear and coherent expression of ideas, while the other favours free association and intuitive randomness.[27] Can we in any case have exciting, stimulating use of writing frames and templates? Drawing on Bruner again, it should be borne in mind that intuitive thinking was also vital to Bruner's theory, and his notion of structured learning was about exploring how teachers and schools might create the conditions for intuition to flourish. We might feel that the attraction of this approach to some educationalists today is that it seems to offer a 'quick fix' for the significant proportion of children whose standards of writing lag behind their reading. The key to self-directed progress is in the capacity and confidence to progress beyond the frameworks, to use and adapt them rather than just to fill them in. The idea of the template then is not to show 'how to do it', but to give learners confidence to explore within a sufficiently structured environment. It's for the teacher to decide how much is too much structuring, but of course there is always some.

What seems clear is that the 'mapping' of concepts in relation to a central point is itself only the first stage of an organization process, or the construction of coherently expressed ideas. Meanwhile mapping introduces that other important part of the process, intuitive thinking, so these two approaches would seem to complement each other very well. At Cramlington Community High School, where the headteacher promotes accelerated learning across the curriculum, they recommend using graphic organizer software (*Inspiration*) to help create structured stories in English, but in conjunction with a template rather than using the mind mapping methodology.[28] This is a nice conjunction of the two applications of ICT to whole text structure and cohesion.

WEBSITE

WEBSITE

Part 2

New types of text

▌ Why do it?

Hypertext and non-linearity

Most English teachers are interested in writing, and in text, and so when a putatively new form of text appears out of the ether – or out of hyperspace – as happened in the 1980s, their curiosity is going to be particularly exercised. Since the 1980s there have been high expectations in some quarters of 'hypertext', and often those have come from academics in the area of English studies. Theodore H. Nelson introduced the term describing it as 'non-sequential' writing, composed of 'chunks' of text or 'nodes'.[29] Talk of 'non-linear' and 'multilinear' text became commonplace, and extensive theorizing accompanied these terms. It seemed at times that there was a desire to turn what is just a functionality of the hyperlink (the interactive connection between nodes) into some radically new way of perceiving the world. Nelson's radical, crusading approach, promoting the idea that hypertext has revolutionary and subversive possibilities for publishing, still has a strong and wide appeal. Peter Foltz quotes G.P. Landow's claim that 'because hypertext has the power to change the way we understand and experience texts, it offers radical promises and challenges to students, teachers and theorists of literature.'[30] This kind of grand claim was certainly common among theorists of literature: there was analogy to be found in the non-linear narratives of modernism, and it seemed in sympathy with post-modern notions of unstructured 'play', or radical notions of 'de-centred' meaning. It was exactly such appropriation by theorists which seems to have made the average English teacher a bit wary of the whole topic, but there are simpler, more practical things to note about hypertext in an educational context, as Foltz goes on to remark:

> Using associative retrieval paths is similar to the way retrieval is performed from human memory, and this may be part of the appeal of hypertext to researchers and developers when they state that hypertext systems will improve a user's ability to find and use information.[31]

The notion of an 'associative retrieval path' is a helpful one in making clear what hyperlinking does: it helps us to connect, and therefore practice in creating and using hyperlinks will focus attention on that connecting of ideas. It has also, perhaps, a special appeal to the right-brained thinker, which would relate this to mind-mapping practice. Hyperlinking does not, however,

WEBSITE

WEBSITE

supersede organization or structure in some way, as will be clear from the examples in this chapter. Foltz's reporting on research into the readability of hypertext makes it clear that effective, coherent use of hyperlinks is in itself a challenge. It might, however, be a cognitive challenge worth presenting to learners at an early age so that they can work out for themselves exactly what usefully hyperlinked information is.

Other new text types

Email

There is something to be said for exploiting and examining the most commonly used new text type, the email. At the least one can do interesting comparison work between letter-writing conventions and email conventions, insofar as the latter can be established. There is plenty of work being done in schools to utilize emailing actively and creatively across the curriculum, but as far as English teaching is concerned it still has a status which at best is 'undecided'. In spite of its ubiquitous presence in our lives, and the fact that letter-writing is becoming ever less common, email is not yet an accepted 'text type' to teach or assess in English.

'Intertexts'

On a more esoteric level, there is also a developing appreciation of how the use of hyperlinking together with multimedia authoring tools can make real the notion of 'intertextuality', that is to say, the connections in culture between the different media expressed as various kinds of text. The European project which ended its first phase in 2003, brought together academics from both IT and the arts to produce a multimedia authoring tool, called CULTOS, which enables text, image, sound and video all to be linked in complex relations.[32] The intention is to seek educational applications for this system in schools, and it could take the idea of mind mapping to new levels of sophistication, showing links between 'texts' understood as crossing the full range of media.

WEBSITE

Fig 1.12

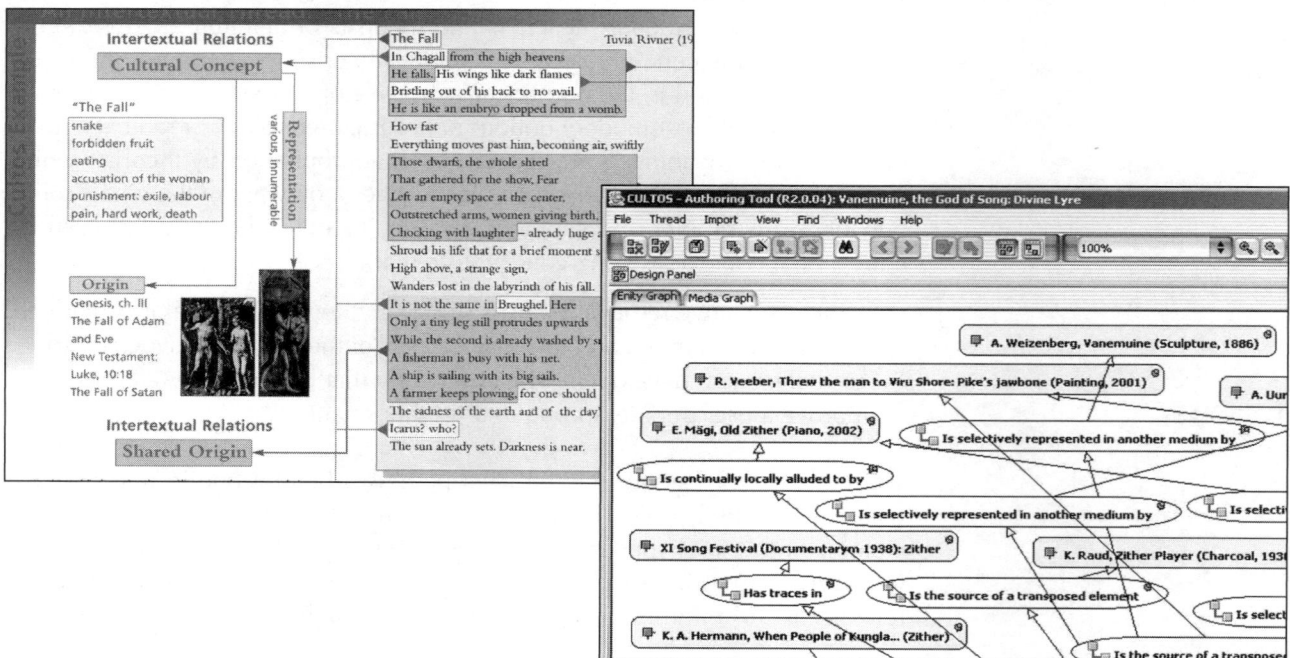

Visual Thesaurus

There is a similar approach taken in this interesting piece of software designed for schools use, which shows relationships between words visually.[33] It's rather like the CULTOS tool without the multimedia aspect. It also has elements of the mind-mapping software about it, but with 3D effects (except that as yet this is not itself an authoring tool). Mouse-over pop-ups on the linking lines explain the relationship (actually this always seems to be 'is similar to' therefore the pop-up seems rather redundant) in between words displayed in a strikingly minimalist fashion.

Fig 1.13

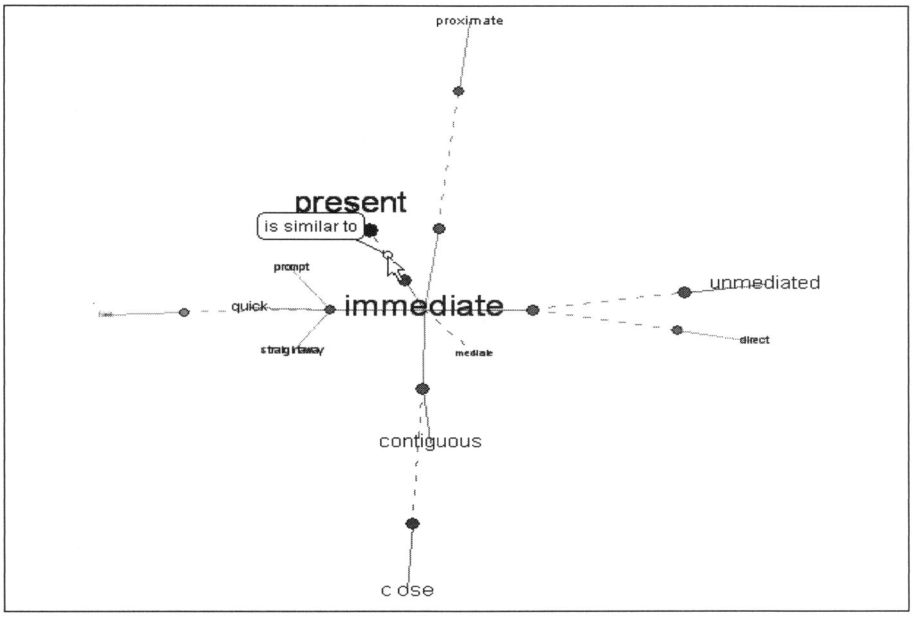

When you click on one of the major words, meanings explode from the centre in a disconcerting but rather beautiful manner. As you can see from this example, while 'immediate' produced an easily graspable set of connections, the linked word 'close' produced such a profusion in 3D virtual space that, however visually alluring it may be, taking it all in is far from easy.

Fig 1.14

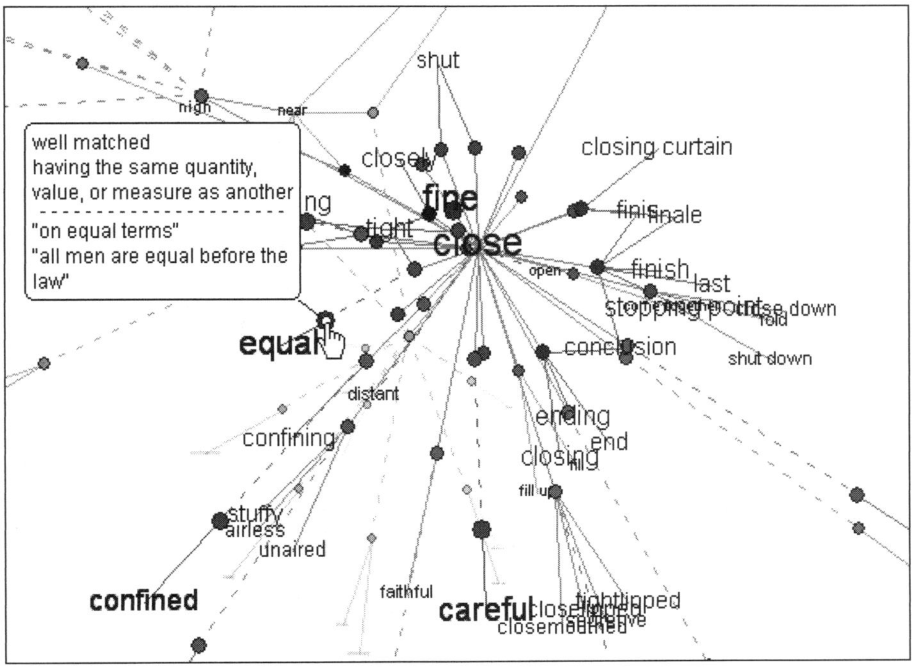

General teaching approaches

Hypertext

One of Foltz's proposals for the successful use of hypertext seems very useful in an educational context – he suggests that used well it can make the reading experience automatically differentiated:

> … hypertexts could include additional background knowledge to readers with little knowledge and make the text more coherent for readers with low reading abilities. For readers with general reading goals or trying to get an overview, the text could be presented as a single path through the text. For readers trying to find specific information, the text could provide search capabilities and appropriate background context of any relevant items.[34]

That close attention to the differentiated needs of the reader is surely a feature of hypertext worth promoting, and not only in providing learners with such texts to read, but in showing them how to modify their own texts to cater for different readers.

Email

There are suggestions from the literacy strategy about areas which emails could address:

At Year 5

➡ to read and evaluate letters intended to inform, protest, complain, persuade;

➡ to draft and write individual, group or class letters for real purposes.

At Year 6

➡ to review a range of non-fiction text types and their characteristics;

➡ to select the appropriate style and form to suit a specific purpose and audience, drawing on knowledge of different non-fiction text types.[35]

WEBSITE

You can find a page of ideas on emails and literacy from the Primary section of RM Learning called 'Imaginative ICT':

Using email children can:

➡ Learn.

➡ Question and investigate.

➡ Inform and instruct.

➡ Report and recount.

➡ Share jokes, puns and word plays.

➡ Collaborate and create stories.

➡ Share reading reviews and preferences.

➡ Exchange files of work.

WEBSITE

➡ Be involved in email adventures and simulations.[36]

Going beyond these ideas for *using* email in literacy teaching, Tim Shortis has provided useful research on attitudes to email, and ideas for work on 'the language of email', detailed later in this chapter.[37] The NAACE document on ICT and literacy tentatively describes the pertinent features of email as a text type and makes some modest claims for its teaching potential:

Sending and receiving emails:

➡ Emails have developed a style of their own and continue to develop as the writer responds to the tone and style of the message.

➡ The communication is characterized by short, informal messages. When longer communications are required to be circulated, these are usually 'attached' to an email and opened in a word processor by the receiver.

➡ In order for the communication system to work efficiently, users need to 'check their mailbox' and send responses promptly. Working economically, emails should be drafted and messages should be read 'offline'.

➡ Children can begin to send emails to 'ask an expert' or make contact with peers in another school.

➡ School links via email can share information and resources.

➡ Comparing data on weather and environmental conditions can be achieved more easily and more quickly via email.

➡ When you receive an email and send a reply, the original message is normally included. This is one of several options that the writer can change.[38]

Teaching ideas, examples and advice

1. Using hyperlinks in text

The method of hyperlinking in Microsoft Word is straightforward enough for pupils to learn, and can be used for a variety of purposes in their writing. In extended informative writing one can link from a contents list at the top to different parts of the document (this is also a common use of the hyperlink in simple web pages, avoiding the need for arduous scrolling down a page). The hyperlinking process has two stages:

1. Create a bookmark (Insert > Bookmark from the menu bar) at the point in the text to which you wish to link (the 'target'). This might be a highlighted word or a sub-title of a section, or it might be the point in the text at which the cursor is placed.

2. Highlight the word or words (for example, the heading in the contents) from which you wish to link (the 'anchor'), and then using Insert > Hyperlink, select the bookmark you have just created. This will create the link within the document.

Providing additional information for different readers

This is an ideal way of children showing off/exploiting their own specialist knowledge while showing an awareness of different readers' needs.

Establish a scenario where they have a specialist knowledge or vocabulary which might not be shared by others, for example, their parents, or adults in general; younger children; or it might even be a gendered scenario.

Suggested scenarios

➡ Describing a computer game, where both the characters in the game, and its rules or conventions, might need explanation to an uninitiated adult.

➡ Relating the plot of a TV soap opera, where characters or incidents mentioned will need background information for those unfamiliar with the storyline.

➡ Explaining how to do something technical (for example, changing a bicycle tyre, wiring a plug, burning a CD) where technical words need glossing.

➡ Telling about a skill or hobby with specialist terms (for example, netball, skateboarding, stamp collecting).

➡ Writing an instruction manual on social etiquette for teenagers, with facetious explanatory glosses for the opposite sex.

The idea is to add explanatory glosses at key points where some readers might need extra information: this can also be done easily with the Insert > Comment function in MS Word.

2. Alternative endings to narratives

One of Vivi Lachs' key ideas for creating multimedia learning materials is interactivity, and when it comes to narrative the chief exemplar is the alternative ending. The example described in the book and viewable on the accompanying CD-ROM is a story in words, pictures and recorded talk by Year 1 children. It is nothing short of astounding, and leaves you wondering what must be possible with Year 6 pupils or older.[39]

CD-ROM Ch 1/Computer Children Children Hyperstudio file

Fig 1.15   **The choice of endings to the story**

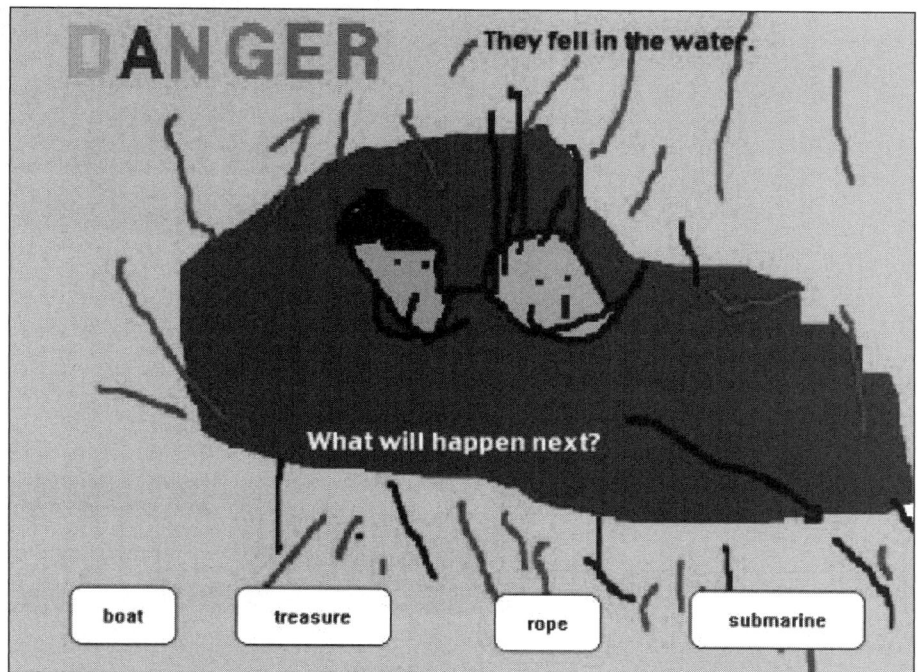

Not only are there four alternative endings, but there is also enactment of the story by children taking the parts of the characters: when you click on the head of the character you hear the child's voice acting out the scene.

These are created using linked HTML pages, but similar effects could be achieved with PowerPoint by making use of forward and back buttons, and if the focus is on the writing, alternative endings could even be achieved within a single Word document, by using its Hyperlink function. Simply create a bookmark (Insert > Bookmark from the menu bar) at the point in the story to which you wish to be able to jump forward, then using Insert > Hyperlink, select the bookmark you have just created.

3. Cloze procedure

Cloze is a method of encouraging learning via the desire to complete unfinished text. Devised in the 1950s as an outcome of psychological studies, it has long been revealed as a particularly apt use of ICT, with its addition of a simple interactive dimension to reading. After being used as a measure of, or as an exercise in, reading comprehension for several decades, software has made it a very easy procedure to present to learners, and there is much cloze material relevant to English teaching available online: a search of 'cloze' and 'English' will bring up plenty of resources. There are also cloze texts

WEBSITE

downloadable from the NAACE site.[40]

Fig 1.16

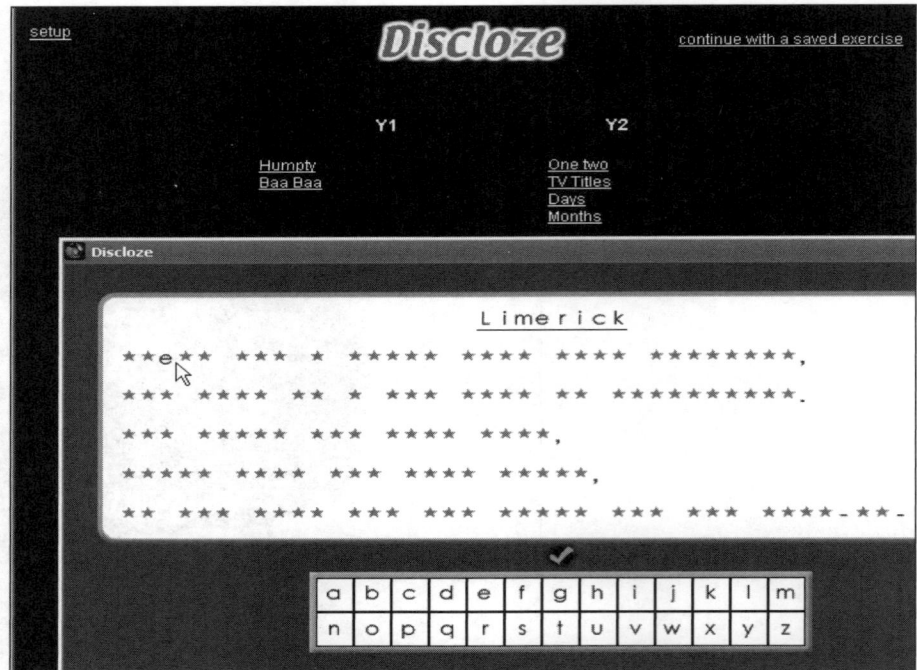

4. Mini-sagas

A tried and tested lesson I devised for QCA's exemplification of ICT in English utilizes various features of electronic text to enable reflection on the structure of narrative.[41] Taking the 'mini-saga' idea, which simply imposes a size constraint on the story, you concentrate attention on the structural process of storymaking.

An extra dimension can be added by focusing on endings of stories prior to the writing, since the crucial thing in such a piece of writing is that end. Find some examples, taken either from films or from appropriate fiction, to demonstrate different strategies for ending stories. I chose:

Open – cliff-hangers or mysterious endings.
Closed – moralistic or happy-ever-after endings.
Unexpected – a twist in the tale.
Cyclical – a resolution of something from the beginning.

Discussion of these can precede actual writing, but once they have decided on a strategy for their story the pupils then have a set amount of time to complete their mini-saga, either individually or as pairs.[42]

Using the word count tool, the pupils monitor the length of their story. Suggest removing or adding adjectives, or rephrasing, to get it to the appropriate length.

The time-restriction has a double function: it concentrates the mind, and also enables the pupils to save copies of their work at set intervals (for example, if the writing time is 15 minutes, then stop and save as a new file every five minutes). Aside from the finished product, each pupil or pair will have several copies of a story at different stages.

WEBSITE

WEBSITE

Below is an example of one of the stories, *Money Problems*, illustrating the kind of outcome obtainable with nine-year-old pupils. They chose an 'open' ending, and after ten minutes, their mini-saga looked like this:

> It was midday when her mom went shopping, she opened the safe and took It out. By the bus station she met her friends. She paid for all of them, (six altogether.) [32 words]

Five minutes later, their second draft looked like this:

> It was midday when her mum went shopping; I opened the safe and took it. At the bus station I met my friends. I paid for all six of them. Her mother was walking towards the house, the safe was open. How was I going to explain this to my mom? [51 words]

After a further five minutes they produced their final version:

> It was midday when mom went shopping; I opened the safe and took it. At the bus station I met my friends. I paid for all six of them. My mother was walking towards the house, the safe was open. How was I going to explain this to my mom? [50 words]

These versions now become a resource to re-examine, and can provide material for subsequent work investigating the decisions made at each stage of the story writing and editing process. Older or more able pupils can write their own commentaries explaining their changes. Here we see the way ICT can shed new light on the writing process, merely because of the capability of saving versions and quickly checking word-length.

5. Emails

Tim Shortis provides useful research into 'the language of email' and attitudes to it. He also makes a number of suggestions for language studies which can be adapted for younger pupils. One of his suggestions, pursuing the idea that emails combine features of both writing and speech, is to take David Crystal's points of contrast between speech and writing as reference-points for describing emails.[43]

If we adapted Shortis's table of contrasts to produce questions for Key Stage 3 pupils to use in reference to emails, we might get something like this:

1. These are usually thought of as features of speech, not writing:
   - loudness
   - intonation
   - tempo
   - rhythm
   - pronunciation
   - tone [of voice].

Do we get any impression of these from the emails, and if so, how?

2. Difficult or complex grammar is more commonly a feature of writing than speech. What are the most difficult grammatical structures in the emails?

3. Informal language/slang is more common in spoken language than in writing. Are there any examples in the emails?

4. Writing is usually more carefully expressed, perhaps because it has been edited and corrected, whereas speech is often casually expressed. Do the emails show careful and exact, or loose and vague expression?

5. Writing can include graphic material such as tables or graphs that aren't possible with speech. Is there any use of 'graphics' in the emails? (do emoticons count as graphics?)

An obvious follow-up and consolidation of this is to get students to produce standard written English versions of emails which include some features of spoken English. These can be shown alongside each other in tables in Word, or the standard English version might be inserted as a mouse-over pop-up 'comment'.

Case study 1

g8way project: SMS poetry

WEBSITE

WEBSITE

WEBSITE

▌Background

This project was the brainchild of Andrew Wilson who provided both the infrastructure, via the Centrifugal Forces community arts project, and the inspiration with his idea of text message poetry.[1] Peter and Ann Sansom went into schools to do poetry workshops, and the follow-up process of receiving texted poems, then assessing and publishing them, was led by Andrew.[2] This collaboration happened first at four schools in the Kirklees district of West Yorkshire, and then in the Fenland district of Cambridgeshire under the aegis of the g8way project.[3]

Teaching and learning objectives

➡ To write imaginatively, drawing on knowledge of good poetic forms and style.

➡ To think about readers and audiences when writing poetry.

➡ To make use of and explore new forms of expression in new media.

How it was done

In the classroom two different approaches were taken:

➡ Choose from 'brainstormed' written materials – write a great deal then 'quarry' from the results just 160 characters' worth of writing.

➡ Write specifically with 160 characters as objective and focus.

Peter and Ann Sansom used tried-and-tested creative writing warm-ups and poetry games to get the students in the mood for writing. Then, when it came to that writing, time limits were set to increase focus.

As a follow-up to this, the finished poems from the Kirklees and Fenland schools were submitted both on paper and by text to judges at the community arts organizations Centrifugal Forces and g8way respectively. Money prizes were awarded to those judged to have produced the best poems.

Classroom issues: incentives to write poetry

To Peter, the incentives are threefold, and were very important in motivating Year 9 pupils to write poetry:

1. Prizes
2. The medium
3. The audience.

1. Prizes and rewards

The prizes available in this case were not the sort of rewards likely to be offered to pupils in school, but the competition element might be helpful, especially since the poetry can be appraised in terms of achievement relative to ability. Incentives and rewards are all too frequently neglected as an issue, as though we find it hard to accept that pupils will not always appreciate the intrinsic value of activities. Bruner makes 'motives for learning' one of his four key factors in the learning process, and long-term goals are rarely as persuasive as short-term rewards.

2. The appeal of the medium

To Peter, texting and poetry have something in common – both are marginalized discourses – 'rebellious' he calls them – and this is part of the attraction for him. He also sees this marginalization as a route into poetry for young people who might otherwise find the conventional learning of poetry rather institutionalized. 'They decide whether it is understandable' Peter says, and that knowledge-power nexus means that the use of a private language like texting is empowering for young people. This may be so but whether this is carried through into poetry writing is another question. The private language element may be an attraction on one level, but of course once it is turned into poetry it is no longer private, so there is a fine line to tread, and unlike a visiting poet, a classroom teacher might not be a convincing champion of marginalized discourses.

The formal constraints of the medium – in particular the shortness, but also the possibilities of abbreviations – makes for a condensed, often pithy, epigrammatic style of verse. The shortness is also inherently attractive to young writers.

The history of written English poetry has always been one of tension between formalistic constraints and expressive subversion of those constraints. The text message poem has this exciting feel of radical departure from convention, while being in some respects quite conventional. It is noteworthy that the young poets often used standard English, and would draft verses in lines in spite of the impossibility (at the time) of these being read as such. And yet there is scope for extensive verbal play and linguistic inventiveness here.

3. Audience and texting

There is a real issue here which arises from the 'one-to-one' nature of the typical text message. You are unlikely (at least intentionally) to find a large audience with a text message. Given that poetry must be a more public activity in order to give it meaning, it seems that we need to introduce a third party, and perhaps a second medium, in order to create that audience:

➡ In the case of Huddersfield the poems were shown on a digital display outside the Media Centre in central Huddersfield.

WEBSITE

➡ We can send texts to a website or intranet where they might be viewed.

➡ Messages can be accessed by people using certain systems such as SMS Bug.[4]

Outcomes

CD-ROM Ch 1/SMS Poems
Word doc

Here are some of the poems produced by pupils in Leeds and Cambridgeshire schools. (Further examples can be found on the CD-ROM.)

1. **MY UNCLE**
I look over my shoulder
and see my auntie
bringing another pot of tea.
How can it be
that this man can drink so much tea.

2. **CAT**
I've been waiting for you
Dinner time at long last
A shame you've hurt your wing
Easier for me to catch my prey
It'll be less painful for you
If you don't struggle

3. **HEAD**
humdrum
a Britney video
an eagle soaring
swimming
the depth of the sea
the ache of my hand
a map of March
the scribble of a pen
the idea for a poem

A range of different poetic approaches is demonstrated here: the epigrammatic, whimsical and rhyming 'My Uncle'; the reflexive, contemplative series of thoughts in 'Head'; the anthropomorphic free verse of 'Cat'. It is worth considering the absence of punctuation here and the role of lines, which would not be viewed as such in a text message.

Doing this in the classroom
Incentives
In a sense, the fact that winning entries were displayed proudly and publicly was of course part of the reward, and therefore part of the incentive, so making an effort to ensure that there is this sort of recognition for effort is going to be useful. It might be possible to display the poems for a time in continuous slideshow on a monitor in the school library, or even on a larger screen. If there is a school intranet or website, it might be possible to publish them there. Alternatively, they could be submitted to a poetry website such as Poetry Zone.[5]

WEBSITE

Preparation

In terms of the preparation for writing, how you go about it will depend on the age and ability of the students. Setting time limits to increase concentration is likely to be useful, as is choosing one of the two methods used by Peter and Ann Sansom.

Reading examples of text message poetry may well prove attractive, not least because of the brevity of the form, and it's worth starting with Andrew Wilson's book of poetry *Text Messages*.[6] There is also online SMS poetry at Centrifugal Forces, including the online magazine Onesixty and 'Thumb Love', a collection of love poems that could be sent by text.[7]

WEBSITE

As a stimulus you might try some website poetry created by children themselves – the thematic groupings on Poetry Zone might provide a starting point, or searchable collections aimed at young people, such as the US site Giggle Poetry.[8]

WEBSITE

Teaching methods

Using exemplars such as the three poems above is a useful method of directing pupils: ask for close observation about a relative, or ask the question, 'What would it be like to be …?' The third example, using a series of juxtaposed ideas or images, might be the result of adopting the 'brainstorm then quarry' approach: write for five minutes in a free association way, then choose and put in order selected words and phrases.

When using a word processor to imitate the way a text message poem might be viewed, you can take two approaches: increase the font size on the page (48pt is about right) so that only two or three words per line are possible, and one poem per page, or of course shrink the page by adjusting the margins.

You can also limit the exact number of characters the student can write by use of the protected fields function in Word:

View > Toolbars > Forms > Insert frame > Insert Text form field, then edit field, set as 160 characters only, and protect field.

Chapter 2

Beyond words

Part 1: Interactive and multimedia approaches to language study

In this section you will:

- look at why interactive and multimedia tools might be useful in English language teaching;
- consider *WordRoot* as a model for this kind of teaching and learning;
- look at ways of applying these principles in the classroom.

Part 2: Text messaging and language study

In this section you will:

- look at the background to and issues surrounding SMS and literacy;
- consider why SMS/text messaging can be a useful focus for English language teaching;
- look at some good practice and general approaches to teaching about SMS language;
- suggest classroom tasks relating to SMS appropriate for Year 6 to Year 9 students.

Part 1

Interactive and multimedia approaches to language study

Why do it?

Interactivity and multimedia are key features of ICT when it comes to teaching and learning in general, and particularly in the area of language learning. With regard to vocabulary it seems obvious why we would want to use multimedia tools: with early learners we use visual, auditory and kinesthetic stimuli all the time to teach reading and writing, so why suddenly abandon that approach with older learners? The teaching of language, except where children are visually or hearing impaired, is initially about sounds and pictures and then increasingly about written words. Typically, words are learned, usually as heard sounds and perhaps in conjunction with pictures, before the spelling is tackled. If we are to set such high store by spelling as a measure of linguistic achievement then we certainly should employ all the strategies available to help children spell accurately. There is evidence that not only spelling but also vocabulary can be improved by using multimedia stimuli.

The interactivity in learning is typically predicated on the idea that we need somehow to 'replace' the activity of a real teacher in the virtual environment. The principle is easily seen in an online interactive 'Look, cover, write and check' tool devised by Ambleside Primary School in conjunction with Digitalbrain, see figure 2.1.[1]

WEBSITE

Fig 2.1

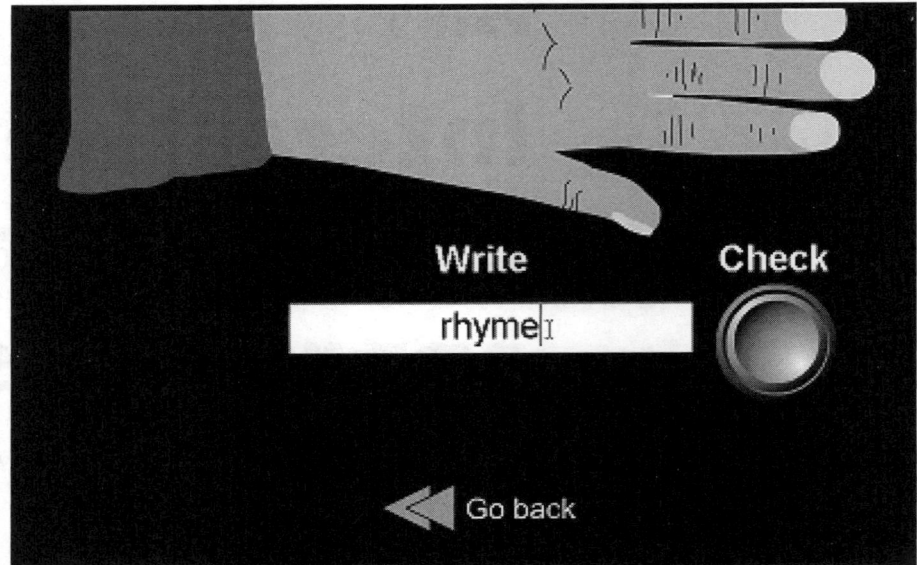

This cleverly reproduces the effect of one flash card activity: you select from either mixed word groups or groups with the same spelling pattern, and the words are selected randomly from those groups. It is this randomness factor (the appeal to right-brain thinking, if you like) rather than the simple graphics that makes it compulsive. If we can utilize these two aspects of ICT imaginatively we will certainly provide possibilities for accelerated learning of language.

General teaching approaches

WEBSITE

A language learning tool that utilizes not only the vital randomness factor in its interactivity, but also the full range of multimedia, is *WordRoot*, which comes as a CD-ROM. This was the brainchild of John Davitt, who now specializes in accelerated learning teaching methods but began his career as an English teacher.[2] The trouble with 'interactive' learning tools can be that after a short time they 'use up' their interactivity. Typically they have a linear (if sometimes 'multi-linear') structure, and before long the student will get to the end of it, with little incentive to return. *WordRoot* is different because it introduces the element of randomness, and therefore excitement, to electronic learning. It relies for its dynamism on stirring the inquisitive instincts of the user rather than taking them by the hand through a sequence of things to learn. The random factor gives the learner a feeling of exploration before discovery, and this is crucial to engaging interest, while the multimedia aspects stimulate in various ways, across the range of learning styles. Tim Shortis, whose book *The Language of ICT* has mapped out the ground for language study related to electronic text, saw that *WordRoot* made a significant contribution to the learning of 'hard words' and the development of a broad vocabulary.[3] It was he who instigated the Bristol project case study carried out by Dan Sutch, and made explicit some of the theoretical underpinning to the *WordRoot* methodology. That methodology can be imitated with widely available software and there are various aspects of it which can be used as the basis for exciting language work, mainly at 'word level', and using VAK learning approaches. Though the graphics on *WordRoot* suggest that it is aimed at quite young learners, the interesting thing is that the vocabulary it uses would typically be considered 'hard words'. The success of the software reminds us not to underestimate children and their capacity to learn when motivated appropriately.

▌Teaching ideas, examples and advice

As far as using a *WordRoot*-style approach to language teaching is concerned, the follow-up work is crucial. The combination of text, sound, and colourful moving images with a random generation of links, has a special appeal to right-brain learners. The teacher's task in the classroom is to pull together and consolidate the learning that has gone on in this virtual environment. Most people will prefer to use PowerPoint for this, but Macromedia Flash[4] is even more versatile if you have the know-how. HyperStudio[5] is also suitable, and a particularly child-friendly multimedia package is Softease.[6] The examples I am going to show are in PowerPoint because this is most commonly used and easily available. One of the ideas we can take from *WordRoot*, and apply in teaching approaches to language learning, is attaching some sort of visual 'tag' – whether text or image – to heard speech. ICT enables the 'tagging' of speech in a way never before possible, and we have only just begun to explore the value of this. It seems to be as useful to learners as traditionally 'flash cards' have been, but it is considerably more versatile and less dependent on a single moment of attention to the card-wielding teacher. The learners can keep returning and clicking themselves, to hear and see, in whatever order they wish. How to produce PowerPoint versions of specific *WordRoot* functions will be shown in the case study that accompanies this chapter, but here are some other suggestions for ways in which the principles can be applied:

WEBSITE
WEBSITE
WEBSITE

1. 'Speech tagging'
a) reflecting on spoken English
There are a number of ways you can do 'speech tagging':

➡ Placing sound objects on a scale of formality in Flash;

➡ Using PowerPoint as in the case study;

➡ Inserting sound into the comment box in Word.

The first option is useful if you have access to and know how to operate Macromedia Flash software, which allows you to create objects that can be dragged across the screen. Thus you can have, for example, various greetings both written and spoken which can be arranged on a sliding scale of formality, from 'Hi!' to 'How do you do?' (see the accompanying CD-ROM for an example). This visual representation of the concept of formality can be a useful focus and stimulus for class discussion of spoken English. The same principle could be applied by taking examples of speech as objects and identifying situations or places where they would be appropriate. So you could have four contrasting locations to which 'sound objects' would be dragged: for example, a classroom, a shop, a football match and the home. The third option using Microsoft Word doesn't have the visual dimension provided by Flash or PowerPoint but might be more appropriate for older learners. We will look at PowerPoint examples because this software is most commonly used, and while it does not offer the ability to drag objects, it does enable combinations of image and sound.

CD–ROM Ch 1/Scale of Formaility Flash file

Create a PowerPoint slide with scattered text boxes. Use whatever shape you want, but an obvious one is the speech bubble (see figure 2.2) that you can find among the Autoshapes in PowerPoint (go to Autoshapes > More autoshapes > Miscellaneous).

Introduce variations in register, tone of speech, or regional variations. For example click on a speech bubble containing the word

➡ 'Polite' and hear 'how do you do?' / 'good evening';

➡ 'Friendly' and hear 'nice to meet you' / 'hello there';

➡ 'Matey' and hear 'hiya' / 'alright' / 'hi';

➡ 'Unfriendly' / 'brusque', and hear 'hello' in a less friendly tone;

➡ 'Australian' and hear 'g'day';

➡ 'Cockney' and hear 'wotcher';

and so on ...

b) Apostrophes

This is an obvious way to reinforce teaching about the use of apostrophes of omission, because of course it is primarily a feature of spoken language, though this seems to be forgotten at times.

CD-ROM Ch 2/Apostrophes PowerPoint presentation

Again, create a slide with scattered text boxes and fill them with examples, but introduce an element of the unexpected by having a sound file of 'do not' linked to the typed word 'don't' (see figure 2.2, below, and the CD-ROM for this example).

Fig 2.2

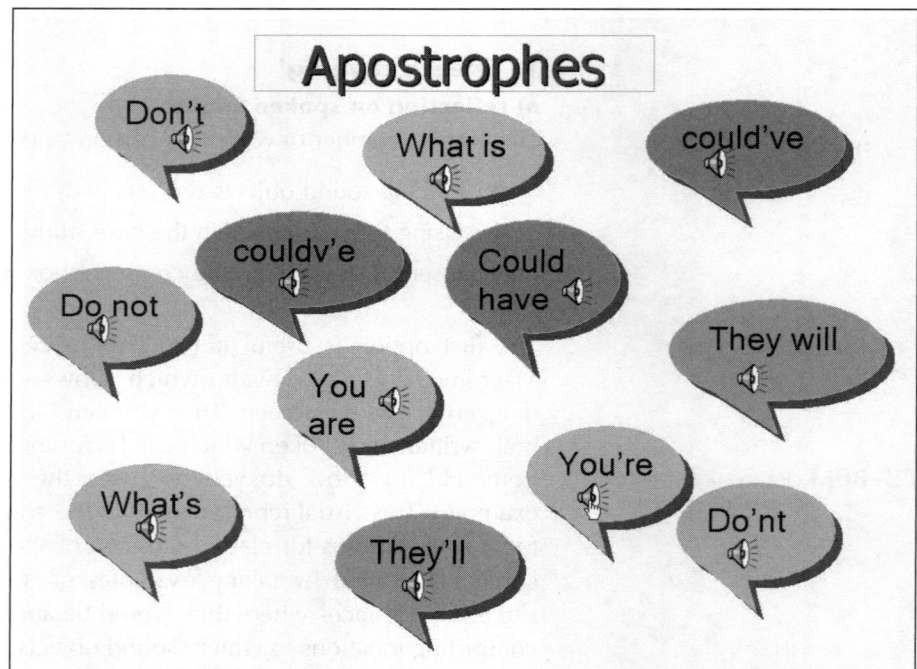

CD-ROM Ch 2/Apostrophe list Word doc

The example included on the CD-ROM shows a selection of frequently occurring written abbreviations and their expanded versions. The trick is to add sound files to the expanded written forms which when clicked will activate voices saying aloud the abbreviated form, and vice versa. Simple colour coding ensures that the visual connection between the two written forms is also maintained.

An optional extra is to throw in a couple of incorrect versions where the apostrophe is misplaced. Use a funny sound effect here to indicate a wrong answer – thus the pupil is forced to look more closely if at first glance it appears to be correct.

Supply your groups with a list of examples of apostrophe use and ask pairs/threes to produce their own selection, using one example from each of the six groups in the word list.

Consolidate this work with lists of the written words and their contractions, and then test the students, both in writing and orally.

2. Word jigsaw wallcharts

Here, non-virtual kinaesthetic input is possible with the physical jigsaw pieces being made and joined together. The end result is visually stimulating too, with the bright contrasting colours drawing the eye and acting as a constant reinforcement to learning. You could also add an extra dimension using a simple colour coding for the suffixes and prefixes from Latin or Greek. The wallchart below (figure 2.3) was produced by Year 6 pupils.

Fig 2.3

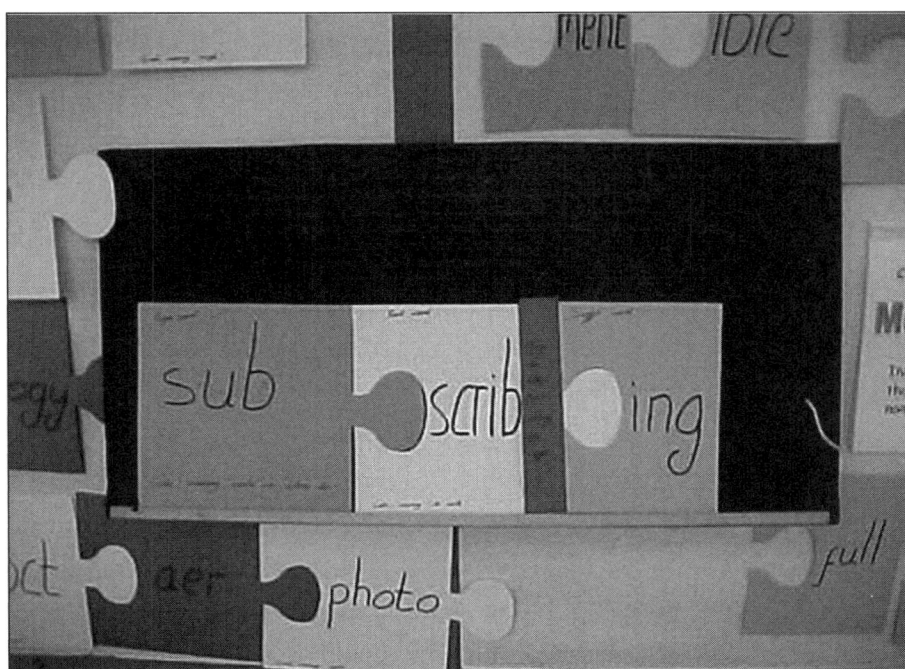

3. Extension work on apostrophes in poetry (for older learners)

The reverse approach to speech tagging is to add speech to text as a gloss, and this can now be done in the commonly available MS Word, which has its own sound recording software built into the 'Insert comment' function. The possible uses of this are various, but in the suggested work below it is a way of reminding students that poetry is, in it origins, a spoken or sung form. Language study is often best done as part of, or as a natural offshoot from, reading or writing, as with this work on apostrophes that combines work on both poetry and language change, with an additional interactive and multimedia dimension.

a) Language study/poetry

Setting language study in either historical or social context is helpful in showing relevance and enabling understanding. Work on apostrophes for abbreviation can be given some contextualization through a project on 'old language' or poetic forms. Since many of these archaic abbreviations lasted longest in poetic language, this might be a good place to start. Consider using a selection or anthology of poems for research, or search for electronic text versions of poems online.

There should be plenty of examples to find in nineteenth-century collections, for example Robert Burns' poem 'To a Mouse':

> *Wee, sleekit, cow'rin', tim'rous beastie,*
> *O, what a panic's in thy breastie!*
> *Thou need na start awa sae hasty,*
> *Wi' bickering brattle!*
> *I wad be laith to rin an' chase thee,*
> *Wi' murd'ring pattle!*

Or Wordsworth's 'The Two April Mornings':

> *Six feet in earth my Emma lay;*
> *And yet I loved her more,*
> *For so it seemed, than till that day*
> *I e'er had loved before.*

Or Walter Scott's 'Rosabelle':

> *O'er Roslin all that dreary night*
> *A wondrous blaze was seen to gleam;*
> *'Twas broader than the watch-fire's light,*
> *And redder than the bright moon-beam.*

Discussion questions:

➡ Why do these abbreviations appear so much in poetry?
➡ Is this a special 'poetic' language, or is it supposed to convey speech?
➡ Why should poetry be more like speech than prose?

b) Research into language change

Visit your library and find an anthology of English poetry and investigate when these poetic abbreviations died out. Online resources can be used too, and might prove easier to search. Try a web search for 'apostrophe'. Or go to a poetry anthology website such as Poem Tree.

The use of an apostrophe in words ending 'ed' to indicate that the last syllable is not pronounced is another feature worth pointing out in much Romantic and Victorian poetry. At some stage it was taken for granted that the 'ed' ending was not pronounced as a separate syllable – when was that?

The turn of the twentieth century is perhaps a useful focus for transitions: look at Hardy, Kipling, Housman and Yeats. 'A Shropshire Lad', published by A.E. Housman in the 1890s, is full of examples partly because of the way he evokes the speech of rural Shropshire of the 'tis and 'twas variety, as in this famous section:

'When I was One-and-Twenty'

WHEN I was one-and-twenty
  I heard a wise man say,
'Give crowns and pounds and guineas
  But not your heart away;
Give pearls away and rubies
  But keep your fancy free.'
But I was one-and-twenty,
  No use to talk to me.

When I was one-and-twenty
  I heard him say again,
'The heart out of the bosom
  Was never given in vain;
'Tis paid with sighs a plenty
  And sold for endless rue.'
And I am two-and-twenty,
  And oh, 'tis true, 'tis true.

➡ See if you can find any later examples of such poetic abbreviations by other poets.

➡ Make a timeline of examples you find (no more than two per poet), citing the line, the poem, the poet and the date (this is good practice for citing quotations).

'Modernism' is often associated with the First World War, so another approach would be to ask if students can find any such examples in poetry from that war.

Discussion questions:

➡ Should poets use this sort of poetic language today?

➡ What should poetic language be like?

➡ Is poetry today more like speech than it was a hundred years ago?

c) Marking up/glossing poems

Finally, you can introduce interactivity and multimedia into learning about such archaic language by inserting an explanatory comment, and even a sound file, using MS Word.

To do this, you simply highlight with your cursor the word or words you want to gloss, and then go to the Insert > Comment option from the main menu bar.

A box appears at the bottom of the page, not unlike the insert footnote facility. Here you can, for example, write the modern/standard English equivalent of the words in the comment box, so that it appears when you 'mouse-over' the words highlighted.

More excitingly, a recently added option within Word is for including a sound file alongside the text comment. To do this click on the 'Insert Sound Object' icon above the comment box.

You can insert a pre-recorded sound here, or use the built-in recording software, which allows you to record something instantly, leaving it stored with your written comment. Students might record themselves saying the abbreviated and expanded forms.

Part 2

Text messaging and language study

▌Why do it?

Text messaging might seem more appropriate as a category in the last chapter, where we looked at new text types, but what this next form of communication has added to our language seems, paradoxically, to go beyond text as it is traditionally understood. Certainly it has been sufficiently influential on the communication habits of young people in recent years to merit the space I have given it. On 3 December, 1992, scientists at Sema, a British technology company, sent the first text message to their counterparts at mobile phone giant Vodafone. At first SMS – or Short Message Service – was just a tool for telephone engineers, and Vodafone's Telenotes service, as it was called, was planned just for businesses. Now figures in the order of one billion text messages per month in the UK are quoted. This is a communication phenomenon which cannot be ignored by English teachers. It is easy to find press reports relating the possible negative effects of texting on literacy, but these are not based on any close examination of evidence, and would seem to be a tabloid-friendly combination of technophobia and anxiety about young people having a private language. There seems to have been an annual round of such scare stories for the past few years across the English-speaking world (and no doubt in other languages too). One such story arose in Scotland in March 2003 after an examiners' report highlighted inappropriate use of text message language in essays. The response from a teachers' union representative was to bemoan the demise of 'the Queen's English'.[7] Meanwhile research is increasing into the educational value and role of texting, as is the number of projects which might harness the enthusiasm for texting shown by young people. Research is tending to support positive interpretations of texting in relation to literacy; there are several aspects to this:

a) The volume of written communication happening between young people is surely a positive thing.

b) There appear to be links between linguistic ability and competence at texting.

c) There is evidence that the medium encourages invention and creativity.

The text messaging issue is only one aspect of a wider and developing interest in the educational potential of mobile phones and other hand-held devices. The European m-learning project, which ended in 2004, investigated whether the use of mobile technologies in the hands of young adults (aged 16–24) might engage them in learning activities, start to change their attitudes to learning and contribute towards improving their literacy, numeracy and life chances. The target audience was young adults not currently taking part in education or training, and the idea was to assist them with their lifelong learning objectives. As part of this project, learning resources for delivery on or via mobile phones and PDAs were developed, some of which used simply SMS, for example an SMS language course in Italy designed to allow learners to take part even if they owned only a very basic mobile phone. Other more advanced materials and systems such as multimedia or picture messaging (MMS), blogs and collaborative learning activities using a tool called the MediaBoard were also used in the UK and Sweden where the learners were lent 'smartphones' and PDAs. In the main research phase in the UK, young adults from ten collaborating organizations in the UK (20% of them in FE colleges) were given mobiles to try out the various learning materials, guided by mentors. The final outcomes of the research were very encouraging; 62% of learners felt more keen to take part in future learning after trying m-learning, of whom 80% would like to learn again with mobiles; 29% were assessed by their mentors as having developed a more positive attitude towards reading after taking part in the research; 82% of respondents felt the mobile learning games could help them to improve their reading or spelling. Some mentors also

WEBSITE

perceived improvements in their learners' reading (17%) and writing (16%) skills.[8] So if hand-held technology in general has shown potential in a post-16 educational context, then what are specific arguments for SMS messaging being promoted within English teaching in schools?

a) The core of those billion messages per month in the UK are being sent by school-aged mobile phone users. The new medium has generated huge enthusiasm among young people – indeed it is now their staple mode of communication – but it is difficult to see why it should cause anxieties of the sort usually associated with new technologies. Space Invaders in the 1970s, and game consoles in the 1990s, were seen as discouraging 'healthy' social behaviour. In contrast, text messaging clearly encourages social interaction and exchange, with young people typically developing social networks which are more extensive than would have been likely before. Another perspective on this is that given the enthusiasm for the medium, its value might partly be motivational if used in a teaching and learning context. This is an assumption underlying the European M-Learning Project. The project is aimed more at young people post-16 than at schools, which of course often ban the use of mobiles, making their use in the classroom rather problematic.

b) There is also reason to question the assumption that texters are bad spellers or that SMS is a threat to literacy. Given that there are spelling rules within the texting conventions, the ability to use these effectively is a competence which itself requires accuracy. Recent studies of actual text messages have suggested that good spellers/readers tended to be good texters. Furthermore, examination of the abbreviated forms of words used by texters indicates a low rate of error within the established conventions.[9] The detractors forget that young people have to become adept decoders to participate in the 'squeeze-text' conventions of texting, therefore they are effectively exercising their linguistic (and in particular phonetic) knowledge and skills in learning a new set of conventions.[10] And neither can 'predictive texting' be seen as merely lazy, since to get it right you need to know how to spell at least the beginnings of words: it is likely therefore that good spellers will prefer to use it (or perhaps that we are breeding a generation of first syllable spellers!).

c) The creative aspects of text messaging are an extension of the literacy issue. There is plenty of evidence that this new genre has stimulated creativity, famously on a national level with *The Guardian's* text messaging poetry competitions. While this might be seen as a new fad, there is also a way in which the medium dictates form that is not unlike the constraints of poetic convention. Haiku is the most obvious analogy, where the measure is not necessarily in terms of lines, but syllables, while in the case of text poems the constraint is the number of characters (and perhaps lack of control over the formatting). Our case study of the g8way project suggests that school-age children are likely to find text poetry more engaging than other more conventional poetic forms.[11] In some senses it is clear that texting prompts creativity and inventiveness, as texters apply a range of strategies to convey meaning appropriately within the constraints of the medium:

> Good spellers felt confident enough to engage in a kind of linguistic play in their 'textisms'. Their mastery of the language provided them with a better foundation from which to explore phonetics in 'text language'.[12]

The issue of literacy and texting, then, is clearly much more complicated than some media reports would suggest. Among those who would take a positive view of texting are those who speak of 'new literacies' and would suggest that we (presumably English teachers) need to embrace these and re-think our notions of literacy in relation to new texts. This is the attitude taken by Victoria Carrington as a result of her discourse analysis of a notorious example of juvenile text messaging, in her essay 'Txting: The end of civilization (again)?':

> What does it mean to be 'literate' in contemporary post-Fordist economies and cultural landscapes? What kinds of texts will the students in our classrooms find it necessary to 'read' and manipulate and produce in order to effectively participate in civic life?[13]

But it is not necessary to become embroiled in a debate about the relative merits of 'new' and 'old' literacies to see that texting needs to be addressed by English teachers. Surely if text language usage is at times at variance with standard English it is all the more important to include study of texting conventions, and their differences from standard English. This would effectively give texting the same status as spoken English, which would be in sympathy with the way Tim Shortis describes SMS as 'written speech'. The idea that text messaging was 'talk written down' also arose in a 2003 account from ex-head of English Sarah Matthews of a lesson with Year 9 pupils.[14] Matthews reported unusual levels of engagement with questions about language use, and while it was a one-off lesson not informed by academic research in the area, it showed that the instincts of a good English teacher are to engage with this new mode of communication rather than try to stifle it.

General approaches

There are several ways you can approach text messaging as an English teacher:

➡ as a new focus for language study

➡ as a creative medium

➡ as a teaching medium.

WEBSITE

All of these have been tried in recent years, and perhaps all will eventually have a place in English teaching. The third of these – texting as a medium for teaching – is an area I will leave aside, because for one thing, the technology is still in development, and for another, it is not an English-specific application. All subjects might in some ways find use of mobile technologies to teach children outside the four walls of the classroom, and there is plenty of cutting-edge research going on in this area.[15] Probably more practicable in the classroom is to explore both the creative possibilities offered by the new medium, and the way it makes us focus on our use of language because of the restrictions it imposes on us. The creative possibilities were demonstrated by the g8way project case study, so in the rest of this section I will focus on language study. What we need to do here is to make clear to our learners that while there is nothing wrong with text messaging conventions, and in fact they are impressive in their sophistication at times, they are, like spoken English, to be distinguished from 'standard English'.[16]

Words and spelling: understanding language variation and language change

The approaches taken by Tim Shortis to texting can lead to productive work in reading and writing, vocabulary and spelling. One can look at:

➡ how meanings are changed when texts are adapted to different media;

➡ how language is used in imaginative, original and diverse ways;

➡ how techniques, structure, forms and styles vary.

WEBSITE

All of these are elements of the UK national curriculum for English.[17] Tim Shortis's work is not dissimilar in approach to that of Crispin Thurlow, whose 2003 paper on the topic is well worth reading, particularly if you are working with older students.[18] His sociolinguistic conclusions about the text messaging of young people were based on study of the usage of 159 teenagers in the United States. In the online journal *Discourse Analysis Online*, you can read discussion of his article alongside the text. Please be warned that the table of non-standard orthographic forms does contain some vocabulary in the 'g-clippings' section that is not suitable for classroom use.

There is also room for comparative study of language structure, and the use of text message conventions as a pupil-friendly way into more general language study, for example, of:

1. consonants and vowels

2. homophones

3. acronyms

4. signs and symbols.

Some practical thoughts on each of these are given below.

▌Teaching ideas, examples and advice

WEBSITE

The suggestions below are based on and inspired by the ideas on the Netting IT website which are aimed primarily at A level or undergraduate students but have wider applicability.[19] The basic approach is for students to collect their own corpus of text messages in order to conduct analyses of various kinds. The work which has been done by A level English students using this methodology has included:

➡ grouping and analysing messages according to their purpose and social context;

➡ examining the use of affective language, emoticons and exclamation marks;

➡ examining the extent and use of homophones;

➡ considering the similarities to speech;

➡ considering the reasons why texters use abbreviations;

➡ investigating the relationship between text messaging and accuracy in spelling.

Each of these, to a lesser or greater degree, might be addressed with much younger learners.

1. Surveys and questionnaires: gathering a corpus

In a Year 9 context, Sarah Matthews used a questionnaire as a preliminary to text language study, and this was no doubt a helpful way to start: beginning from and therefore validating their own practice and experience.[20] English teachers planning work with younger learners might draw from both of these approaches. A corpus might be collected by a group of students rather than an individual, or from a group of people such as family members, and it might be much smaller than the 100 messages suggested on the Netting IT website – perhaps the aim would be for the whole class to collect 100. I think this sort of work might be done with pupils in Years 6 to 9, but modifications will need to be made according to the viability of phones actually being used. If we assume that most pupils will have a mobile phone of their own, or a mobile phone user at home, then these tasks might be done either entirely as homework, or with messages being transcribed from phones and brought into class. Pupils who do not have a phone of their own could involve family or friends, or they could be paired with a pupil who does have a phone.

Suggested prompt sheet or questionnaire:

Starter questions:

- Do you have a phone?
- Which generation is it?
- How many people in your family have phones?
- How many times a day do you use it for texting?
- How many times a day do you use it for making phone calls?

Statistics:

Make a note of:
- Total words sent in texts.
- Total paragraphs/'message length' of texts.
- Total characters (excluding spaces) sent in texts.

Make simple calculations to establish the following:

➡ average number of words per message;
➡ average number of characters per message;
➡ average word length.

An easy way to highlight all the differences between usage in texts and standard/grammatical English is to run a spellchecker/grammar-checker on a message and write a commentary on all the things it finds 'wrong'. Ask how many are really 'wrong' as opposed to being SMS conventions.

2. Looking at context and style

Even in text messaging people use different styles, so conduct a survey of:

1. How many contacts you have in your phone.

2. Of these contacts how many/what proportion are
   - School friends?
   - Friends from outside school?
   - Relatives?
   - Other?

3. How many friends do you have who are not in your contacts?

4. Compare ways of texting to friends and family:
   - Do you always use the same abbreviations?
   - Do you write in more grammatical sentences?
   - Do you have a different way of opening a text/greeting or closing it?
   - Do you 'sign' your name at the end? Do you just use an initial? Do you sign off in the same way to everyone?
   - Which sort of smiley convention(s) do you use?

Use these questions as discussion starters and record the exchanges.

3. Thinking about the rules for text message spelling

Although there are clearly rules to be followed, they are many and varied, and a single word might produce several different variations following different rules. One could start with 'love' as an example, which can be abbreviated to luv or lv, or the use of 'x' in 'thanx' compared to 'x' in 'xpect'. Ask pupils to describe the rule being applied in each case, then discuss a few examples such as these:

Text	Standard English	Rule
bout	about	omitting the unpronounced vowel
goin	going	omitting the unpronounced consonant
wot	what	1. omitting the silent letter 2. making the spelling of the vowel phonic
ful	full	not doubling the consonant

Of course there are many more rules to the spelling conventions of texting than those four in the table, but rather than try to dictate what they are, why not ask the pupils themselves to investigate the rules? Extend this table with some other words suggested by the pupils, then ask them to analyse a selection of other words, putting them under headings that describe the rules. Dan Sutch found that this approach worked very well even with 9–10 year olds, giving pupils the feeling that they were explorers of the rules of language rather than simply followers of them.

To consolidate this work, create a grid of words with speech inserted in comment boxes to illustrate the 'phonic' spellings.

4. Related language topics

Here are some specific thoughts about how to use SMS messages as a springboard into areas of language study which might normally seem rather dull:

a) vowels and consonants

b) homophones

c) acronyms

d) signs and symbols.

a) Vowels and consonants

'Abbreviation' is not a sufficiently precise word to describe the peculiar style of compressed language seen in texting. This is mainly because of the phonemic tricks that are played within certain words, notably the use of the numbers 2, 4 and 8, and various letters but perhaps most commonly c and u. Such rules combine with the omission of vowels to produce a quite complex code.

Examples:

Abbreviation	Standard English spelling
Cya or c u	See you
Xlnt	excellent
2mrw	tomorrow

If we separate out these two features of texting we can use them as a focus for spelling work:

➡ Compare conventionally used abbreviations which omit vowels such as Ltd, Slctr, Dr.

➡ Take a selection of words which have vowel omission and ask pupils to fill in the missing vowels.

➡ Ask pupils to produce a list of ten or more of their own abbreviations and afterwards test a partner, or the class, on the missing vowels.

➡ Mix up text messaging and conventional abbreviations and double the learning.

b) Homophones

The phonic spellings are sometimes quite complicated because phonic abbreviations are used not only for whole words as in these phonic letters:

Y = why

X = ex

B = be

U = you

C = see

or these phonic numbers:

2 = too, to, two

4 = for, four

but also for parts of words, for example 'neway' for 'anyway', 'l8r for 'later' and 'str8' for 'straight'.

Here is another obvious opportunity for a 'word wall' of homophones, that includes not only text messaging homophones but others too, and this time perhaps using animated GIFs (Graphic Interchange Format) for a really dynamic feel:

WEBSITE

Use PaintShop Pro to create frames showing the letters and words. Images found from internet searches, or the Microsoft Office proprietary 'Clipart' (best used sparingly) can be combined in Animation Shop[21] to produce an impressive animated sequence, as in figure 2.4.

Fig 2.4

CD–ROM Ch 2/Homophones PowerPoint presentation

You can then link your animated GIF to a sound file by inserting it into a single PowerPoint slide, so that both the image and the sound appear at the same time, as you can see from the example on the CD-ROM. When you insert your sound file (figures 2.5 and 2.6, overleaf) it will ask whether you want the file to play automatically or when you click on the icon.

Fig 2.5

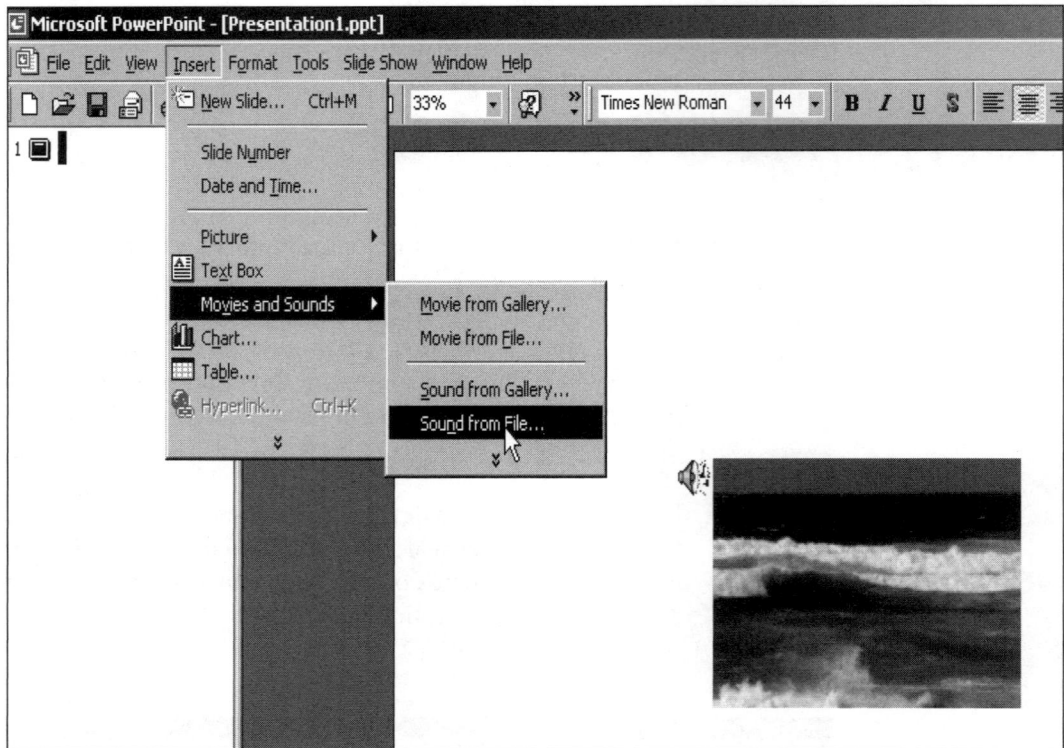

What might the sound file be? Perhaps just the sound of the homophone being made once, or perhaps someone reciting the playground rhyme 'A sailor went to sea'? If the animation is looped, the visual stimulus of words and images will continue rotating while the audio runs. If you want it as part of an automated sequence of slides, make sure the slideshow transition time is greater than the duration of the audio file so that the sound is not clipped (figure 2.6).

Fig 2.6

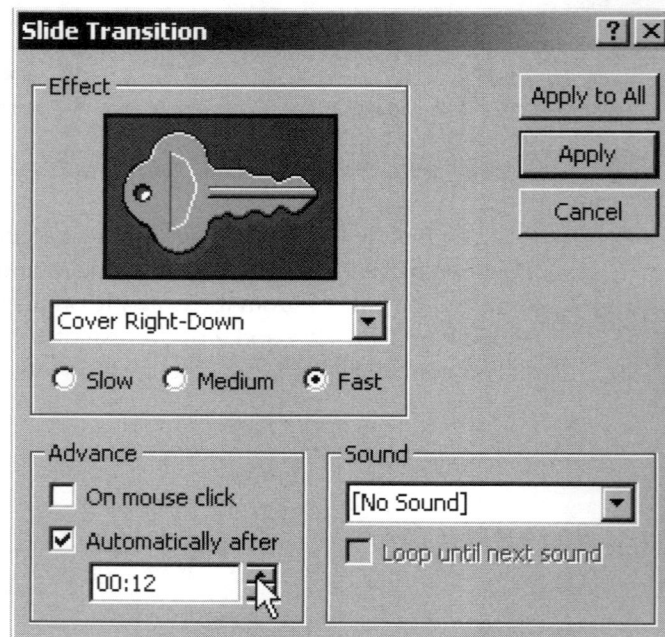

c) Acronyms

Text messaging 'initialisms' remind us that acronyms are not just a written form. Even before messaging, terms like ETA (estimated time of arrival) had moved from a written abbreviation of a commonly used phrase (in this case used first in the air industry) to a spoken idiom. Other examples are:

➡ SP – starting price, from horse-racing.

➡ LBW – leg before wicket, from cricket.

➡ AWOL – absent without leave, from the military forces.

➡ TTFN – ta ta for now, from colloquial English.

And there are many recent ones from new technologies:

TV, DVD, CD, VCD.

Popular texting acronyms/initialisms:		
AFK	=	away from keyboard
ATK	=	at the keyboard
BAK	=	back at keyboard
BBL	=	be back later
BFN or B4N	=	bye for now
BRB	=	be right back
BTW	=	by the way
FWIW	=	for what it's worth
GMTA	=	great minds think alike
IMHO	=	in my humble opinion
IRL	=	in real life
LOL	=	laughing out loud
LTNS	=	long time no see
TBH	=	to be honest
TTYL	=	talk to you later
ROFL	=	rolling on the floor laughing
WTG	=	way to go!
OIC	=	Oh, I see

WEBSITE

WEBSITE

See how many can be collected from shared knowledge, and invent new acronyms for other three-word phrases that people use, for example CUS for 'see you soon', JAM for 'just a minute', and so on.[22] This requires awareness of what constitutes colloquial English, and is interesting to highlight how formulaic spoken English can be. Many more current examples can be found online at dedicated sites such as Lingo2Word, which allows you to search for and translate acronyms.[23]

d) Signs and symbols

WEBSITE

Emoticons are interesting starting points for discussion of symbols and language. They originated it seems from the simple smiley face :) first used by Scott Fahlman in the early 1980s.[24] While the smiley and the emoticon have a shared lineage (see the Smiley World and Smiley Dictionary websites), animations like those found on Emoticons4u show how the genre has

WEBSITE

developed from punctuation marks denoting emotions into a wider use of pictorial symbolism.[25]

Ask pupils what exactly the different faces mean, and how/when they would use them. For example, :-p or :p (tongue sticking out) – what might this mean? Is it rude? Does it imply embarrassment? Or is it just a funny face? Ask a series of different people what they think it means, record their answers, then attach the sound files to the icons.

You can also do this with a range of emoticons and/or groupings of them. More recent variations on these do not always derive from punctuation marks but are modifications of the yellow 'smiley' face. This is an ideal exercise to do in Word using the Insert Comment feature, adding not only the sound file of those recorded answers, but also transcriptions/edited paraphrases of the responses in the text comment box. First create a table in which to hold the graphic icons, the punctuation marks where relevant, and perhaps a simple explanation of their meaning, as in figure 2.7:

Fig 2.7

Emoticon	punctuation	signifies
😊	:) or :-)	happy
😢	:(	sad
😑	:o	bored [yawning]
😣	:e	very unhappy [crying]
😠	>:/	annoyed / angry / irritated
😲	:o	surprised / shocked
😉	;) or ;-)	winking
😀	:D	laughing

Then produce sequences of them. Add comments showing what pupils think they might mean, by highlighting them then adding text with the Insert Comment command, as in figure 2.8. Also add sound files, either at the time using Word's recording software, or by inserting a sound file recorded separately.

Fig 2.8

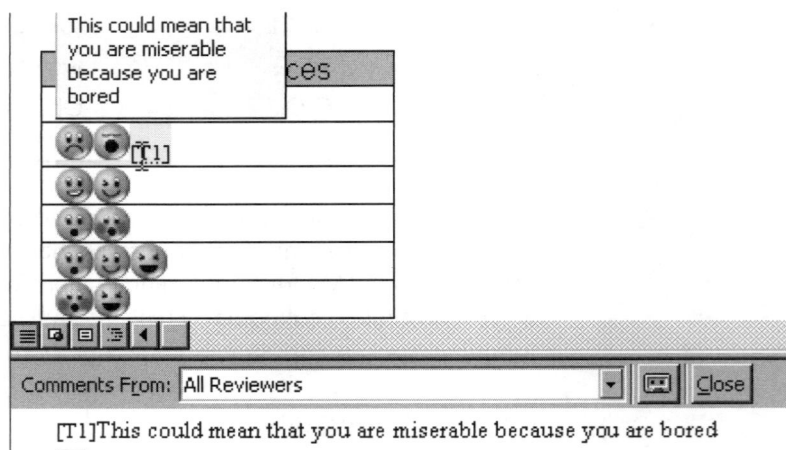

[T1]This could mean that you are miserable because you are bored

Further discussion and research topics:

→ Are words signs?

→ Why do we use symbols instead of words?

→ Find out more about icons/hieroglyphics/graffiti.

Case study 2

Tim Shortis: VAK teaching of spelling

WEBSITE

Background

This case study is a particularly interesting one because it involved a partnership between an academic tutor interested in the teaching and learning of spelling, and a recently qualified primary school teacher with an interest in ICT. The work was with a Year 6 class, and it demonstrates the way that ICT can raise both the teacher's and pupils' interest in literacy. While the features of teaching and learning used here are reproducible with generic software packages, the starting point for the work was a particular software package on CD-ROM called *WordRoot*.[1] This is an interactive, multimedia learning tool which engages the user with visual and auditory stimuli in order to aid learning of the origins of words – mainly those with Greek or Latin roots which are often considered difficult vocabulary for primary level. University tutor Tim Shortis introduced the teacher both to the *WordRoot* CD-ROM and to the principles which he saw as making the software effective as a learning tool. Some of the aspects which he wanted to focus on were:

➡ The kinesthetic learning involved via interactivity;

➡ The visual element;

➡ The 'language approach to spelling'.

The last of these is key to the *WordRoot* approach, where spelling is learned as a by-product of learning about the language, rather than as a stand-alone, memory-test operation. So, not only should the memory be enhanced by VAK approaches, it should also be reinforced by understanding.

Some key statements from Bruner underpin this approach (see figure 2.9):

➡ 'Educational encounters, to begin with, should result in understanding, not mere performance.'[2]

➡ ...learning is 'best when it is participatory, proactive, communal, collaborative, and given over to the constructing of meanings rather than the receiving of them'.[3]

Fig 2.9

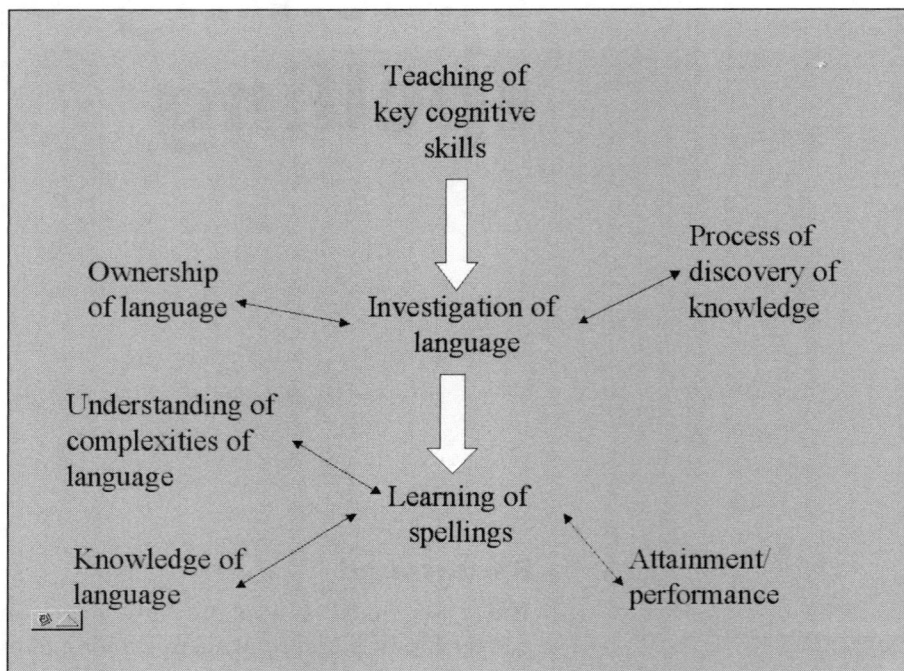

By this model the teacher is a guide to understanding who helps students discover knowledge for themselves rather than simply receive it.

Dan Sutch, the classroom teacher, engaged with the pedagogic theory as well as the classroom practice and highlighted the following aspects as being vital to the success of the experiment:

➡ easily malleable texts;

➡ a visually stimulating environment with animated texts and pictures;

➡ sound effects and voices, creating a multisensory interface;

➡ kinesthetic learning – hand movement to individual letters;

➡ the 'wow!' factor.

Teaching and learning objectives
The objectives for pupils were:

➡ To learn about the relation between spoken and written English by looking and listening.

➡ To investigate connections between cognate or related words in order to expand vocabulary and deepen understanding of language.

How it was done
The kinesthetic element was transferred from the virtual to the real with giant word jigsaws which were created by the pupils themselves and then pieced

together for wall display (see figure 2.10). The visual aspect was accentuated by the use of large-screen projection of the words and word-parts being studied.

Fig 2.10

To the classroom teacher, the 'wow factor' for learners was the use of ICT itself. He produced his own teaching materials using PowerPoint, focusing initially on individual words. The slideshow facility meant that he could create a great deal of visual stimulation simply through use of font size and type, and colour of both font and background. The slideshow (figure 2.11 and CD-ROM) projected onto a screen or whiteboard magnified the impact when teaching a whole class.

CD-ROM Ch 2/Word Meanings
PowerPoint
presentation

Fig 2.11

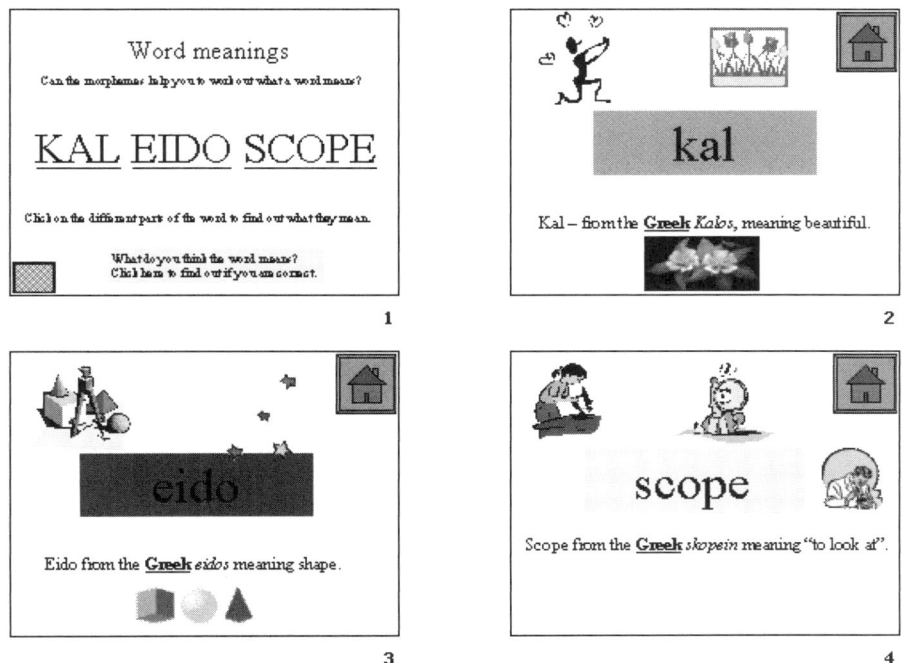

CD-ROM Ch 2/Changing Words
PowerPoint
presentation

Inspired by the 'Wall of Talk' from *WordRoot*, Dan Sutch got the pupils to produce 'word walls' using PowerPoint with a variety of approaches, including this mixture of vocabulary and key words relevant to language change (figure 2.12 and CD-ROM). Pupils explaining different terms can be heard when you click on the icons. Both the production of this material and then the re-use of it involves all-round VAK learning.

Fig 2.12

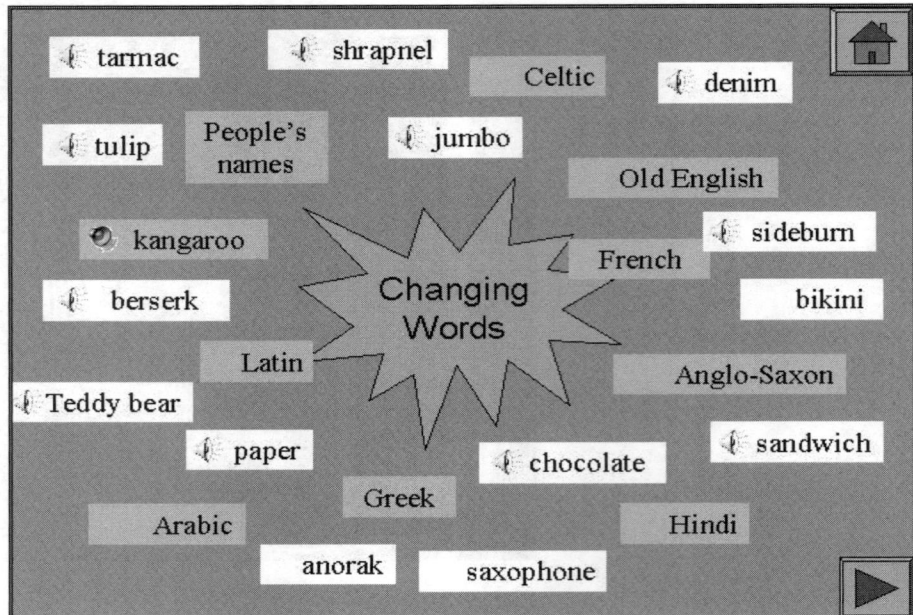

You can see from the example above that Dan imitated the randomness of John Davitt's 'Wall of Talk' (figure 2.13) in his choice of key terms to click on.

Traditional methods for learning spellings, including mnemonics and syllable breakdown, can also be applied to this software and used in the classroom, an example of which can be seen on the CD-ROM.

CD-ROM Ch 2/Word Walls –
Spellings PowerPoint
presentation

Outcomes

The class teacher found clear evidence of significant improvements from the class in a variety of areas, including:

- ➡ spelling
- ➡ vocabulary
- ➡ presentation
- ➡ extended writing
- ➡ understanding of etymology
- ➡ interest in language
- ➡ understanding of language use in relation to purpose and audience.

As Dan Sutch put it:

> Beyond improved test scores, the students also benefited from being involved with the projects. Their ease with trying out new words and their interest in actively searching for new knowledge was amazing to observe. Over time they became active learners, searching for new words, new contexts; investigating language and testing their hypotheses.

CD-ROM Ch 2/Word Walls

The impressive 'Word Wall' presentations which the children produced (see the CD-ROM), are evidence of the energetic involvement in understanding of the English language that this approach generated.

Doing this in the classroom

1. A PowerPoint version of *WordRoot* links

Take a compound word and create links to slides showing its component parts. On each slide have:

1. the word in writing
2. the word being spoken
3. a written definition
4. someone using the word in a sentence (context) or explaining what it means to them (ask an adult).
5. image(s) to represent the meaning (clip art or web-searched image).

2. Wall of Talk

Fig 2.13

You can develop your own versions of the Wall of Talk (see figure 2.13) in a variety of ways. The exciting thing about the original is that there are no fixed rules in terms of the relation between the visual and aural content. The unexpected element is part of the pleasure and also inspires the learner to think, particularly encouraging holistic right-brain thinking. Creating a Wall of Talk can be as much a learning process as using one, so it is a worthwhile collaborative task if you have the facilities for sound recording.

CD-ROM

For further inspiration take a look at some of the examples Dan Sutch produced with his students, which can be found on the CD-ROM.

Chapter 3

Information and English

Part 1: Information handling with ICT

In this section you will:

- consider the role of ICT in information handling as part of English teaching;
- look at good practice and general approaches to using ICT in this area;
- consider practical ways to make information retrieval exciting to students.

Part 2: Databases, thinking skills and writing

In this section you will:

- look at what databases are;
- consider why the study of databases is relevant and useful in English teaching;
- look at some general approaches to teaching about databases;
- suggest practical ways you can introduce databases into your English teaching.

Part 1

Information handling with ICT

WEBSITE

▌ Why do it?

There has always been an uneasy but necessary collaboration between English teachers and school librarians. Whether teaching the basics of the Dewey decimal system, or information retrieval, English teachers have been expected to teach research and study skills that will be applicable across the curriculum. Anyone who was a teacher in the late 1980s when CD-ROMs were introduced to school libraries will appreciate that information retrieval, and now information 'handling', has become a largely electronic process. Unless a school has an extraordinarily well-stocked reference section on the bookshelves, the CD-ROM and online resources will be the most effective way to practise those skills. Only a decade ago, you would have been unlikely to resort to the internet for educational research, though CD-ROMs were becoming available at major libraries containing resources such as encyclopedias, or the Chadwyck-Healey poetry archives. Now, much can be found online, whether by subscription or for free. Over the past decade Microsoft's online encyclopedia Encarta became a standard source for school homework, to the concern of many who saw this as a lazy approach to research. At least now there is a range of options, including the impressively omni-lingual Wikipedia and the Columbia encyclopaedia.[1] As it was before this electronic revolution, it is up to English departments in consultation with librarians to decide what are the best online resources to subscribe to, but we can at least consider some of the best ways to utilize those resources which are available.

Of course there is a problem with data handling in English teaching, in terms of our knowledge and skills base, and in terms of the curriculum. In the UK curriculum for English there is indeed room for it to exist: elements of the statutory requirements for teaching reading can be mapped against key 'information handling' skills, and national literacy strategy at Key Stage 3 features similar skills under the heading of research and study skills. There are also proponents of 'information literacy' for whom information retrieval and using information for problem solving is central to ICT. Mike Eisenberg and Bob Berkowitz, who developed the 'Big Six' stages of information problem solving,

WEBSITE

refer to this as a 'metacognitive scaffold'.[2] This suggests that, though they might be presented as such, these are not ICT-specific skills, but rather general research and problem-solving skills. As such they are still of interest to English teachers, who have long acted as a 'service industry' to other curriculum subjects by focusing on generic study skills.

General teaching approaches
The best practice would seem to be to build an electronic resource centre using a school intranet and drawing together various electronic resources. Of course, this will normally be done in conjunction with the school library. A prime example of this is the resource centre built up by a head of English, Duncan Grey, at Hinchingbrooke School. This includes audio-visual resources and databases on video, CD-ROM and DVD, and software shared across the school network.[3]

WEBSITE

WEBSITE

There is also a valuable online resource centre, the VLRC Directory, designed for schools use.[4] It makes searches of numerous online directories selected by librarians and teachers, for materials relevant to a wide range of topics. It provides a good starting point for extended writing and also for research on literature. It does have an American slant, because most of the directories are US-based, and this will be particularly obvious on current affairs topics. British history, however, can be searched separately.

The Virtual Learning Resource Center is a valuable way of making controlled, pre-limited searches of the internet, but often searching and browsing is not like that – it is much more random and unpredictable. Understanding 'browsing' is in itself a cognitive challenge for children (and for that matter adults!). The fact that there are so many variants on browsing methods across different sites shows that this is still a developing science. But search engines are the most common way of searching for material on the web, and the rules for these are now fairly standardized.

WEBSITE

WEBSITE

WEBSITE

Everyone knows about Google, but there are numerous options for searching, with many other search-dedicated sites which are also well established, for example AltaVista, Hot Bot and Ask Jeeves.[5] There are also 'metasearch' engines such as Metacrawler and Mamma which will provide you with the search returns of several different engines.[6] There are browsing options too for people with various disabilities. People with visual impairment or reading difficulties rely on speech output, Braille displays or screen magnification; and in many cases use the keyboard instead of the mouse. People who can't use a keyboard rely either on voice recognition of spoken commands, or on switch devices which can be controlled by head, mouth or eye movements. There are online browsing solutions for each of these scenarios.[7]

So what are the problems with these search engines as research tools if we are to encourage children to learn how to use them?

➡ Value and reliability is an obvious concern, and it is not uncommon to find yourself reading a discussion board thread on the topic you are interested in, and suddenly realizing that it was all uninformed nonsense.

➡ Out of date material: the same thread on a discussion board might be several years old: web pages returned from searches might contain out of date information.

➡ Redundant returns: unless you are searching for something that can be uniquely identified with a word or two, you are likely to be presented with a great deal of unwanted information.

While the simple word-search is the most commonly used, all of these sites will have 'advanced' search options which address at least some of these difficulties, allowing the user to modify or 'refine' the search by a range of means, according to

➡ the type of internet domain, for example .gov or .ac.uk sites;

➡ the last update date of the page;

➡ language.

WEBSITE

While these are likely to be catered for by drop-down lists or tick-boxes, all major search engines offer the function of Boolean logic. Even though this is mathematical logic, it seems to be perfectly sensible to include the basics of these logical terms when teaching research skills.[8] This is not nearly as daunting as it sounds: while some search engines will allow use of 'or' and other Boolean operators in advanced search options, all now utilize the options below in their general search boxes:

Function	How
Must include the term	+
Must exclude the term	-
Must include the whole phrase	' '

Introducing pupils to web retrieval skills via Boolean logic probably doesn't sound the best strategy except for the most left-brain-oriented learners, but there are plenty of fun ways to stimulate interest and develop skills in web-searching.

Teaching ideas, examples and advice

WEBSITE

In June 2004, the first of the lesson plans produced on behalf of the DfES by NATE began to appear on the Standards Site, and interestingly one of these was a Year 7 unit on 'Searching and selecting'.[9] The end-products of these information-retrieval and presentation ideas are PowerPoint slideshows. In the context of this book's advocacy of visual, auditory and kinesthetic learning approaches, it is difficult to recommend these materials as anything but a starting point or framework. To be fair to the lesson plans, they do make reference to pupils saving 'text, pictures and/or sound' from internet downloads, but the example slideshows present purely textual information and the underlying premise seems to be that data are 'facts about things'. The sample information sheets and questions about Christianity and Islam are worthy but also wordy. Yet the lesson plans are a laudable attempt to combine English and ICT teaching and learning objectives, so one could use them as a basis for more adventurous work, perhaps incorporating some of the ideas below to offset the alienating effects of word-heavy information.

1. Googlewhacking

Before looking at image searching it is worth mentioning the phenomenon of 'Googlewhacking' in our search for exciting approaches to online information retrieval. Googlewhacking is about trying to devise a combination of two search terms that will return only a single web page (even without speech-marks around them). This now has its own website for fans of this hobby, producing such 'whacks' as 'ambidextrous scallywags' and 'assonant octosyllable' which apparently produced only a single result, at least before they appeared on the front page of the Googlewhack site.[10] Words which have potential for whacking are, as those examples suggest, likely to be interesting vocabulary, so this site might be a useful starting place for English teachers. After looking at the amusing collection in the 'whack stack' and deciphering some of them, pupils can download the rules and try to discover their own. They can even check online their pairs of words which, if they really produce only one result, can be submitted to the online list.

WEBSITE

2. Image searching with Google

Several search engines, including Google and AltaVista, now provide image searches as well as text. Of course there are worries about children trawling the web for images, but filters are provided to stop any indecent images being returned on a search. Taking Google as our example, the default will be 'moderate filtering' which prevents sexually explicit images being returned; for extra caution you can adjust the 'safe search' options by going to Preferences and setting them to 'strict filtering', which also cuts out the chance of linking to any dubious text.

Your initial search will return rows of 'thumbnail' images (see figure 3.1).

Fig 3.1

You can use these images at this size, but if you want to enlarge them you will need to click on the image you have selected, which will give you details of the page on which it was located. Often you will still have to expand the image further to see its full size (see figure 3.2)

Fig 3.2

Google™

Health Makes You Smile!

Image has been scaled down. See full-size image.

www.chiro.org/chimages/ logos/logo.jpg
364 x 322 pixels - 23k
This image may be subject to copyright.

When you are happy with the scale of the image save it by simply right clicking and selecting 'save picture as' (see figure 3.3).

Fig 3.3

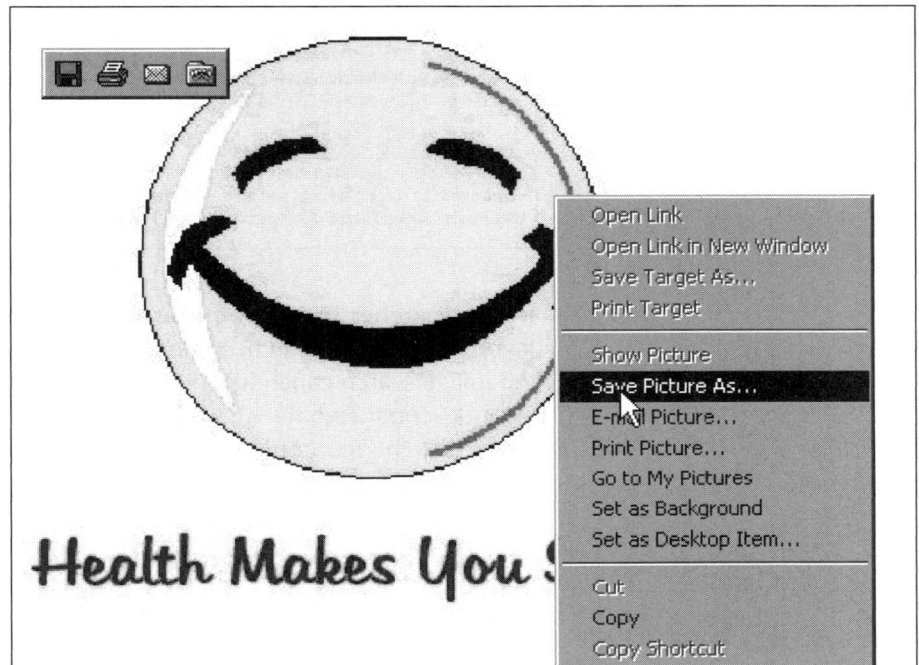

3. Boolean searching

Silly searches for must include

In an ordinary text search you can have fun by devising the most absurd and unlikely connections and then writing down the interesting results. 'Ostrich +hailstones' returned a fascinating selection (see figure 3.4 overleaf). (It's worth noting that, because of the way most major search engines work, it will make little difference whether or not the + sign is used since they will search for all terms entered in the box.)

Fig 3.4

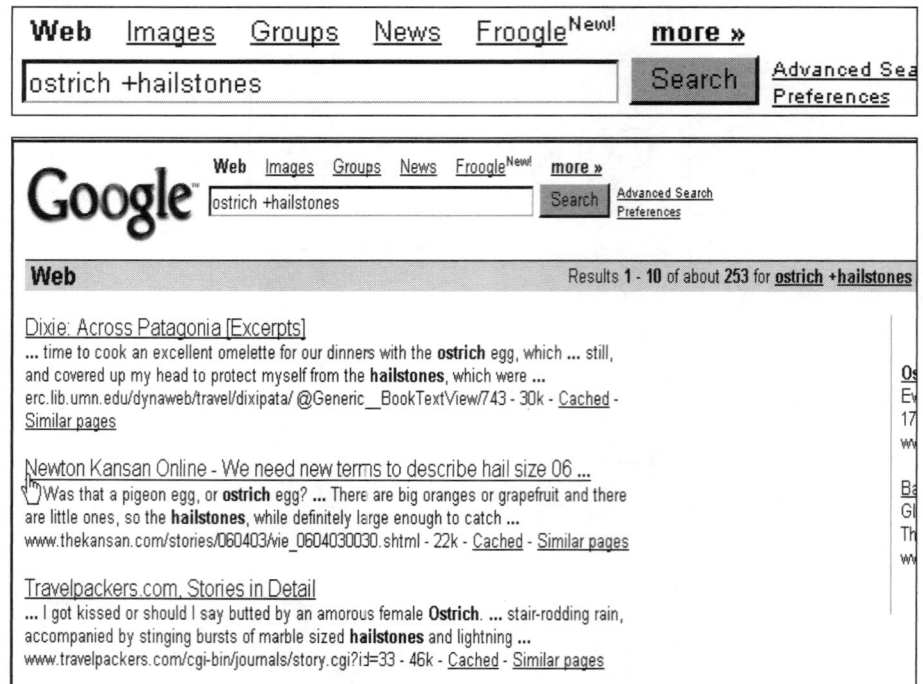

Image searches for must exclude

If you feel that text searches are unlikely to grab the attention of pupils, try using the image search capability, which is a fun way to learn. To produce the 'must exclude' command, the minus sign must immediately precede the second term in the search. You could start by demonstrating the principle with 'cats -cats' which will of course produce no results at all. Then try a search for 'cats-siamese' or 'cats -tigers' which would narrow down the search a little, excluding Siamese cats or tigers from the returned material. Illustrating the point is perhaps better achieved with idiosyncratic searches using pairs of words which are often found together:

➡ 'Potter -Harry' (this worked better for me in a text search than with images).

➡ 'Manchester -United' (even this will not purge the return of football-related images, but it filters some out. See figure 3.5).

➡ 'pop -music'.

Fig 3.5

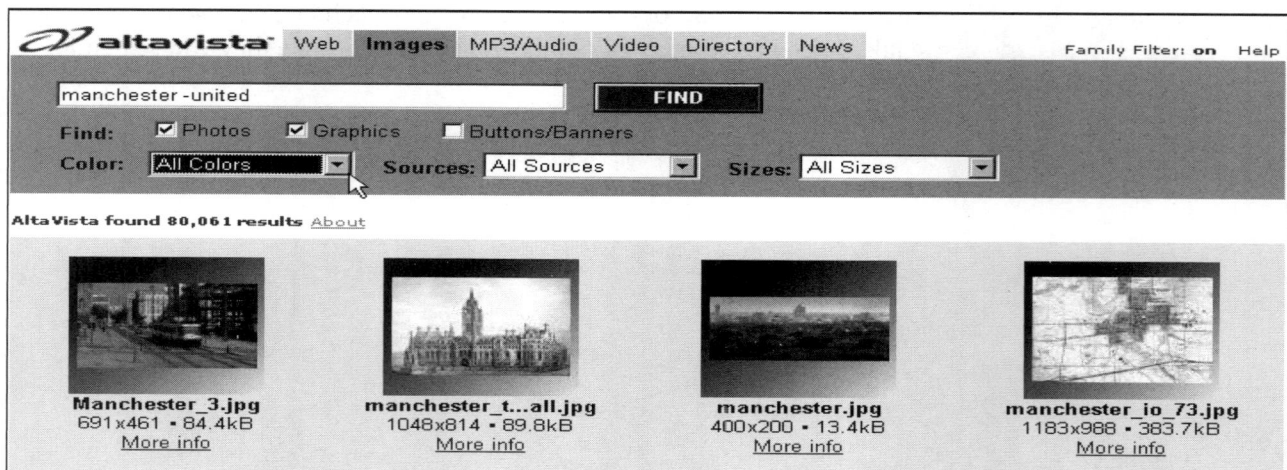

WEBSITE

Compare these results to searches made with the first word alone. Ask pupils to think up their own illustrative word pairs and test them with a search engine.

Set exercises such as trying to find the best search terms to use to return pictures of the Queen without any of the famous rock band, and so on.

Searches for must include phrase

Use famous quotations or proverbs: these can be found in profusion on the web.[11] For some carefully selected lines the search might even return audio files (you can use AltaVista to limit your search to MP3 files – see sub-section 5. Audio-visual searching).

Searches might seem to work much the same whether or not you use quotation marks, but using them ensures that all the words are searched. This can be useful as some search engines omit short, common linking words. For example if you were to search for 'I had a dream' without quotation marks the search engine might well omit 'I' and 'a'.

4. Image searching for thinking skills

As with word searches for Googlewhacking, web image searches done imaginatively can build vocabulary and make children think about words and language.

Let's imagine a group is performing a variation on the 'speech tagging' exercise (already described in Chapter 2): saying 'Hello' in different tones of voice. The process itself will become part of the learning exercise. Lateral thinking, as well as synonyms, might be required in order to come up with an appropriate image.

Ask pairs to find images to go with ways of saying 'Hello'. The likelihood is that the most appropriate images will be ones showing facial expressions, but one might allow poetic licence for older or more able pupils, as in the examples below:

Example 1. *For younger learners:* find an image to go with a happy voice. For differentiation, more able learners are not allowed to use the word 'happy' in their searches. Create a folder called 'happy' to save your images in and try

➡ 'joyful' or other synonyms and see which gets best results.
➡ 'smiling'.
➡ 'hooray', 'yippee' or 'great'.
➡ adding the word 'face' if the single word is not producing good enough results.

Example 2. *For older learners:* find an image to go with a 'quizzical' tone of voice.

➡ Try 'quizzical' (adjective).
➡ Try 'question' (noun).
➡ Try 'why?' 'what?' 'who?' 'where?' and so on (interrogative adverbs).
➡ Given that question marks are ignored by most search engines, which is best of the above to use?
➡ See which produces best results, and consider why.

By searching for the images, they are understanding the principles of searching, and understanding language use; both its descriptive and 'performative' aspects.

5. Audio-visual searching

AltaVista will search separately for images, MP3 files (a compressed audio file format which is smaller than other types and therefore convenient for downloading), other audio files and for video. While Google goes for simplicity, AltaVista provides a number of ways of refining the search, for example with sound files you can define the file-type and playback duration:

Fig 3.6

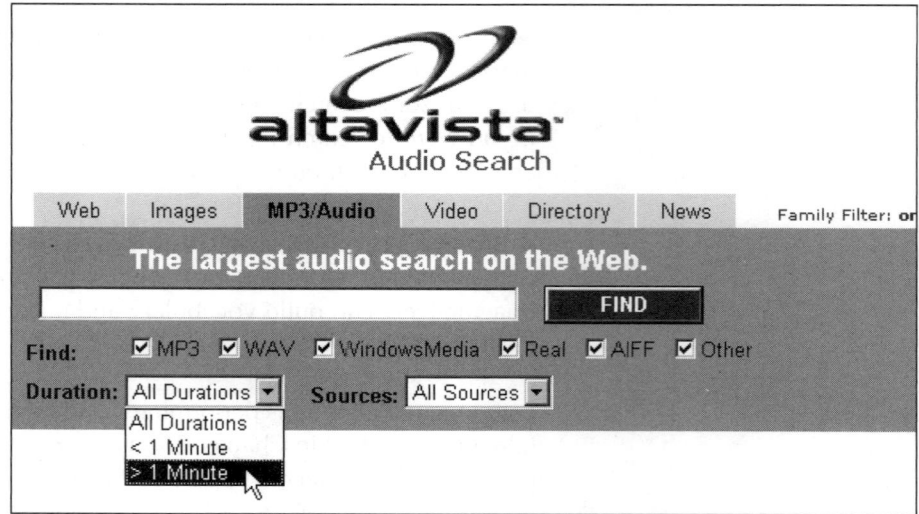

Try searches for video or sound files of famous people from the twentieth century. You should be prepared for a few dead ends in the search returns, but a search on 'Mandela' for example can return some wonderful material. A project where students had to find video or audio material on a hero (or maybe villain?) would be a good stimulus here. Unfortunately, it will not always be possible for students to save and re-use video if it is in Real Media format, but where it is saveable, it can be incorporated into a presentation along with an explanation of why this person is a hero to them.

WEBSITE

The example opposite (figure 3.7), which uses facts about Mandela's life from a searched website, a video[12] and an image from a search for the South African flag, took only a few minutes to produce in PowerPoint:

Fig 3.7

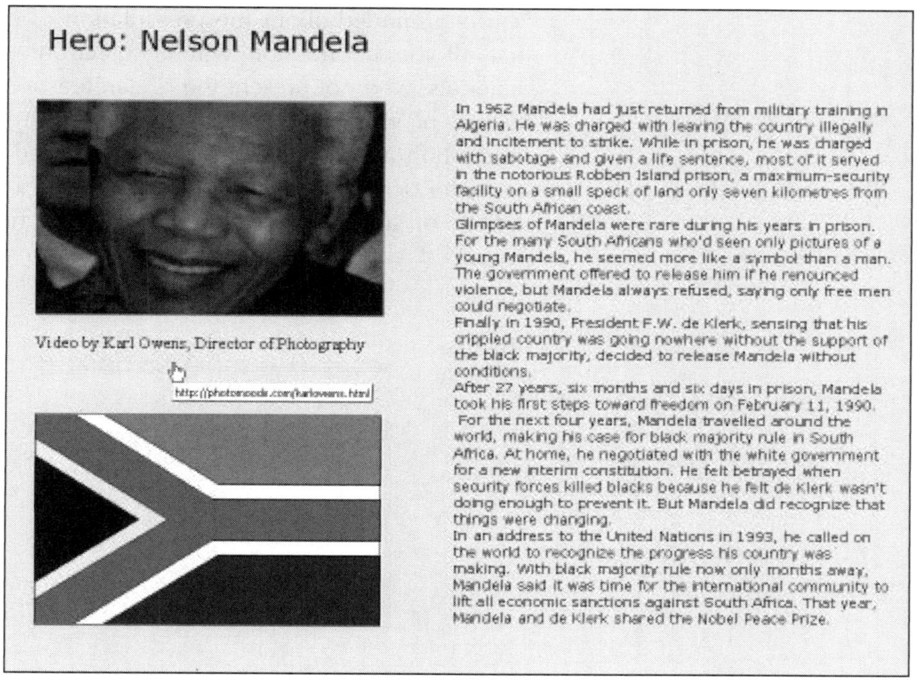

CD—ROM Ch 3/Nelson Mandela
PowerPoint
presentation

Hero: Nelson Mandela

Video by Karl Owens, Director of Photography

http://photoneeds.com/karlowens.html

In 1962 Mandela had just returned from military training in Algeria. He was charged with leaving the country illegally and incitement to strike. While in prison, he was charged with sabotage and given a life sentence, most of it served in the notorious Robben Island prison, a maximum-security facility on a small speck of land only seven kilometres from the South African coast.

Glimpses of Mandela were rare during his years in prison. For the many South Africans who'd seen only pictures of a young Mandela, he seemed more like a symbol than a man. The government offered to release him if he renounced violence, but Mandela always refused, saying only free men could negotiate.

Finally in 1990, President F.W. de Klerk, sensing that his crippled country was going nowhere without the support of the black majority, decided to release Mandela without conditions.

After 27 years, six months and six days in prison, Mandela took his first steps toward freedom on February 11, 1990. For the next four years, Mandela travelled around the world, making his case for black majority rule in South Africa. At home, he negotiated with the white government for a new interim constitution. He felt betrayed when security forces killed blacks because he felt de Klerk wasn't doing enough to prevent it. But Mandela did recognize that things were changing.

In an address to the United Nations in 1993, he called on the world to recognize the progress his country was making. With black majority rule now only months away, Mandela said it was time for the international community to lift all economic sanctions against South Africa. That year, Mandela and de Klerk shared the Nobel Peace Prize.

More ideas about producing this kind of multimedia presentation can be found in the next chapter.

6. Online research projects

An obvious way to consolidate data retrieval and handling skills is a project which will require use of electronic information. The scope here for English teachers is almost unlimited. It could be about current affairs or a topical issue, or even a literary topic (see Chapter 7 for more ideas). A helpful model is Duncan Grey's outline for a series of lessons on planning a holiday, aimed at Key Stage 4 students. He includes references to the ICT skills learned as well as relevant English assessment objectives (see figure 3.8).[13]

WEBSITE

Fig 3.8

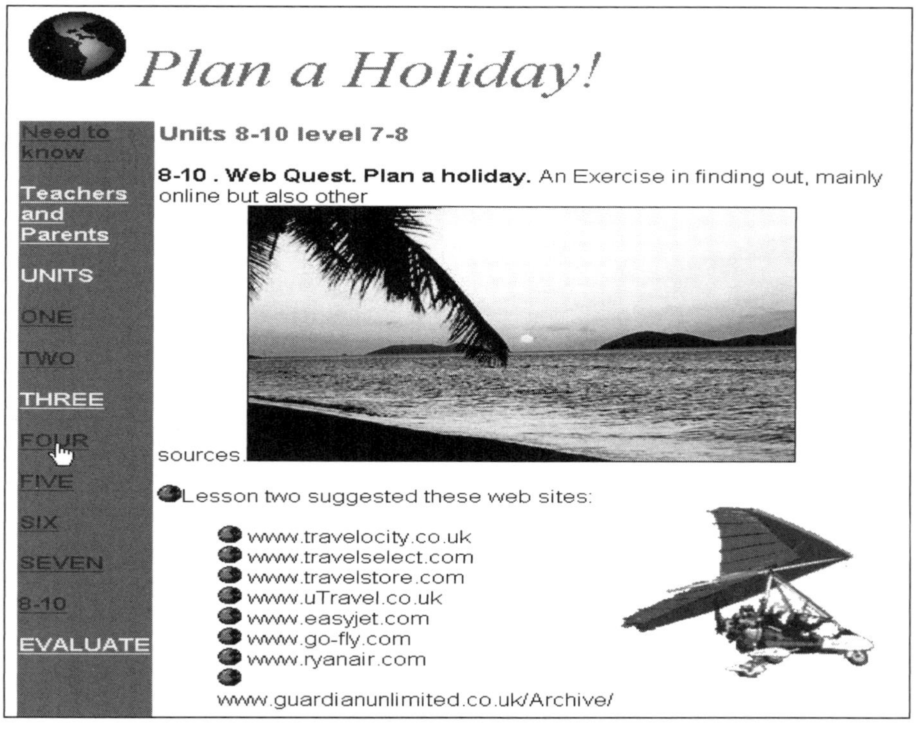

Plan a Holiday!

Need to know

Teachers and Parents

UNITS

ONE

TWO

THREE

FOUR

FIVE

SIX

SEVEN

8-10

EVALUATE

Units 8-10 level 7-8

8-10 . Web Quest. Plan a holiday. An Exercise in finding out, mainly online but also other

sources

Lesson two suggested these web sites:

www.travelocity.co.uk
www.travelselect.com
www.travelstore.com
www.uTravel.co.uk
www.easyjet.com
www.go-fly.com
www.ryanair.com

www.guardianunlimited.co.uk/Archive/

Be open-minded about the presentation of outcomes of this research. Given that all the information will be electronic, and may include audio-visual materials, why not present the research as a multimedia text or as web pages? Instead of writing a report, students might script a review of their holiday destination and present it to camera; instead of the transcript of an interview, an audio or video file can be inserted into a presentation. Some ideas for the variety of approaches you might take, and the way multimedia can be presented, can be found in Chapter 4: 'New ways of writing'.

Part 2

Databases, thinking skills and writing

Why do it?

There are two ways of thinking about information in relation to English. One is a fairly traditional way, which brings what might in the past have been called 'library skills' under the aegis of the English teacher. In this respect English has been a service industry to other subjects, often focusing on research and study skills. More recently we talk in terms of 'information retrieval', which is seen as a component skill within reading itself, so there is an obvious way here for English to put the 'I' into ICT. The other way of thinking about information in relation to English perhaps puts the 'C' into ICT: thinking about how the organization of 'data' helps us to communicate clearly. Understanding database and management principles will help learners organize their thoughts, and by extension could aid the ability to organize material in non-fiction writing of various kinds. It might seem a very functional approach to language, but in simple terms, data management and handling are about putting things in categories, just as writing in paragraphs is.

I think we need to get beyond thinking of databases as just a tool for us, or as electronic reference books. When I first encountered databases in the mid-1990s, having been involved in research for several years, their potential was immediately obvious. By the time I had finished that research I wished I had known about databases from the start, and not just because I was able to find various databases containing material that was useful. Beyond that usefulness in searching, there was a feeling that understanding databases a little earlier would have made easier the whole process of organizing my own research material.

Databases are typically used to store and make accessible large amounts of information. Their use is appropriate only when there are multiple similar bits of information, which can be arranged for easy searching or 'querying'. The similar or related pieces of information are shaped, or 'normalized', into 'records' which constitute recurrences of the same groupings of 'fields' which are populated with a certain category of information. The difficulty of trying to explain this simply in words is exactly why we prefer the spatial arrangement of records and fields that databases offer us. The process, though, is analogous to asking pupils to gather material to present in an ordered way in an essay – it is basically about the organizing of things, where 'things' can include words and ideas. Constructing a database of even the simplest kind exercises critical thinking skills which can surely contribute to improved discursive speaking and listening, and writing skills.

The language of the database could and perhaps should be taught by English teachers, just as the Dewey decimal system was a decade or two ago. It has always baffled me that database work is typically thought of as exclusively the realm of scientists and statisticians. There are new breeds of experts such as 'data managers' and 'content managers' emerging from a background of technical or scientific subject specialism, yet it seems clear that where the units of data are words, we need word specialists involved. The reason for this is that the skills it takes to 'normalize' textual information, reducing it to the categories needed for establishing fields and creating tables, are the sort of analytical reading skills taught and learned in English.

General teaching approaches

There are two common ways in which data handling is approached: spreadsheets and databases. The spreadsheet itself, used for collecting and sorting data, can be a real asset in terms of visual representation of information because of the automatic graph production. Pie charts and English lessons are not incompatible: understanding alternative, visual ways of presenting information has long been within the remit of the English teacher. Now you can do wonderful things with a few lines of data, including stylish three-dimensional charts, as in figure 3.9 below:

Fig 3.9

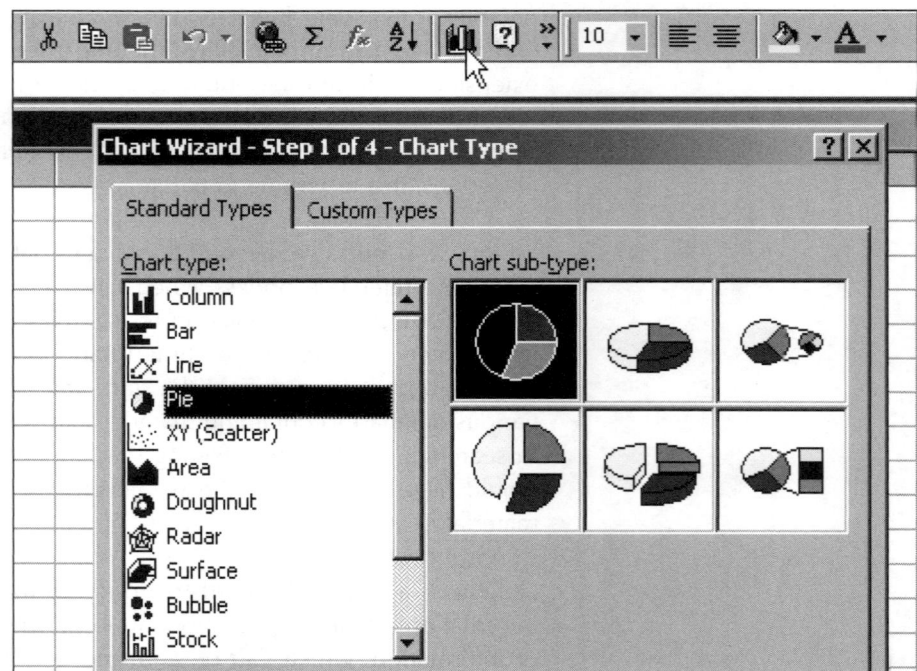

True databases, as opposed to spreadsheets, can be queried because of the way tables are composed of 'fields' and 'records'. The simplest database would be just two fields, with two records:

Fig 3.10

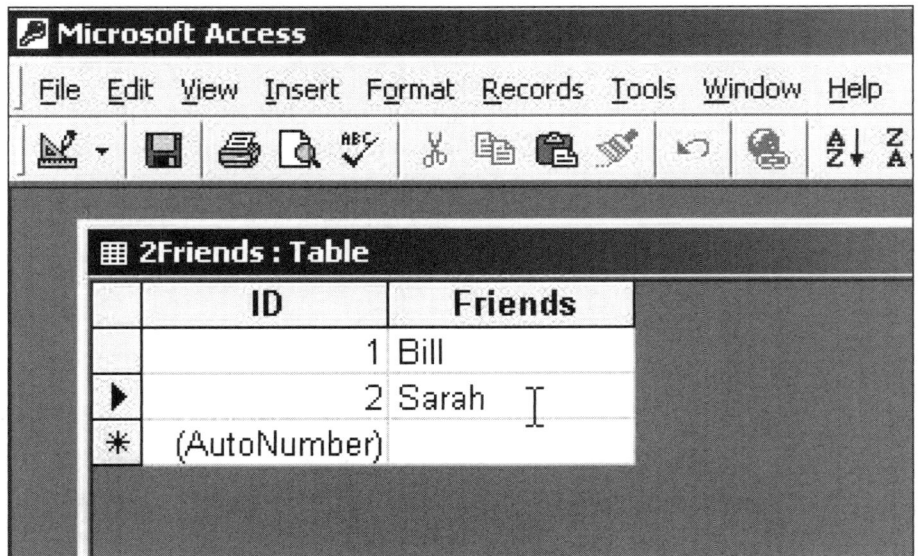

In the case of the example in figure 3.10 the automatically assigned ID number is the 'primary key', which is going to stay constant, and the second field is the list of names. Now this is not the most exciting of databases, since all we have is a list of names and numbers, and in reality a database will rarely be so simple. Beyond our unique identifier (the assigned number) and the name we are likely to want some further information associated with the person – perhaps their hair colour:

Fig 3.11

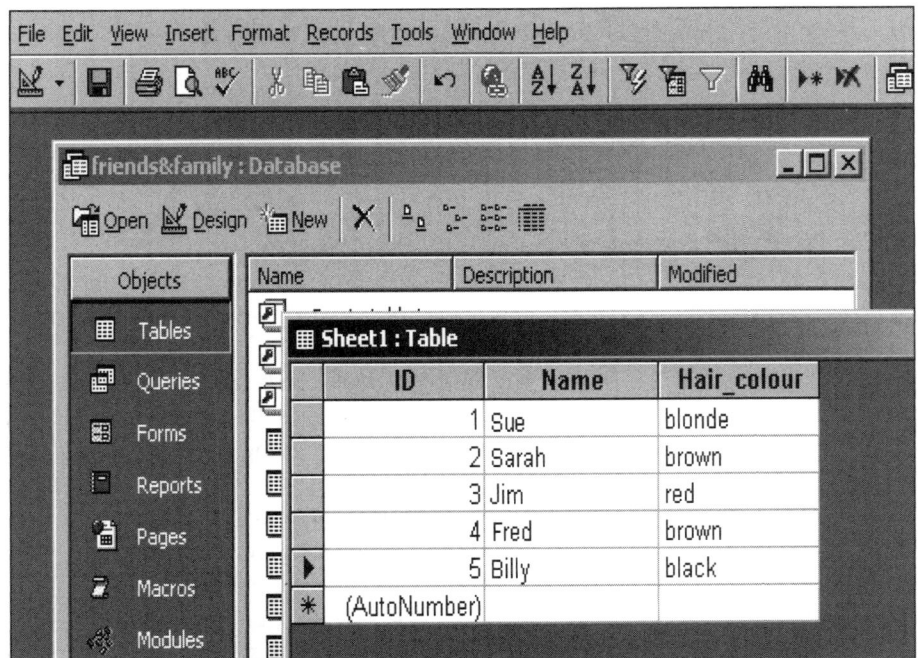

A record (or row) transects the fields (or columns), and this constitutes a table. It's the linking of associated tables that constitutes a relational database, which is where databases become something cognitively different from spreadsheets. The key thing to having linked tables is that this makes them more searchable, because if the data in one of your fields is being taken from a column in another table, this enables you to query (or in effect search) according to the fixed value in that second table. In terms of thinking skills, understanding databases means understanding interrelations, connections and complex organization of material. Keeping to our simple example, if we expand our table to include musical tastes in a new column, we can link a second table as a 'look-up' list of music styles – a fixed set of options. As a result you would then be able to run a query that gave you a list of all the people who liked a particular style of music.

The problem that needs solving before we get to the stage of handling issues specific to databases is the lack of a vocabulary for English teachers to deal with the issues. If we are going to address our deficiency in skills here, we first need to fill that language gap. We don't need to explain the principles of Standard Query Language or relational databases, but we need some key terms to be commonly understood, and perhaps some database software applications to be commonly used by English teachers.

The sort of terms which need to be understood include:
- data/dataset
- importing and exporting data
- 'content'
- table (not in the same sense as tables in MS Word)

➡ fields (and 'populating' them)

➡ records

➡ primary key.

What we also need to do is get past the dull, grey image of databases (literally grey, in many cases!) and show that they can provide exciting ways of ordering information, and therefore ideas. Recent developments in software are beginning to make that possible, as we will see.

Teaching ideas, examples and advice

What software?

The kinds of software applications which might be used for simple databases include the child-friendly Textease, and Lotus Approach, which has a more intuitive approach to creating a new database than most (see figure 3.12):

Fig 3.12

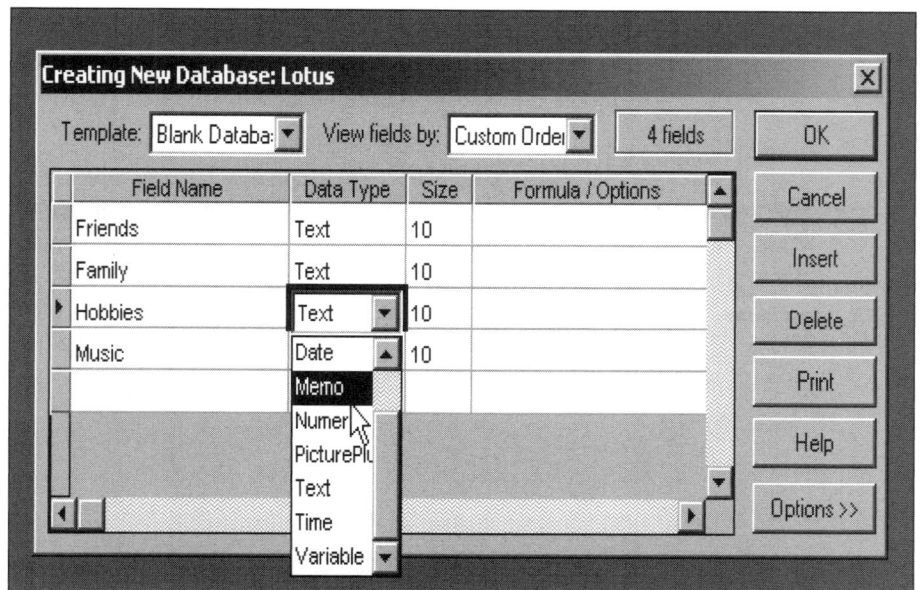

This software is compatible with Microsoft, so that you can import data from MS Excel or text files.

WEBSITE

Microsoft Access is certainly worth looking at, although its development history means that it is by no means a user-friendly application for beginners.[14] The crucial difference between Lotus Approach and MS Access is the fact that you can link tables in Access. It may be that you would want to introduce the basic vocabulary of databases via one of the more straightforward applications where a database is constituted of a single table of columns/fields. Even in the subject of ICT itself, teaching the use of a relational database is uncommon in the age range we are concerned with. Data handling is often addressed using spreadsheets which can be turned easily into graphs, but each sheet is one 'table' of information, and linking tables is the essence of databases.

A simple linked 'look-up' table using Access

I am going to show how easy it is with MS Access to at least begin to appreciate the structure of a relational database, without getting into the area of complex queries. Before looking at how to link tables using Flexidata, we can look at how, in MS Access, you can effectively link a single-field table to a field in your main table using the 'look-up wizard'.

Ask pupils to create a simple database of their friends, deciding first on the criteria by which they would like to sort the data. Ask them how they would like to be able to search for their friends – presumably not by age, but perhaps according to their interests, hobbies, and so on. Our main table will contain names of friends and one of the ways you might want to classify them is by their musical interests. A quick survey of musical tastes can provide you with the data for a table of musical genres. So as well as creating a field in the first table called 'Music', create a second table of just one field listing the types of music, name it appropriately and save it alongside your main table. Then, so that for each friend you can select their favourite music, link them using the look-up wizard, which is a straightforward procedure. Open the main table in Design view, and open the wizard by clicking on the Data Type column for the field. The wizard (which can alternatively be used to enter look-up data directly) allows you to select the second table for linking as illustrated in figure 3.13 below.

Fig 3.13

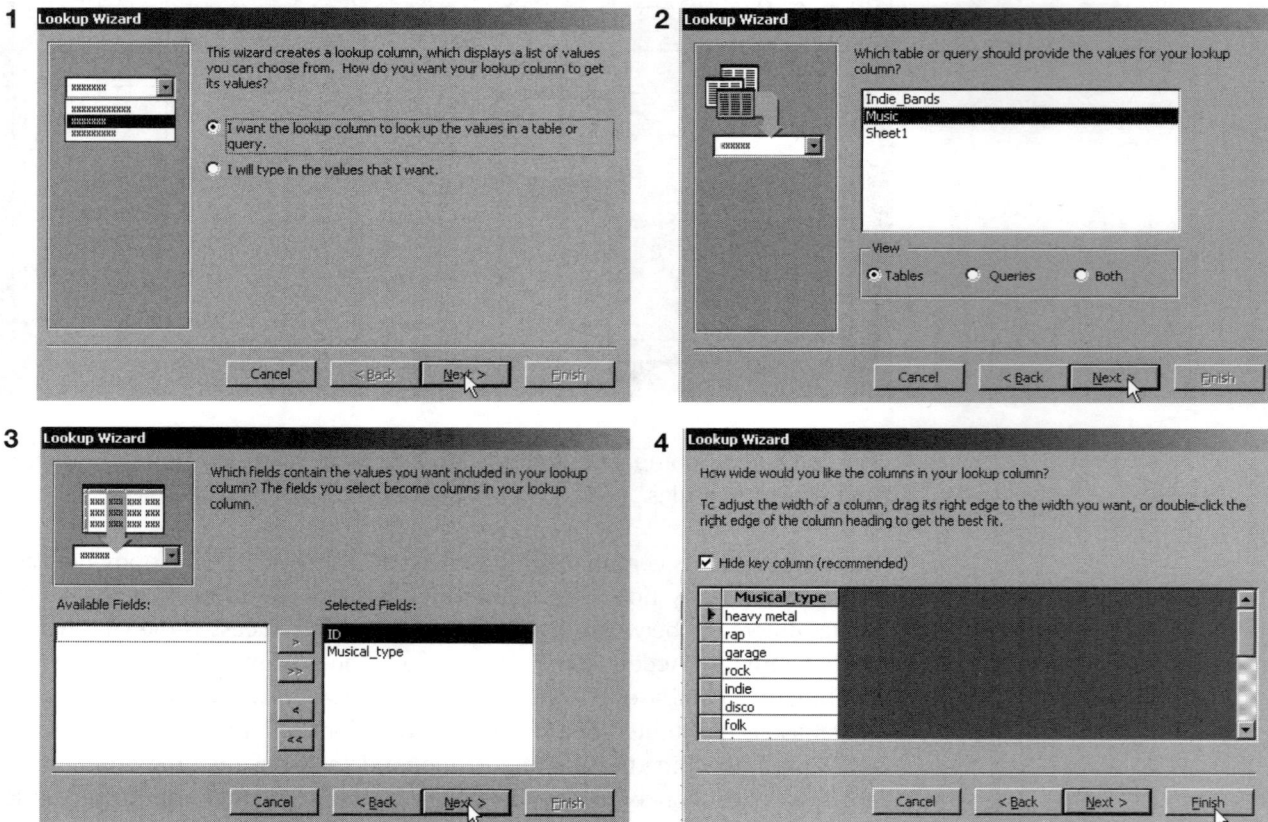

So that finally you have two tables, the second providing a look-up table for one of the fields in the first (see figure 3.14).

Fig 3.14

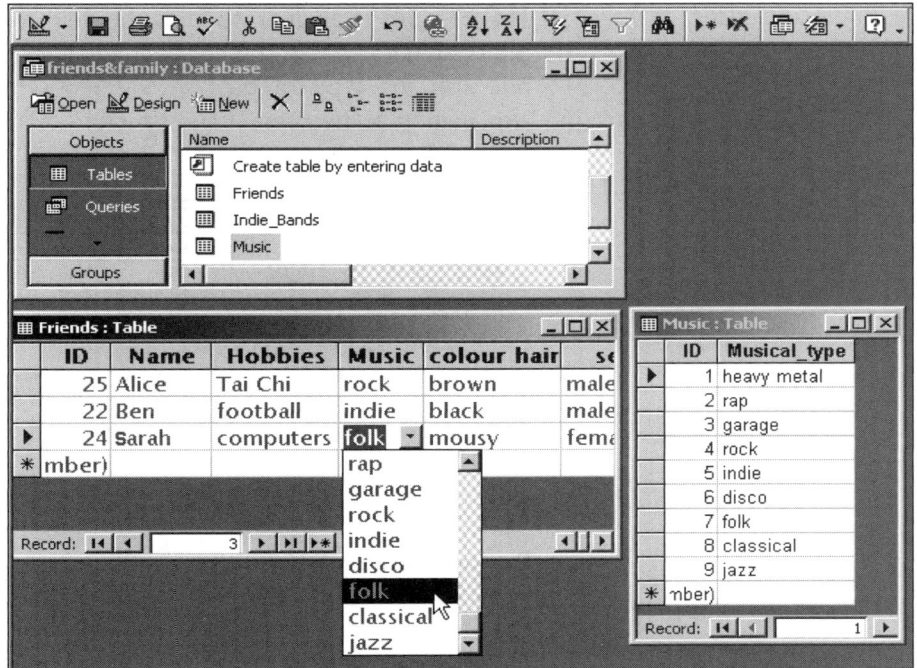

Using Flexidata

WEBSITE

If MS Access is well-established and sophisticated, it is still basically about storing alphanumeric data, which is why Flexidata[15] is innovative and progressive. One of the problems for someone with a preference for visual learning is the way databases can be visually unstimulating: in fact every record on a database will necessarily look the same in terms of the raw data. Flexidata adds a variety of visual elements to make databases more engaging to learners. It also combines the user-friendliness of a system designed for schools with the ability to link tables, so as to demonstrate the potential of a relational database. This makes it quite unlike any other system as yet available for teaching use, and is why it is worth looking at in some detail.

Linking tables

WEBSITE

Linking tables with Flexidata is a more visually comprehensible process than with Access.[16] In figure 3.15 you can see how the relations of the two sub-tables of this cottage holiday bookings database are shown with colour-coded highlighting and lines. You will also see that these sub-tables themselves, unlike the one linked using Access, have multiple fields, giving more detail regarding the content of the link fields, that is, the customers and the cottages.

Fig 3.15

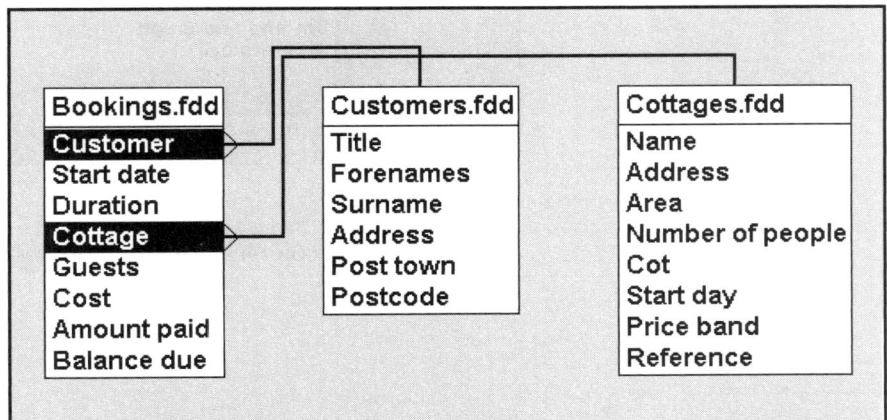

There is also the option to view the field type alongside the field (see figure 3.16) so that you can see not only what are the 'link fields' in the main table, but also the type of data in the other fields. This gives an at-a-glance explanation of the content and structure of the database.

Fig 3.16

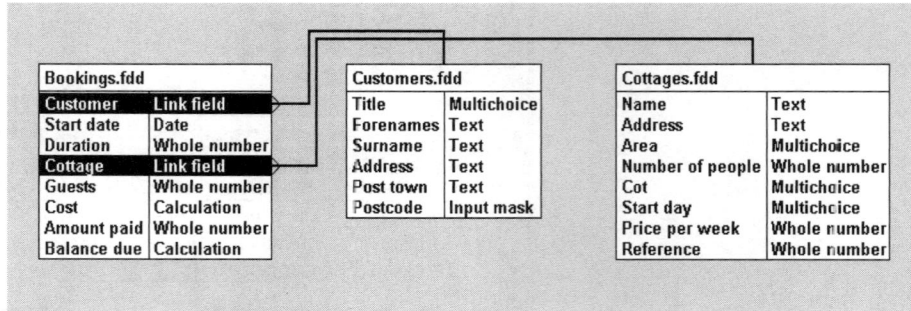

Bookings.fdd			Customers.fdd			Cottages.fdd	
Customer	Link field		Title	Multichoice		Name	Text
Start date	Date		Forenames	Text		Address	Text
Duration	Whole number		Surname	Text		Area	Multichoice
Cottage	Link field		Address	Text		Number of people	Whole number
Guests	Whole number		Post town	Text		Cot	Multichoice
Cost	Calculation		Postcode	Input mask		Start day	Multichoice
Amount paid	Whole number					Price per week	Whole number
Balance due	Calculation					Reference	Whole number

Report views of the data

What particularly distinguishes Flexidata from Access or Lotus database software is seen in the 'report' views of data. Various graphic ways of showing the data are available, in a way familiar from MS Excel but going beyond the functionality of that software. It comes with some ready-loaded datasets, such as the elements, and you can see how easily graphs can be produced from these data with the example below.

After viewing the raw data, simply select the type of graph you want:

Fig 3.17

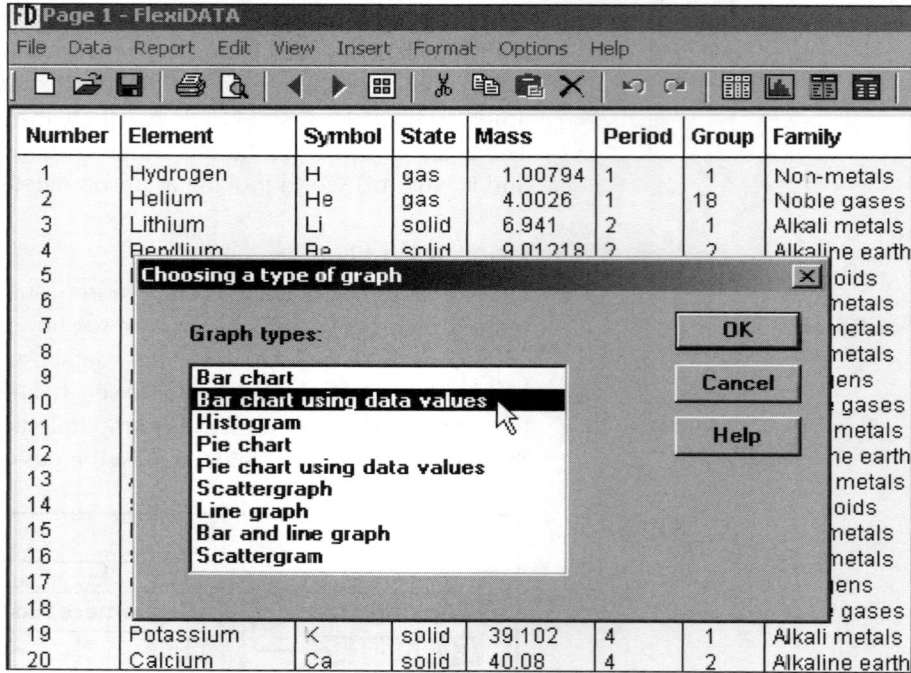

Then choose the columns or fields whose data you want to present:

Fig 3.18

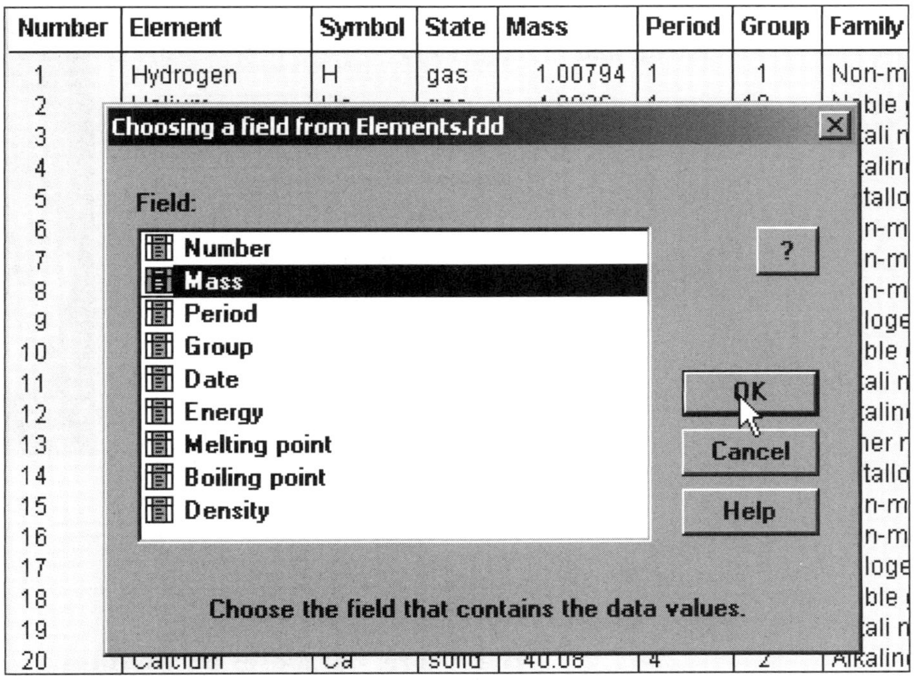

Number	Element	Symbol	State	Mass	Period	Group	Family
1	Hydrogen	H	gas	1.00794	1	1	Non-m
2							ble
3							ali n
4							alin(
5							tallo
6							n-m
7							n-m
8							n-m
9							loge
10							ble
11							ali n
12							alin(
13							er r
14							tallo
15							n-m
16							n-m
17							loge
18							ble
19							ali n
20	Calcium	Ca	solid	40.08	4	2	Alkalin

Choosing a field from Elements.fdd

Field:
- Number
- **Mass**
- Period
- Group
- Date
- Energy
- Melting point
- Boiling point
- Density

OK Cancel Help ?

Choose the field that contains the data values.

The graph will appear alongside; as in this example of a bar graph showing the mass of the elements:

Fig 3.19

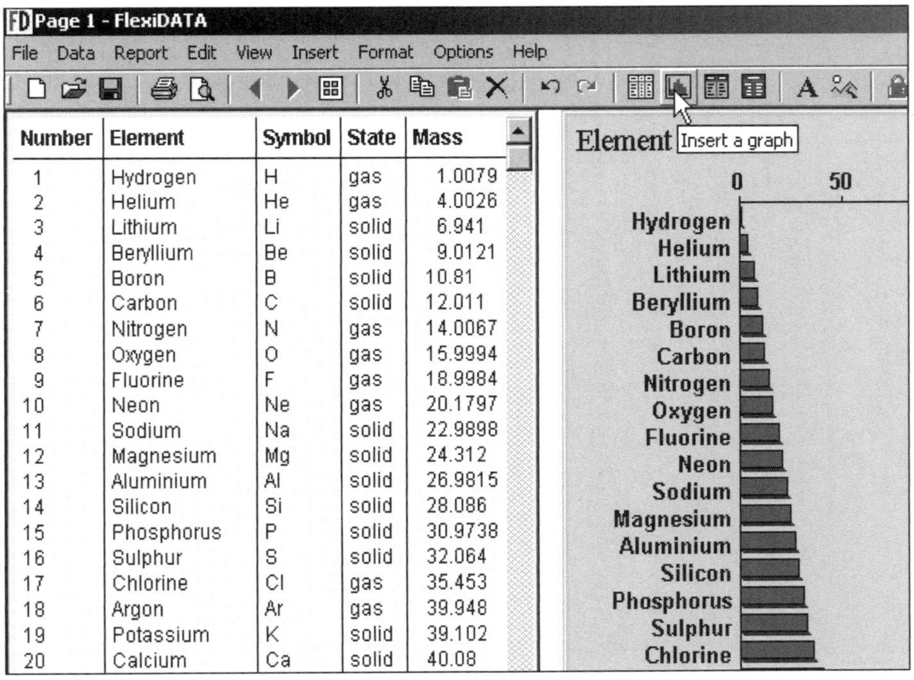

Page 1 - FlexiDATA

File Data Report Edit View Insert Format Options Help

Number	Element	Symbol	State	Mass
1	Hydrogen	H	gas	1.0079
2	Helium	He	gas	4.0026
3	Lithium	Li	solid	6.941
4	Beryllium	Be	solid	9.0121
5	Boron	B	solid	10.81
6	Carbon	C	solid	12.011
7	Nitrogen	N	gas	14.0067
8	Oxygen	O	gas	15.9994
9	Fluorine	F	gas	18.9984
10	Neon	Ne	gas	20.1797
11	Sodium	Na	solid	22.9898
12	Magnesium	Mg	solid	24.312
13	Aluminium	Al	solid	26.9815
14	Silicon	Si	solid	28.086
15	Phosphorus	P	solid	30.9738
16	Sulphur	S	solid	32.064
17	Chlorine	Cl	gas	35.453
18	Argon	Ar	gas	39.948
19	Potassium	K	solid	39.102
20	Calcium	Ca	solid	40.08

Element [Insert a graph]   0   50
Hydrogen Helium Lithium Beryllium Boron Carbon Nitrogen Oxygen Fluorine Neon Sodium Magnesium Aluminium Silicon Phosphorus Sulphur Chlorine

You can change background colour, font type, colour and size, and modify the report design in various ways. The real boon from a visual learning perspective is that individual records can have images inserted, so there is a visual mnemonic alongside the typed data, distinguishing one record from another. The example below is from one of the sample reports provided with the software, the planets of the solar system, in which each of the planet records has its own image attached.

Fig 3.20

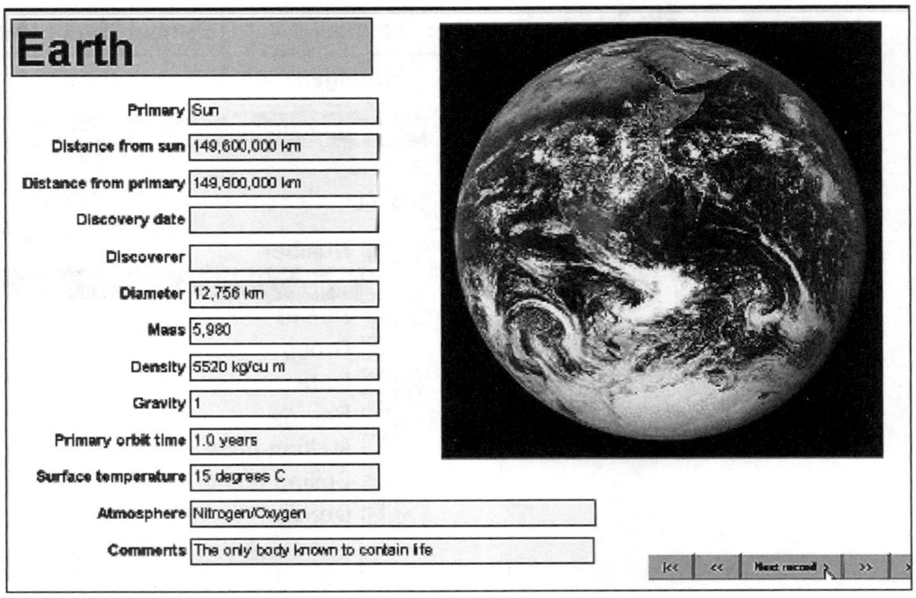

Earth

Primary	Sun
Distance from sun	149,600,000 km
Distance from primary	149,600,000 km
Discovery date	
Discoverer	
Diameter	12,756 km
Mass	5,980
Density	5520 kg/cu m
Gravity	1
Primary orbit time	1.0 years
Surface temperature	15 degrees C
Atmosphere	Nitrogen/Oxygen
Comments	The only body known to contain life

The future: databases on websites

If we are to teach about how websites are built, as I will suggest we should in the next chapter, at some stage the notion of databases will need to be introduced. Many sites these days, and no doubt increasingly in the future, are effectively run by databases – when you click on a link it calls up/searches pages from a database rather than transferring you to a static, hyperlinked page. This will also require teaching about the 'meta-tagging' of content for search purposes (and if this seems way beyond the ken of pupils, of course that is quite wrong: if they know how to use multiple search options, then they already know the principles of tagging). In the long term, these skills may well come within the scope of the English teacher, as notions of literacy constantly broaden in the age of new media.

Case study 3

Census at School Project: building databases

WEBSITE

Background

This project, which has resulted in impressive work across the curriculum both in the UK and beyond, is certainly worth noting by English teachers. The Census at School project was initiated by Professor Neville Davies of the Nottingham Trent University, here in the UK, but now has become an international project involving South Africa, Australia, New Zealand and Canada.[1] The project comes under the aegis of the Royal Statistical Society's Centre for Statistical Education, but it should not be seen as being just about statistics.

Between autumn 2000 and March 2001, across England, Wales and Northern Ireland, thousands of young people between the ages of 7 and 16 participated in the project. Over 2000 primary, secondary and special schools registered to take part, and over 60,000 school children were involved via the website. The original Census at School questionnaire consisted of a single A4 sheet of simple questions covering information about pupils, their households and their school life. While some of the questions were identical to those in the UK population census, others were designed to appeal to the pupil's own interests and enthusiasms. Since then many other countries have embraced the project with necessary adjustments to reflect local culture and traditions.

By 2004 the UK branch of the project had progressed to Phase 4, with the RSS Centre using questionnaires which are downloaded as Word or PDF (Adobe Acrobat – Portable Document Format) files then data returned as Excel or CSV (Comma Separated Variable) files. The project is frequently used by the DfES

(Department for Education and Skills) in their Key Stage 3 national strategy training documents for teachers. In Kent, the Kent Schools' Passport uses the Census at School idea to develop cross-phase links between primary and secondary schools. Guidance on getting involved in the project is provided through lesson plans by the national strategy (ICT strand), that involves a detailed examination of database use and construction.

Relevant teaching and learning objectives

The project's stated aims are:

➡ Providing real data for data-handling activities across the national curriculum.

➡ Increasing awareness of what a national census is, and what it is for.

➡ Showing how ICT can be used effectively to enhance learning and teaching resources for good practice in data handling.

So this project's objectives were strongly ICT-biased, though data handling will always overlap with English, as we saw in Chapter 3. But the fact that the raw data at the heart of this project are data about pupils themselves means that it opens up all kinds of possibilities for interesting and engaging work in English.

How it was done

It starts with questionnaires – with separate ones in the UK for Key Stage 2 and Key Stage 3 – and then involves a variety of activities. The large-scale effect is to produce a massive databank enabling people to compare the lives of English-speaking school children across four continents.

The 'Curriculum Activities' suggested on the Census at School website do not, strangely, include English, but in a sense most of the activities that are suggested could fall within the scope of English teaching – this is particularly so when looking at the citizenship tasks about 'People to look up to', 'Healthy Eating' or 'What's Your Opinion?'.

The project has been used as the basis for two case studies exemplifying ICT progression into and through Year 9 by the Key Stage 3 strategy, and comes with extensive electronic supporting materials, including Excel data spreadsheets and Access databases.[2]

WEBSITE

WEBSITE

Interestingly, Case Study 9.2a has the teacher using Flexidata[3] for creating fields and doing simple and complex queries, as well as graphs (see Teacher resource 6, for Lessons 2 and 5) though raw sample data is provided in Access tables.

Outcomes

The worldwide database now contains over 800,000 responses, which can be accessed via the internet by teachers and students.

Fig 3.21   **The Census at School website homepage**

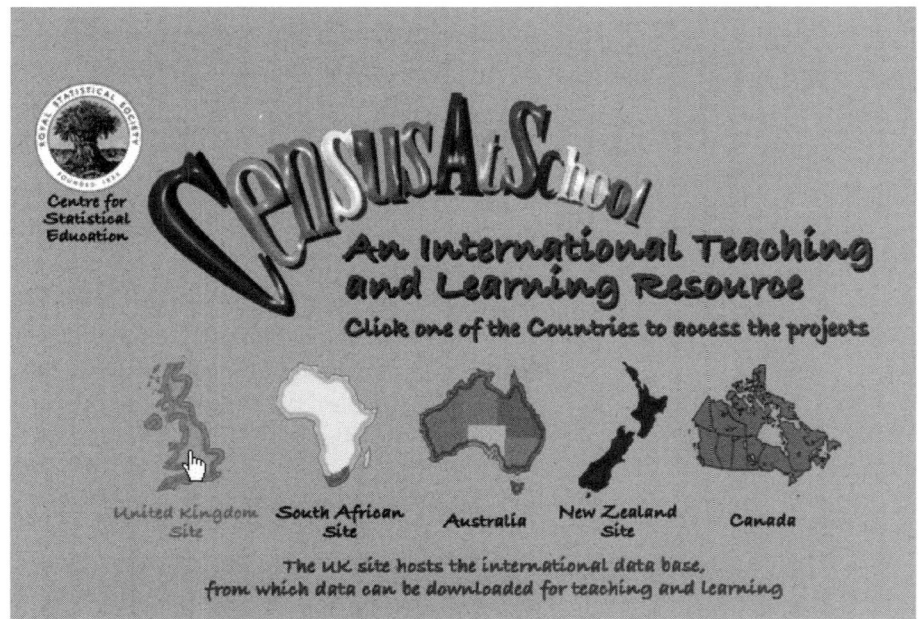

On the UK part of the site you can find a whole range of results for the census, through the first four phases. On request, via the 'Random Data Selector' pages, schools can also receive emailed selections of raw data from any of the five participating countries as CSV files.

Fig 3.22

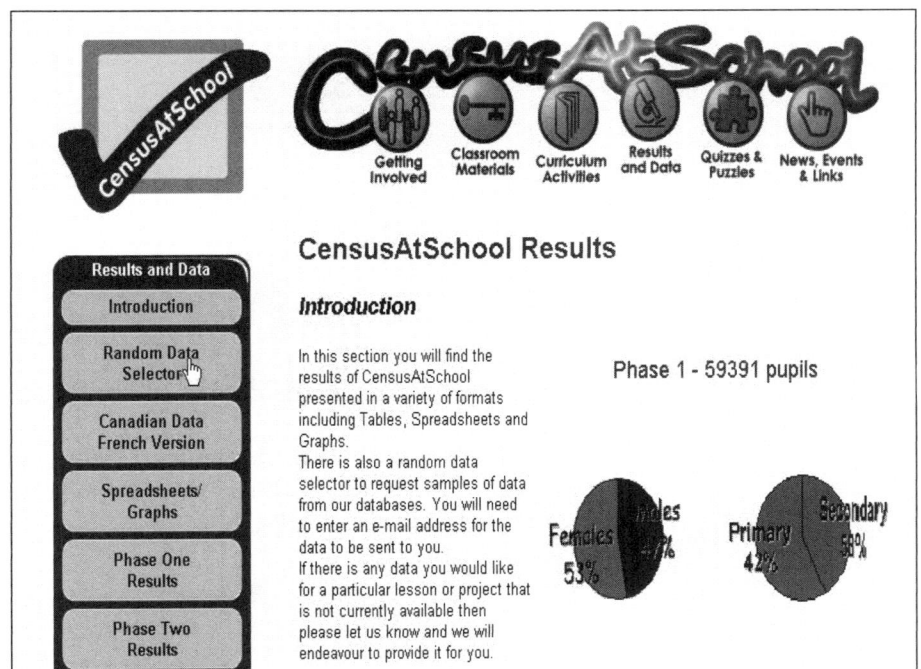

The outcomes of this project have been extensive, as you can glimpse from the evidence of example work and ideas from numerous schools on the UK website. As well as enabling teachers and pupils to enhance their data-handling skills, it is also potentially a route to social and cultural exchange across the world, alongside more local comparisons or communications between regions.

Doing this in the classroom

For use in English, Flexidata would provide greatest versatility, so you will need to convert data that you have created in response to the questionnaire. If your data is in an Excel file, save it as a CSV (Comma Separated Variable) file and you will then be able to open it in Flexidata. If your data is in an Access table you will need to export it as an Excel file first, and thence as a CSV file.

If you do this with the sample Access table provided in the Teacher resources for Case Study 9.3 you can then create another table with, for example, details about the pupil's house. There is no reason why this should not be an occasion for descriptive writing too. There is a common assumption in the use of databases that all the data will be simple facts, but text fields can have as much text as you like, being limited mainly by the difficulty of formatting. So single paragraphs are best, but these could provide descriptive writing about the other people in the household, explanatory writing about why they like their favourite subject, and so on. In the example below (see figure 3.23) an extra field allowing the pupil to describe their bedroom has been added:

Fig 3.23

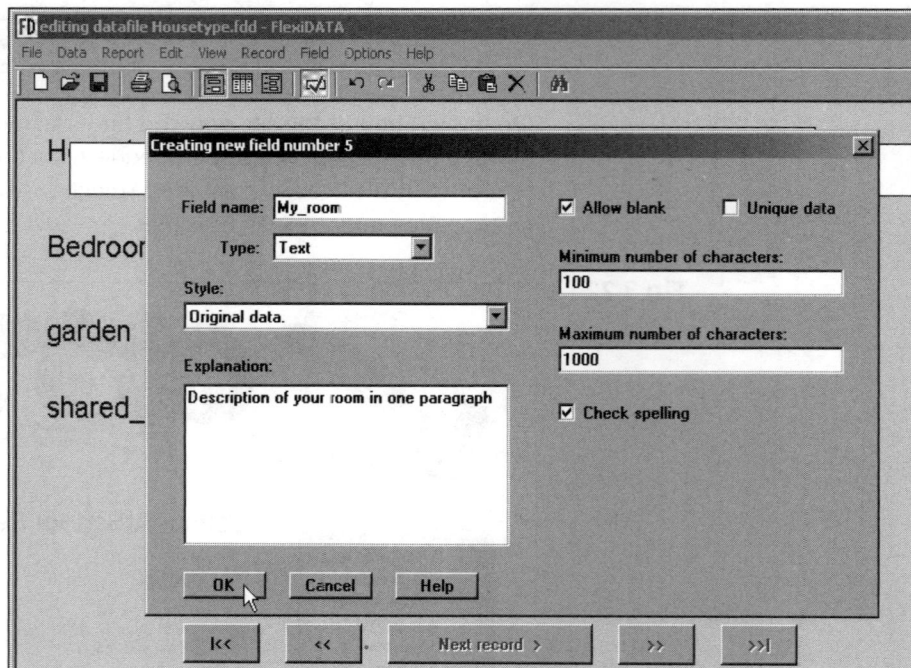

You can now link the two tables together, so that you have extra information about the houses in which the pupils live, beyond whether they are detached or semi-detached, and so on.

Fig 3.24

pupildata.csv	
ID	Number
Key Stage	Number
Gender	Text
Date of Birth	Date
Year Group	Number
Height (cm)	Number
Foot Size (cm)	Number
Mobile	Number
Computer	Number
Internet	Number
Region	Text
Move1yearago	Number
Housetype	**Link field**
Household	Number
Cars	Number
Fav Subject	Text
Travel Type	Text
Travel Time (min)	Number

Housetype.fdd	
Housetype	**Link field**
Bedrooms	Number
garden	Multichoice
shared_bedroom	Multichoice
My_room	Text
House_picture	Picture

What really raises the interest level is that you can have picture fields, in which images are stored as part of a record, and can be shown in the report view. These digital images – taken with a camera or scanned – might be of the pupils themselves, their family, their house, their garden or their bedroom.

Using the Card view of the data report, you can view the images alongside the text, and change colours and fonts, as in the example below:

Fig 3.25

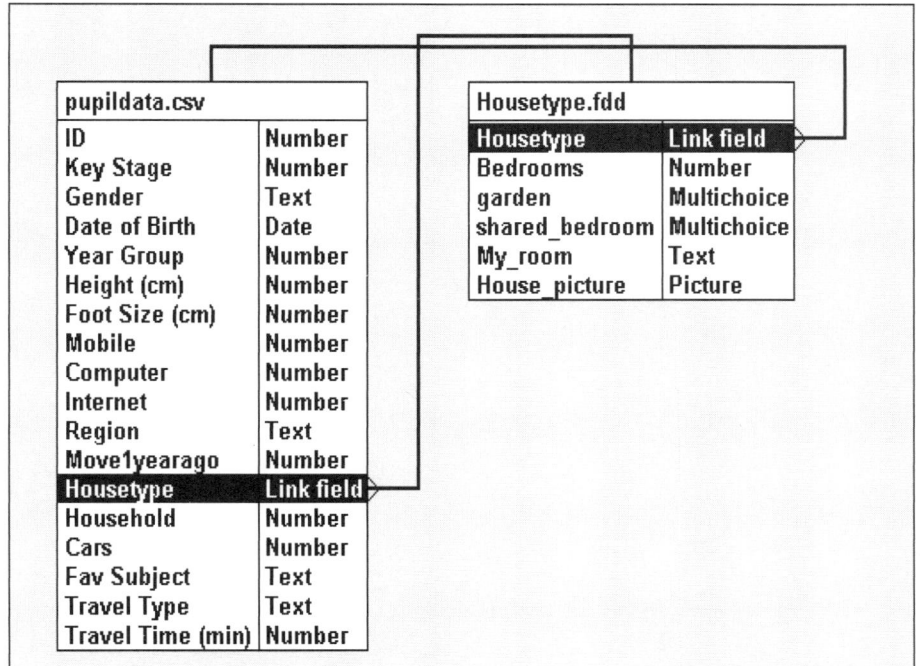

Garden | yes

Bedrooms | 3

Who_in_house | I have two sisters and a brother, and Mum and Dad

Shared_bedroom | have my own room

My room | My room is quite small but I have room for a desk to do my homework. I also have aTV. I decorated the room myself last summer.

Housepic

Chapter 4

New ways of writing

Part 1: Writing for the web

In this section you will:

- examine the nature and value for English teaching of writing for online publication;
- consider websites in terms of 'text structure';
- look at ways of introducing this into your teaching.

Part 2: Whole text work using multimedia

In this section you will:

- consider how multimedia can be useful in teaching writing;
- look at the idea of 'multimodality' and some general approaches to the use of multimedia in whole text work;
- look at examples of good practice and advice in this area;
- consider practical ways you can apply this technology and these approaches in your teaching.

Part 1

Writing for the web

Why do it?

Pupils publishing for new readers

We are witnessing an irreversible revolution in publishing at the moment, and as English teachers we should be involved. In the past we have associated the notion that something is 'worth publishing' with notions of 'quality'. The standards have traditionally been set by English teachers and editors, so the idea that nowadays 'anyone can publish' might seem a threatening one. But if being published used to imply something about standards, it was also about exclusivity. One can see the massive growth of web publishing as a democratization of something which has for centuries been controlled by a few people with power and influence. The social and educational arguments for web publishing are at least as important as the political ones: beyond the anxieties about quality control, there are real positives to be found in the idea of publishing to the web. These positives are about individual empowerment and motivation; about reaching both local and networked communities; about an openness instead of a circumscription or even prescription of audience.

If, as an English teacher, you have any doubt about the value of web publishing, you only need to look at the staggering amount of writing being done for poetry websites and 'blogs' (short for 'web logs', or simple online diaries) around the world.[1] In verse and in prose people all over the world are recording and reflecting on their experiences online, and importantly much of this belongs to youth culture. Young people are constantly presenting and describing themselves to the world, creating their emerging identities, online. Every time they create a profile on one of the many online communities they are practising self-presentation skills; every time they re-edit that profile to modify people's perceptions of them, they are showing what they have learned about readers and meanings.

WEBSITE

Teachers of English have, particularly in recent years, been asked to focus on the notion of audience when setting and assessing writing tasks. The UK national curriculum for English makes it a standard part of the way we approach the teaching of writing: three out of four of the specified 'purposes for writing' refer to 'the reader'. There is a great deal of nonsense talked and written about how the internet provides a 'real' audience for school children, when of course as far as teaching is concerned the reader of pupils' writing is always ultimately the teacher, and all other imagined readers convenient fictions. Close examination of persuasive writing ostensibly addressing a postulated reader suggests that there is actually little perceivable difference from persuasive writing without such an imagined reader.[2] And in any case who is the reader in the age of the internet? What assumptions can we make about web users? When the reader could be in a suburban British home or a cybercafe in South-east Asia, we have a less fixed notion of audience, and notions of 'the reader' seem to become increasingly meaningless.

If pupils will always actually write for the real reader of their work, the teacher, what happens when there are truly other readers provided by the new medium? This can happen thanks to online communities where the readership is known and fixed. One thing we can be confident of is that it will be motivational. We can see from the numerous online poetry sites and competitions that the internet is encouraging verbal self-expression on a scale never before seen.[3] If we worry about dilution of quality this is more a sign of our deferential attitude to traditional publishers' power than genuinely about the merits of publishing.

WEBSITE

The internet enables us to be truly open-minded about the value of the written word and the value of publishing: if as an English teacher you see 'bad' poetry online, do you feel it's a bad thing that it was published? Would we prefer people to keep their unedited thoughts to private diaries? While we might feel there is an element of self-importance about people who publish to the web, it is also an act of sharing and community, and of course it encourages people both to read and to write!

General approaches

It would be good if we could harness the excitement involved in the idea of publishing to a wider, sometimes unlimited, imagined audience, while addressing the unease often associated with this. Thanks to the possibilities of online publishing, imagined readers can be the class, a year group, the whole school community (including, potentially, family and friends of pupils) and groups of schools. The virtual world makes real a readership prescribed by the UK English curriculum: 'The range of readers for writing should include teachers, the class, other children, adults, the wider community and imagined readers.'[4]

Teaching the basics for a new medium

It is surely necessary that we teach young people how to write for the new medium that is the world wide web. The implication of this for us as English teachers is that we need to examine closely the salient features of such writing. We need to be aware of the electronic text as more than just words on a page, and the most obvious difference from conventional writing is in the formalistic qualities of organization and structure. While 'blogging' might be a rather unstructured form of writing, there are some very clear structural and organizational rules about websites in general. If we are going to ask pupils to critically examine web pages, they will need to consider more than the text in isolation. It will need to be considered as 'content', where the receptacle for containing the text, that is, the website, needs to be appreciated too. In a sense, this is not really different from the way we consider conventional writing to be composed of paragraphs and perhaps chapters, but in fact the rules for website structure are probably more rigid and fixed, and therefore easier to teach.

Text structure on the web includes navigational methods such as:

➡ menu bars
➡ drop-downs
➡ hyperlinks
➡ pop-up links.

The way people find their way around (or 'navigate') websites can also be looked at as a way of understanding text organization. Of course, the best way of understanding website structure is in visual and spatial terms, because ever since the invention of 'windows' (or the 'object-oriented' programming principles that it emerged from) we have treated the virtual world as if it were in real space, somewhere beyond the interface of our monitor screens. Schematic representation of a website's structure is not unlike doing a flow chart of the main paragraphs of an essay, but there are some differences. We have seen the way *Inspiration* (see Chapter 1) might be used, creating a linear sequence for the paragraphs of a story with perhaps parallel strands building up characters or other features/details. Websites have some similarities in structure, but understanding the differences is important. The chief of these to remember is that while a story or essay plan will have a beginning and an end, with websites the main, or 'home', page can be seen as both alpha and omega.

A website will follow certain rules which are dictated by the fact that you 'access' all the information via a single page: the home page.

Fig 4.1

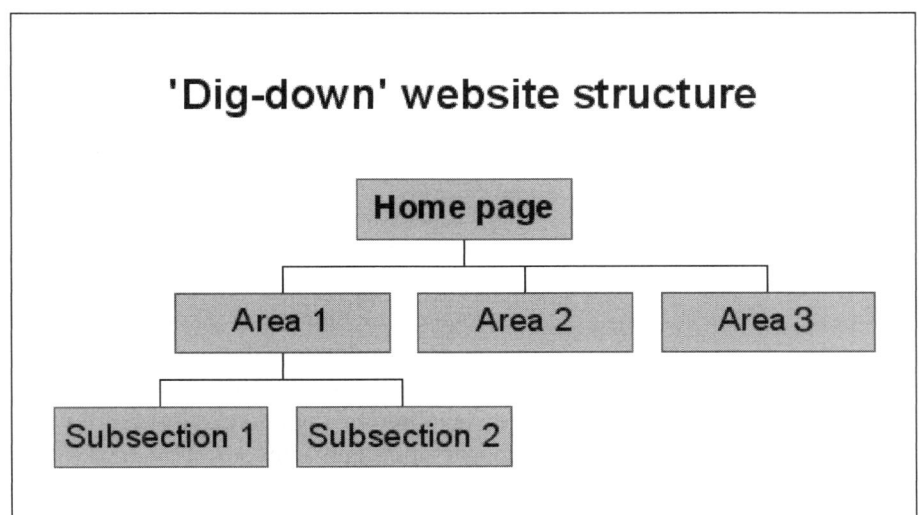

The norm for websites (except those which are database-driven) is what has been called a 'dig-down' navigational structure, by which you go from level to sub-level of the information in stages via hyperlinks, so that the mass of information increases at each level, pushing the structure outwards. In shape terms, we might call it pyramidal, though other, organic metaphors might be used – the roots of a plant perhaps. Like the roots of a plant (or indeed a pyramid) there is both neatness and efficiency in this method of structuring information. Everything on the site can be traced back/upwards to the home page. In theory you should never get 'lost', because a website should always display a link back to the home page no matter what page you are on. Many websites go further than that and keep the 'second level' showing at all times too – that is to say the main headings (or 'areas' since we're speaking spatially) of the site. These headings are typically found in either a 'menu bar' (either along the top or in a left-hand column) or a 'drop-down' list.

Fig 4.2

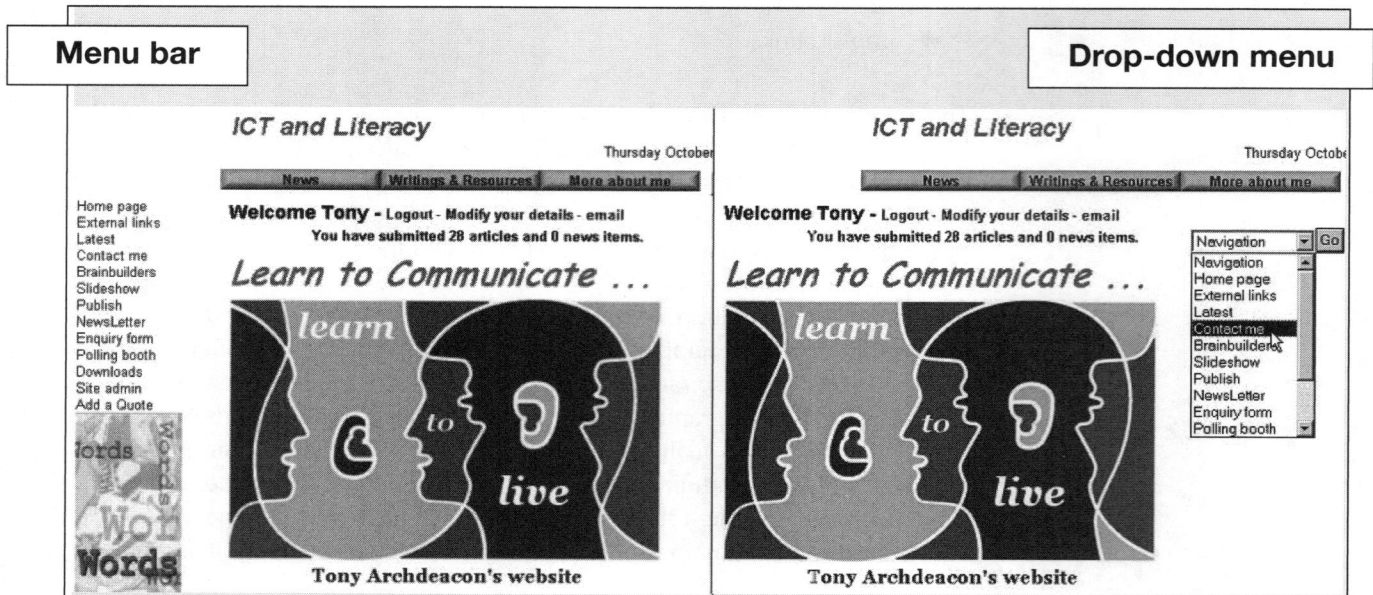

Children who are used to the web will know this to some degree already but perhaps without ever reflecting on it. It's our task to articulate it for them and get young people to appreciate the principles of text structure that they see at work on the web every day. This is particularly valuable in terms of development of thinking skills because of the hierarchical ordering of ideas involved – our missing factor in textual organization and planning from Chapter 2.

WEBSITE

There is also, inevitably, an overlap here with design, and perhaps therefore an opportunity for cross-curricular work. In a sense the principles of good website design are congruent with (and perhaps actually derive from) the principles of 'information architecture'.[5] Though there is more than one approach to web design, many adhere to the principle of having a minimalist home page that is easily grasped visually. This provides a feeling of wholeness and unity, and is often favoured by commercial institutions wishing to present a clear brand. The opposite approach is favoured by news sites that follow a tradition created by the printed newspaper, showing as much as possible on the front page. Looking at issues like usability of websites in an informed way will increase understanding of the way websites work as media for communication.

Teaching ideas, examples and advice

1. Look and learn

Ask a group to look at some sample home pages of websites, perhaps using a projector or interactive whiteboard to help show the main features. Try to pick a couple of sites which are not too 'cluttered' on the home page, with an obvious navigation system (a news site, for example, will not be ideal because there will be too much change on it and probably a lot of distracting links).

WEBSITE

Using UK education sites as examples, you could take the national curriculum site with its left-hand menu of all curriculum subjects, for comparison with the DfES Standards Site (see figure 4.3) which uses a drop-down menu.[6]

Fig 4.3

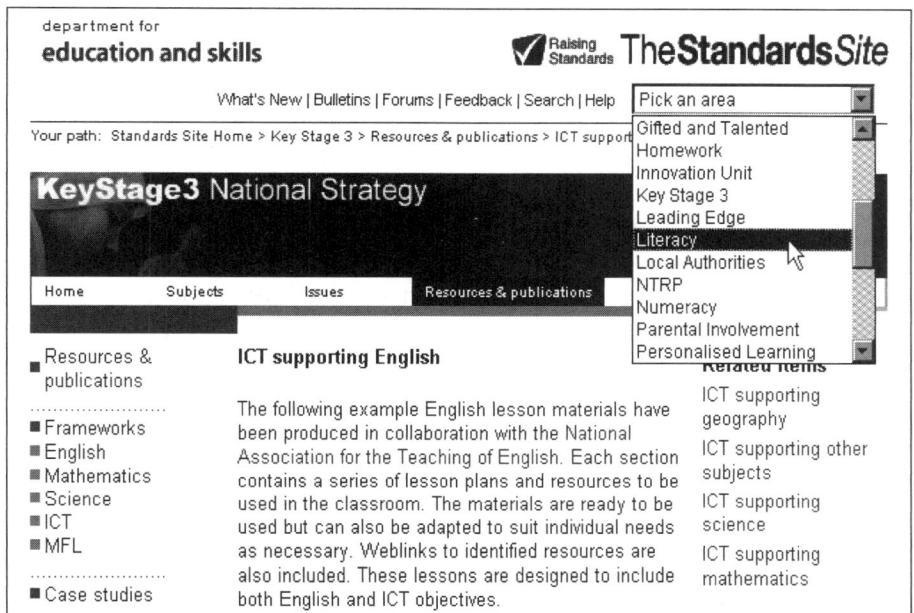

Often a drop-down will be used if there is a large number of links, as on the Standards Site which has over thirty. The national curriculum site has an unusually large number in a side menu – 18 in all – but the subject links on the menu are colour coded too for ease of use:

Fig 4.4

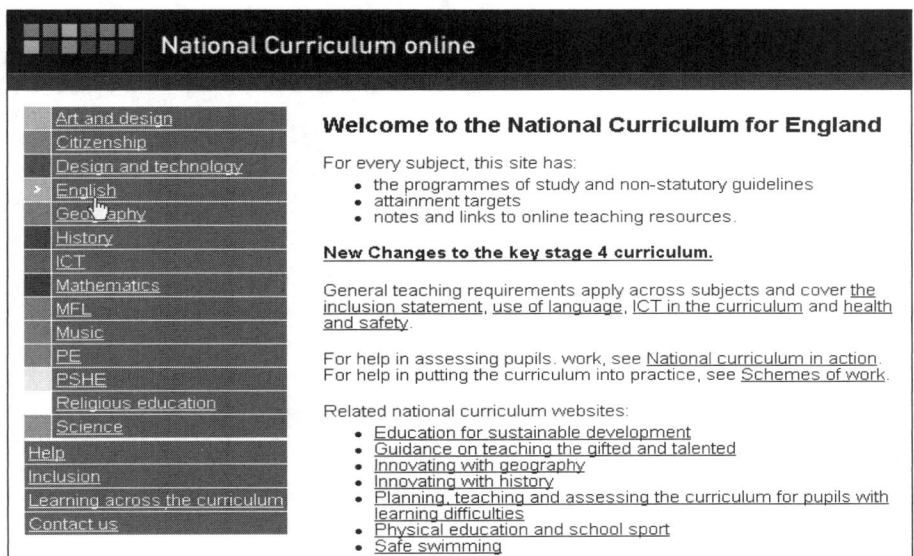

2. Research and explore

If you have internet access, prepare a list of sites for the groups to check out and identify which uses which kind of navigation. A homework project might involve doing a survey of the sites used regularly by students, and getting them to answer a number of key questions:

→ Does the site use a menu bar or drop-down?

→ If it uses a menu bar is it placed at the top, left or both?

→ If there are menus both at the top and on the left, are they using the same headings?

→ How many links are there on the menu bar or drop-down?

→ Are there usually more headings/links on a drop-down than on a menu bar? If so, why?

→ What is the average number of characters in a heading? Is there a noticeable difference in heading length between drop-downs and menu bars?

→ Are there other links on the home page which aren't included in either the menu or drop-down? (these might be 'latest items' links, or 'news' or special features, that is, things which might change regularly, unlike the main structural areas).

→ Are there any colour codes?

→ Are there any 'graphic' links?

If these questions are applied to a selection of sites they already use they can start to understand at a structural level what is already familiar to them in terms of content.

For my two education sites, the answer to the last question on the list would be no, but many of the sites used by children will have graphic links: images which act as links when you click on them. See, for example, the fish cartoons used on the BBC Bitesize learning sites (figure 4.5).[7]

WEBSITE

Fig 4.5

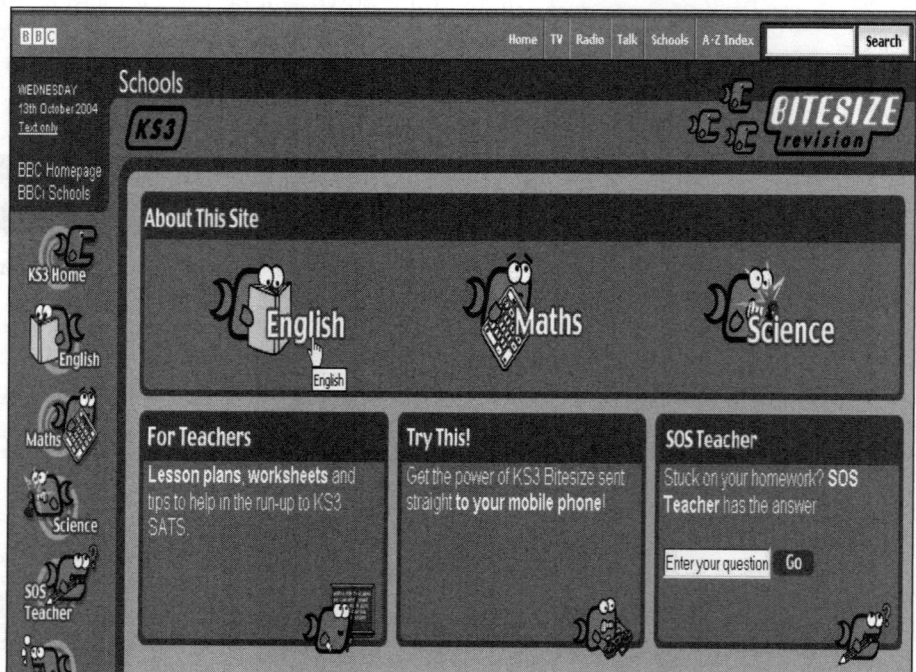

3. Swap words for graphics

A fun exercise is to take a site without graphic links and ask the class to make up their own – one for each of the 14 curriculum subjects for example. The least exciting way would be to resort to clip art, but with an image search, not only will the images be more varied and interesting, but other thinking and language skills will be brought into play as well (see Chapter 3). If they simply search for 'English' they are unlikely to find the image they want, so they will have to work out how to narrow down the search by adding extra words, perhaps just the word 'subject', which helped me find the image below:

Fig 4.6

A good question to ask about this icon would be whether its meaning would be clear without the word 'English' added. Perhaps rather than asking for 14 images, ask them to find appropriate images for their favourite five subjects.

Higher level questions

More advanced questions can be set for older or more able students, looking more closely at perhaps one or two sites:

➡ How many linked 'levels' are there on each site? (Or if you prefer, how many links down from the home page is the 'deepest' level?)

➡ Are there links to other sites, and if so, where are they found? What are they for – extra information? advertising? a 'parent' or 'sister' site owned by the same people?

➡ Are there any other sites which might usefully be linked to the original?

➡ Is the site easy to navigate or not, and why?

➡ Are there graphic links on the front page and are they helpful?

These are just some ideas to get you started when thinking of assignments that might be given to students.

4. Putting it into practice

The next step is for them to apply their new understanding of these principles by planning (and perhaps even making) their own site.

Text form and structure on web pages: navigation

It's simple to show a typical website structure using the 'Organization Chart' template available in PowerPoint. Create a new document from the menu bar New Doc icon (alternatively use File > New > General > Blank document). Then select the hierarchical Organization Chart from the collection of 'AutoLayout' templates. This allows you to create the plan of a website, adding linked pages so that several layers of pages are created below the main or home page (see figure 4.7).

Fig 4.7

Planning my website

This is an exercise in organization of ideas and information, and every bit as demanding and as useful as the conventional English exercise of planning an essay in paragraphs.

Extension work

Incorporate hyperlinks into narrative for collaborative story-telling, or 'branching' storylines. Use the opening of an actual story (not one likely to be familiar to the pupils) and ask them to provide alternative endings. The home page of the site will contain the opening, and all pages linked from it will contain the various endings.

Part 2

Whole text work using multimedia

Why do it?

We have looked at the way multimedia can aid literacy at 'word level', but what about the larger scale of whole text work? This is where a whole range of new criteria start to enter into the matter. Expectations, even for the most recently qualified teachers, of what constitutes a 'composition', an 'essay' or a 'story' are based on handwritten sentences and paragraphs. The idea that 'you can draw a picture with it' might survive a couple of years into secondary school, but the real business of English, we tend to feel, is the written word. As usual there is inconsistency and internal contradiction in our attitudes to visual literacy. Comic books or graphic novels which combine images and text are not considered 'proper literature', and yet film can be treated as a serious artistic medium. Whether it is suspicion of the very notion of 'visual literacy', or just a cultural tendency to degrade hybridity, there will be many English teachers who roll their eyes or grit their teeth at the mention of 'multimodality'. A historical perspective is, as often, instructive. In the fifth century BC, Socrates thought that writing would mean the end of civilization. Why? Because it was superseding speech as the dominant medium for teaching. Today we can scarcely comprehend such an attitude to the innocuous grapheme. It should remind us, however, that writing is in one sense just a refined graphic tool, and we need not see writing and the use of images as two different modes at all. So are we still busy appeasing Socrates, or can we move on and explore the possibilities of literacy in a broader context than simple 'writing'?

It seems that there is a lack of consistency too in some of our attitudes to teaching writing. On the one hand there have been recurrent 'back to basics' movements with regard to literacy, which, precisely because they look backwards, are unlikely to fully engage with new technologies. So the majority of pupils are spending most of their time trying to fill pages with words for their English teacher, and often in the story genre. Yet someone categorized as SEN is likely to be encouraged to produce narratives or other extended texts in whatever mode available. Is this because, as with early learners, we see telling stories in pictures as a preliminary exercise to telling stories in written words? This does not seem to be a sufficient explanation: clearly we have some notion, beyond the realms of written grammar and sentence-structure, that young people expressing their views or feelings or even telling stories is part of the value of the English curriculum subject.

The 'multimodal' narrative case studies are inspirational examples of what can be done with even the most reluctant learners. Though these examples came from a project with SEN pupils, the rationale and the principles behind the approach are more generally applicable to the wider categories of reluctant writers or under-achievers. We're looking at 'whole text work' in a way that is less daunting, and more engaging, for many young people. And at the same time we are accepting an apparently radical redefinition of text, one that includes not only the visual but also the aural.

There are two ways of considering the positive value of this. There are many even within the English teaching community who would argue for a general re-thinking of text so that this sort of work was not considered outlandish at all. BECTA's allusions to 'digital and visual literacy' in their report on research findings for English in ICT (2004) are suggestive of some institutional acknowledgement too.[8] Yet while we might not want to embrace this so wholly that we replace old values of what constitutes a complete text, it can clearly have, at the very least, an enabling role. This is one of the arguments that has been put forward for the study of the moving image in schools:

WEBSITE

> By recognizing the skills children have acquired in story comprehension during their pre-school years through television and video, we can seize a huge opportunity for the development of many more skilled and confident readers.[9]

WEBSITE

If we see some intrinsic, developmental value in young people seeing 'finished product' self-authored work, then we surely should not arbitrarily erect fences that exclude new media. Furthermore, in the specific case of narratives, if they must be required of children then surely we need to facilitate the inventiveness needed to be a story-teller. It seems that these technological developments force us to reassess the position of stories – both the reading and writing of them – in our English teaching. The 'augmented reality' storybook featured in our sixth case study below (see page 163), which makes the reading of printed text almost redundant, is an extreme but indicative example. John McKenzie, who had a leading role in that project, has examined the consequences for 'story' of such innovation, suggesting that modern readers (and children in particular) are accustomed to crossing code and genre boundaries in ways that our English curriculum has not begun to take into account.[10]

General approaches

In narrative, it seems paramount to make completion a priority. We can use spoken delivery to expedite this, so that there is a sense of achievement and 'something to show'. Transcribing the recorded speech later can then be seen as a second stage to the project, focusing on a different set of skills.

In general, think about combining text and image, or moving images, or sound – the spoken word to reinforce the written, the image to reinforce both. The case study accompanying this chapter shows that twelve year olds with learning difficulties and a reluctance to write made startling use of multimedia presentation to produce narratives. Can we not harness that motivational, empowering function of the technology in mainstream teaching? If we see the value in children reading their writing out loud to the class, why not record these spoken versions? Why not combine text with audio readings, sound effects or images, and even images that carry sounds with them? It is worth noting here that, by the time children have reached secondary school, and if not then soon after, the skills required may have already been learned from ICT teaching. This is evidenced by Unit 1 of the government's suggested ICT Scheme of Work for Year 7 pupils:

> In this unit pupils create a multimedia presentation using text, images and sound. In creating their pages, pupils are expected to be sensitive to the needs of their audience.[11]

WEBSITE

The trouble here is that the teaching skills which are appropriate to ensuring sensitivity to the needs of the audience are those of the English teacher as much as the ICT teacher. One approach to this would be to look at 'user requirements' and 'usability' of the content and its medium, another would focus more on the meaning of the 'content', whether textual or graphic. For guidance on the first, one need go no further than Vivi Lachs' section on Audience in *Making Multimedia in the Classroom*.[12] While she is thinking of multimedia projects across the curriculum, there is much that can be learned by an English teacher in this chapter, particularly in her list of factors to be discussed in order to make the piece engaging for the audience:

WEBSITE

➡ The wording matches the level of understanding of the audience.

➡ The sounds and pictures are age appropriate.

➡ The information is as accurate as possible.

➡ It involves an element of humour or personality.

➡ It is clear how to navigate the piece.

➡ It includes interactivity on the screen to give the audience both something to do and something to think about.

This is in a sense almost a QA checklist, except for the mention of 'humour or personality', which perhaps gestures towards the English teacher's notion of the relation between audience and text.

Except in the rare cases where there is collaboration between subject areas, we are unlikely to see much more than the technical skills learned in ICT, but we can take those learned skills and apply them in the English context. This is what the UK's national literacy strategy had to say about multimedia texts:

Purposes for creating a multimedia text:

As with any other writing, there should always be a real purpose for creating a multimedia text. Here are some ideas; however, the possibilities are endless:

➡ Retelling traditional tales.

➡ Presenting fiction for a young audience.

➡ Presenting a history topic.

➡ Personal biography pages.

➡ Creating an anthology of pupils' work – for example a poetry collection.

➡ A guide to the school.

➡ Interactive newspaper.

➡ Local area guides.

Planning the presentation:

➡ Look at examples of other presentations and websites. This will give you ideas for layout and structure, showing different ways in which information can be presented.

Points to consider:

➡ It is helpful to plan everything out on paper first, before going near the computer.

➡ Who is the intended audience? What are their needs?

➡ Define the purpose of the presentation: whether it is to inform, report or entertain (or, of course, a combination of these).

➡ If the presentation has several pages or sections, how will users move between the sections? Will there be a main menu always visible so users don't get 'lost'?

➡ Consider how you can utilize the non-linear nature of multimedia through hyperlinks.

➡ Unlike a conventional printed document, the effective use of hyperlinks on a page should enable the user to move through the information in different ways.

➡ Keep it simple! The more complex the presentation, the harder it is to put together and keep track of where everything should link to.[13]

WEBSITE

Bearing in mind what we have already considered about hypertext and multimedia, this seems like good advice, but much more guidance is needed in the application of these principles.

Teaching ideas, examples and advice

1. BookMaker and VideoBookMaker

WEBSITE

For a quick route to multimedia books there are some excellent resources provided by NAACE on their website for BookMaker and VideoBookMaker.[14] These complement their electronic Big Books, enabling you to insert text and images, or text and video, into HTML templates in order to produce web pages that could be stored locally and viewed using a browser, or even published online. As with the Big Books, you can customize font type and size to suit the reader, with the added facility of choosing your font colour. This is an excellent tool for getting older pupils to produce stories designed for younger readers. The Big Book format is simple, with a two-page spread for each web page, one being text, the other image, and arrow navigation buttons at the bottom of the page (see figure 4.8).

Fig 4.8

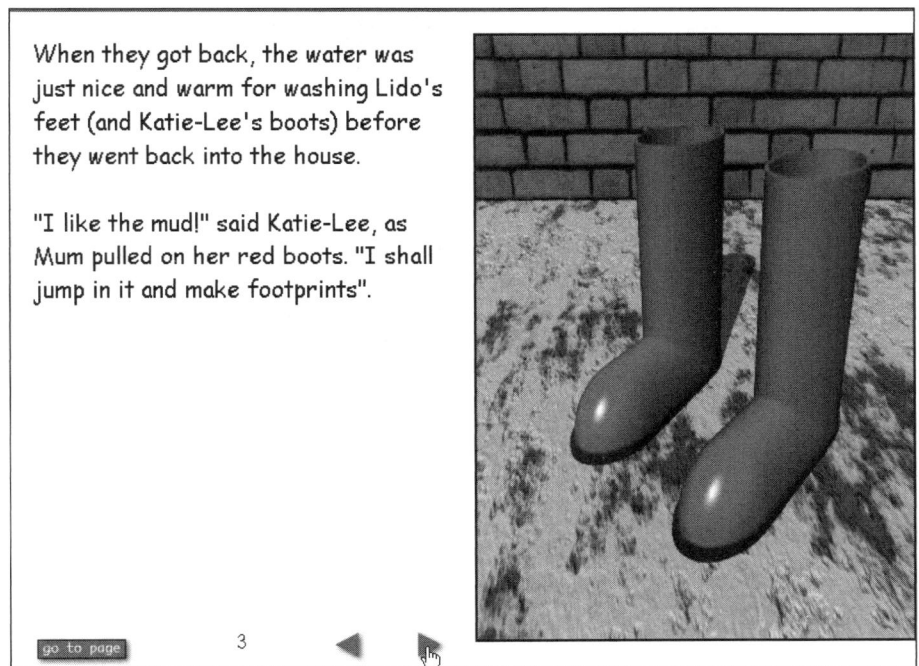

When they got back, the water was just nice and warm for washing Lido's feet (and Katie-Lee's boots) before they went back into the house.

"I like the mud!" said Katie-Lee, as Mum pulled on her red boots. "I shall jump in it and make footprints".

go to page   3

2. Multimedia narratives with 'branched' endings

WEBSITE

One of the leading figures in the UK promoting the use of multimedia is Vivi Lachs. Her book *Making Multimedia in the Classroom* was a ground-breaking one, that mapped out the territory for the first time while rooting all her ideas in actual practice. While the book shows that multimedia approaches to learning are applicable across the curriculum, her teaching experience in English and drama make her work in those areas particularly useful examples to follow.[15] Some of that work has been with very young children and special needs learners, often using their own artwork in combination with text.

CD–ROM Ch 4/Computer Children HyperStudio file

Interactivity is one of her principle ideas, and, when applying this to narrative, the alternative ending is probably the most notable example. She describes a remarkable instance of this created by Year 1 children (see figure 4.9 and the accompanying CD-ROM. After viewing the file on the CD-ROM, you can exit by holding down the 'Alt' key and pressing the 'F4' key.). Using words, pictures and recorded talk, these young children have produced an astonishing interactive story that leaves you wondering what older children might achieve.

Fig 4.9

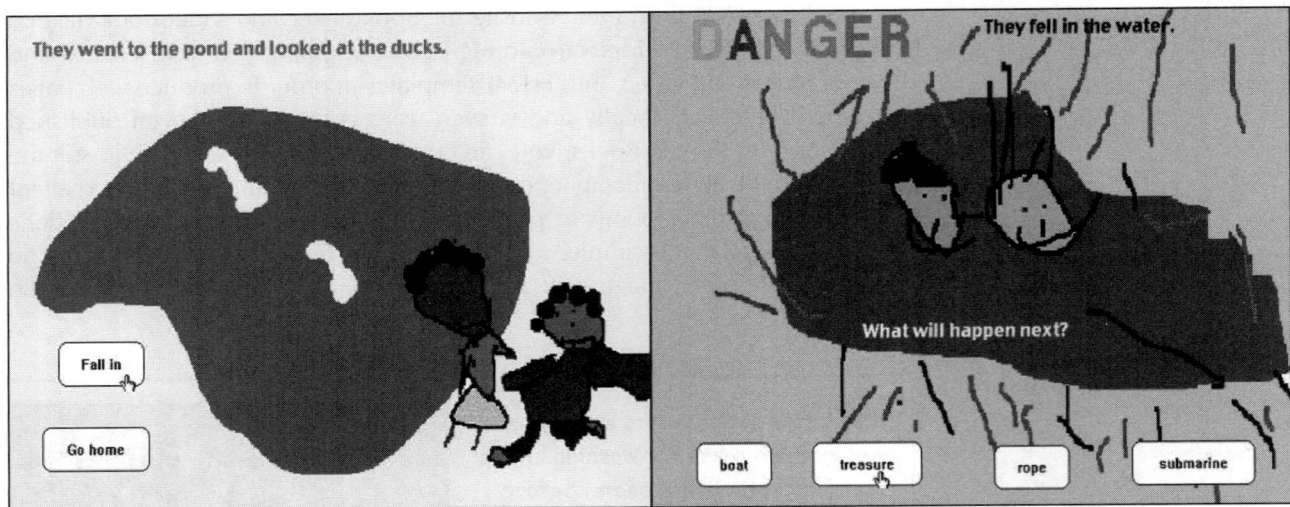

They went to the pond and looked at the ducks.

Fall in

Go home

DANGER   They fell in the water.

What will happen next?

boat   treasure   rope   submarine

Four alternative endings are available to choose from. There is also an enactment of the story with children taking the various character roles: when you click on a character's head you hear the child's voice acting out the scene. This project was created using linked HTML pages, but a similar effect could be achieved using PowerPoint. Various software applications designed to aide 'previsualization' of video productions are also available. These basically allow you to create storyboards, and can be used as an end in themselves for producing multimedia narratives.

3. Animated narratives

Simple but effective animation can be produced using a digital camera, PaintShop and Pro Animation Shop. Using collages, puppets or plasticine figures you can produce simple classroom animation sets to re-tell stories from literature or invent new narratives. Take still images then combine them in series to produce animations. ICT expert John Davitt specializes in this sort of animation, and recommends it especially for younger or special needs learners. The end product can be an animated GIF (Graphic Interchange Format) or an AVI (Audio Video Interleaved) file. GIF files are particularly versatile since they don't require any special media software to be viewed, just a web browser. In the example shown in figure 4.10[16], and available to view on the accompanying CD-ROM, he has simply used toy animals, moving them in a sequence, along with a model of the brain to suggest that the rabbit is thinking of the fox (or is it the other way round?). Opposite you can see the still images in order. Obviously what is needed is a constant light source and some way of keeping the camera in a fixed position. The rest of it is all about your imagination – and patience!

WEBSITE
CD–ROM Ch 4/Rabbit and Fox Animated Gif

Fig 4.10

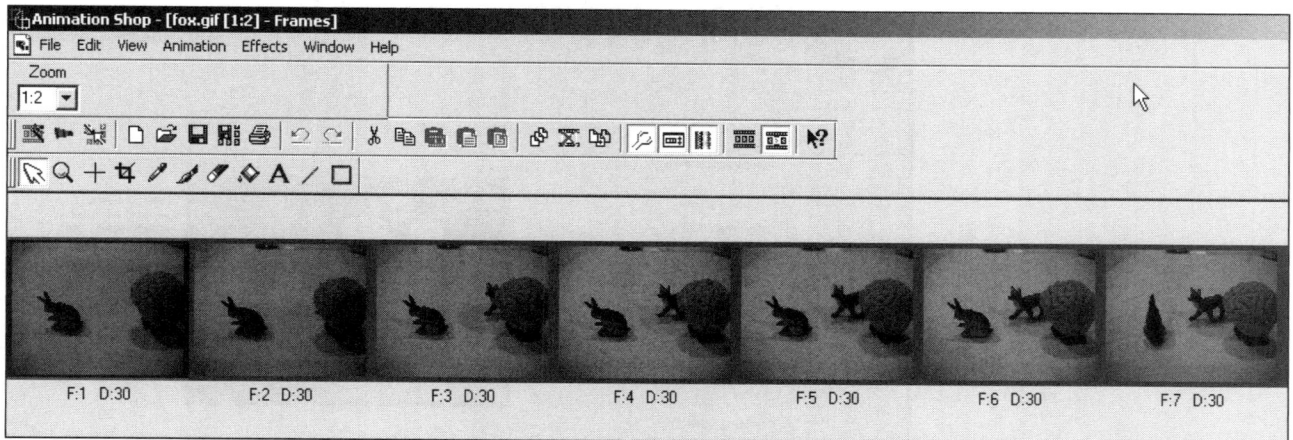

One of the BECTA Digital Video award winners used this method, along with a voice-over narrative and enactment of the dialogue in the story. 'Speccy 4 eyes' (see page 138) was a 2004 winner in the five-to-seven year age range, but it would be a good model for work with older pupils too.[17]

WEBSITE

WEBSITE

4. Immersive environments: Kar2ouche

One of the most impressive developments so far in interactive educational software has been Kar2ouche.[18] This software's application in the study of drama texts has been seen for several years, but now it includes an authoring tool which makes it possible for pupils to devise their own narratives in an 'immersive' virtual environment. They can produce storyboards, animations and publications by choosing a background, giving the stock characters and props different poses, rotating and resizing them, and then adding their own text in speech and thought bubbles. They can record their own voices with built-in software, and add their own sound effects or music.

In terms of the total immersive effect of three-dimensional characterization and manipulation, this is impressive, but it also has limitations, notably the stock of characters from stories and plays which are already loaded into the software. The same tools can be used to do 2-D storyboarding using your own imported images, but in a sense this is not significantly different from other multimedia environments. Certainly, though, Kar2ouche does have an attractive interface for young people, drawing as it does on video game design, with a very graphic approach to navigation (see figure 4.11).

Fig 4.11

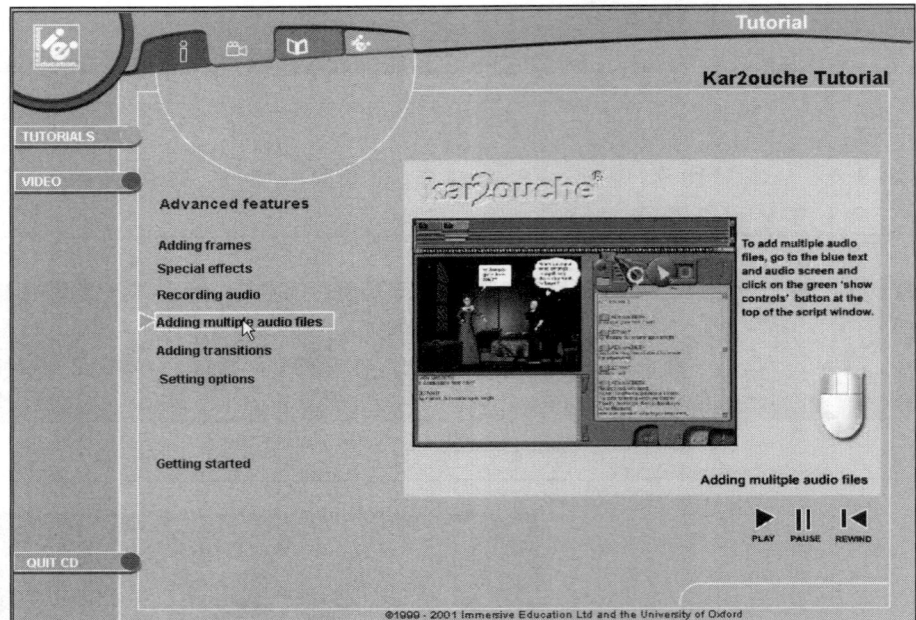

5. Videopapers

A newly emerging genre is the digital videopaper, which integrates DV and/or images with text in a simple page format. It is designed with academic use in mind – for people presenting research papers – but it can be used as an instructional or presentational medium. Where digital video is available to use, this can be a very effective way of combining extended writing with illustrative visual material, or even a simple 'talking head'. Either a related interview or the author speaking to camera alongside the text is very engaging for the reader. VideoPaperBuilder software was produced by TERC in conjunction with the Concord Consortium.[19] It is available as a free download and can be used in a variety of ways:

WEBSITE

- as digital video with subtitles, to be viewed by the user either as a whole or in segments predefined by the author;
- as text with commentaries or information on the video, with buttons to play relevant segments of the video;
- as video with further images shown at pre-determined times providing contextual information about the videotaped events.

Fig 4.12

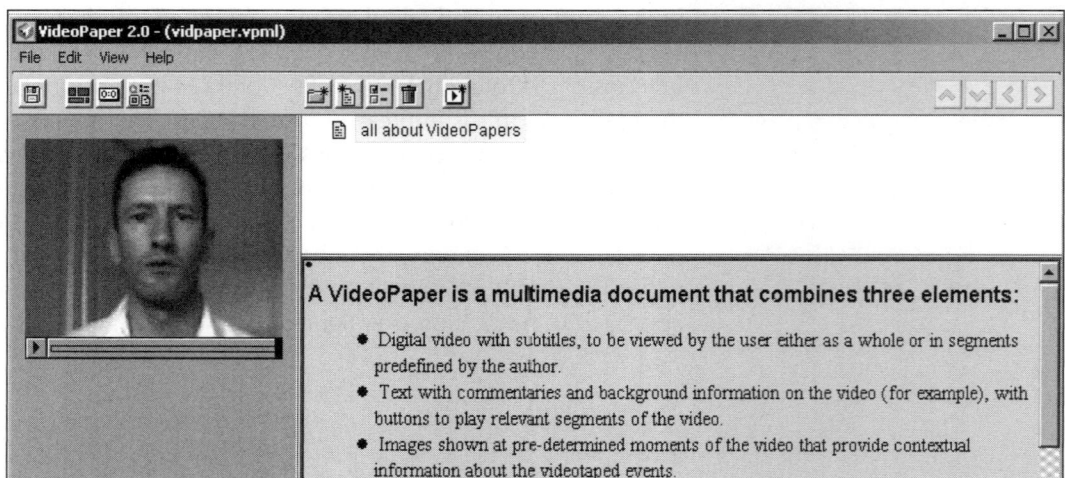

6. Digital photography as stimulus for observation and reporting

Rather than the traditional approach of starting with text first then adding images, why not turn that expectation around and start with images – preferably ones selected or created by your pupils? Get pupils to seek out, choose, or make, an image to write about. Many pupils will have a digital camera at home, so you could ask them to take a picture of something or someone interesting, then explain why they thought it would be interesting. Alternatively they could bring in an existing photograph, or picture from a magazine, which could then be scanned.

If you have the use of digital cameras within school, and can trust your pupils, get them to take a camera around the school and take pictures of interest.

There is a range of ways in which the digital image and text can be presented. Here we will look at just two.

1. You can simply insert the image into a Word document by following the Insert > Picture > From File route via the menu bar, as in figure 4.13. The image will appear where the cursor has been placed on the page, and will be adjustable. To minimize file size first convert the image into JPEG or JPG format (Joint Photographic Experts Group) using picture editing software, and adjust the size of the image before inserting it into Word.

Fig 4.13

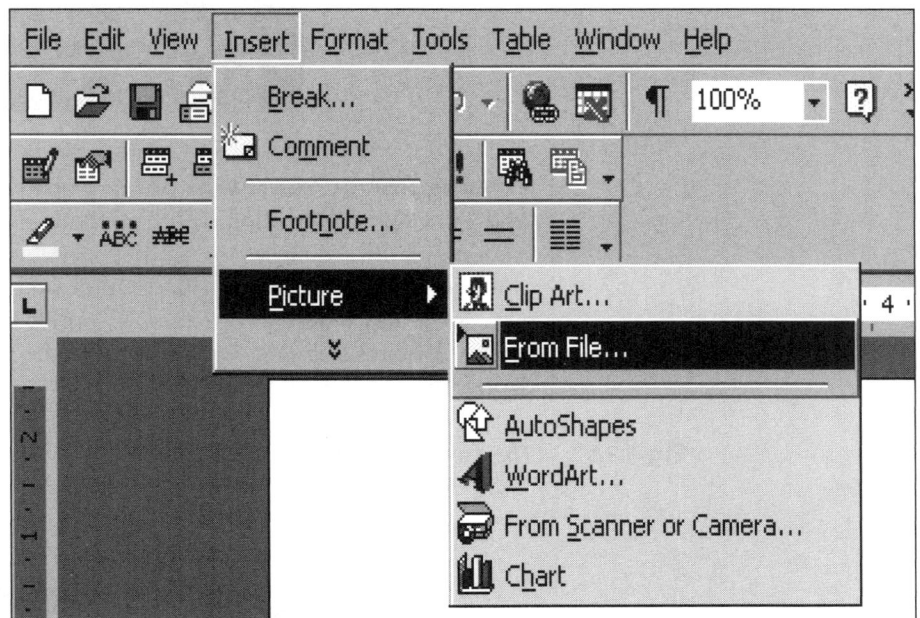

2. By using PaintShop Pro, Adobe Photoshop or similar software, text can be superimposed on an image as a 'layer'. This can result in very attractive end products for pupils who might find producing large amounts of descriptive writing problematic. There are issues of text colour in relation to the background, text size and position to address to ensure legibility and effectiveness (see figure 4.14).

Fig 4.14

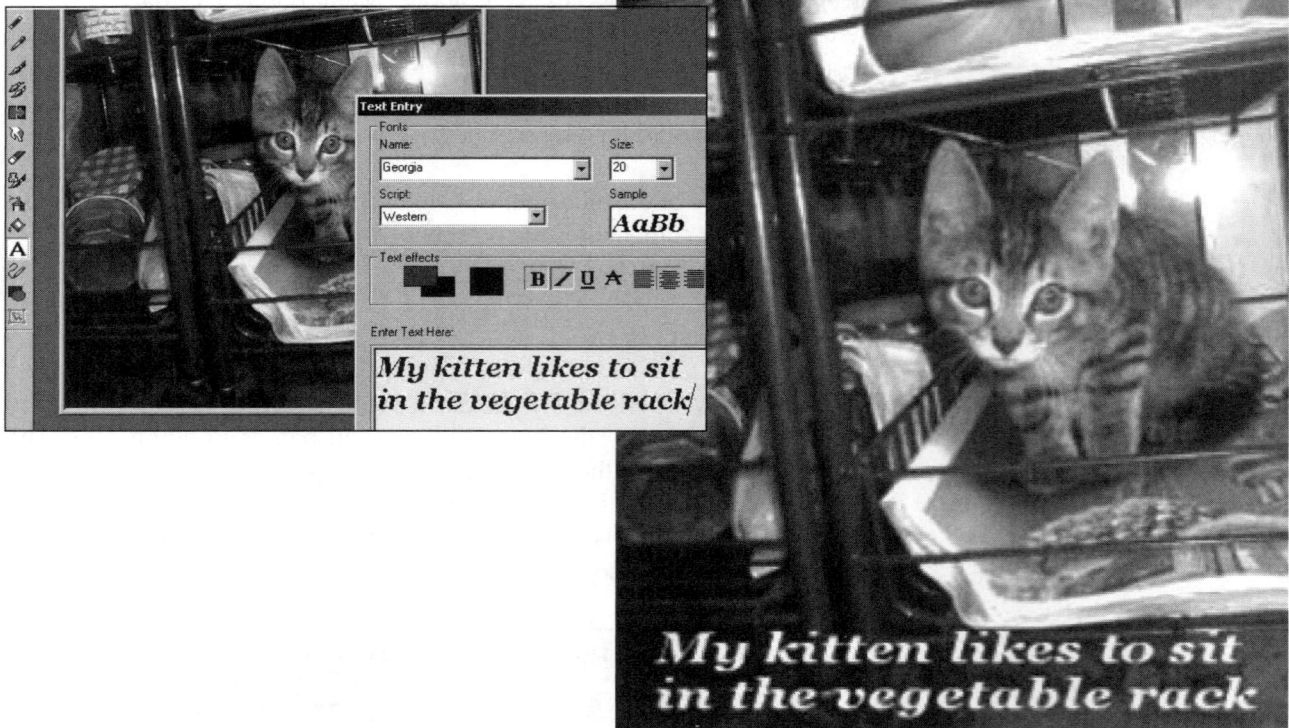

7. Using PowerPoint with older pupils

Neil Shaw has been exploiting the possibilities of English teachers working with PowerPoint for some years, and it remains a versatile tool for producing multimodal texts. He used visual stimuli such as works of art to generate both discussion and writing. For example, pupils began by looking closely at Ford Madox Brown's painting *The Last of England* (an online image search will find digital images of most famous paintings).

Fig 4.15   *The Last of England*

WEBSITE

CD-ROM Ch 4/The Kiss PowerPoint presentation

Publisher software was used in order to allow pupils to scrutinize the painting's fine detail. Pupils put together their versions of the story the painting told using an interrogation sheet, and a mind map of ideas was created. Pupils were then encouraged to write from the point of view of a character in the painting, expressing emotions and giving background information. This could be in either verse or prose.

A number of other images/works of art were stored in a folder for pupils to choose from. They included more contemporary works of art found on 'Artchive'.[20] Students 'interrogated' the images and brainstormed what was suggested by them. Poetry was written and edited in Word then placed in PowerPoint. The images were cropped, copied, animated and customized to suit the writing. A musical soundtrack was added and pupils read out their work along with the presentation. The example provided on the accompanying CD-ROM show pupils working with *The Kiss* by Gustav Klimt, as illustrated in figure 4.16. The poetry fits very naturally with the vibrant and richly coloured images, and deliberately evocative and poignant music could also be used to enhance the atmosphere of the piece.

Fig 4.16

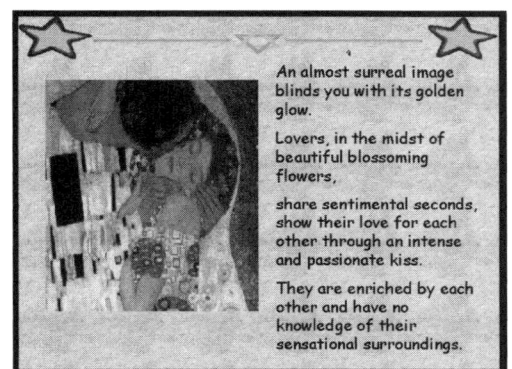

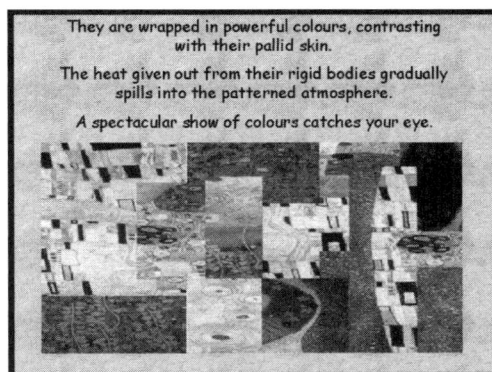

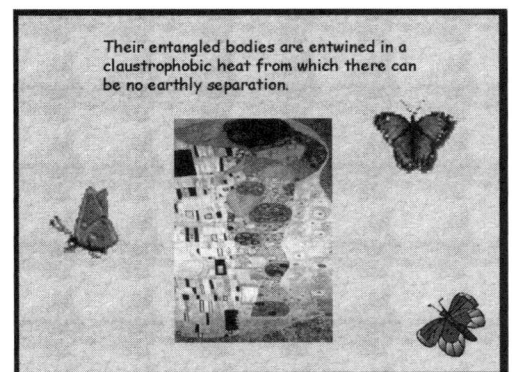

The teacher used this project to assess both ICT and GCSE 'Original Writing' targets. Using multimedia software to achieve a 'writing' grade was motivational for pupils and they thoroughly enjoyed looking at works of art and choosing a piece to explore further.

To Neil Shaw the development of visual literacy is an important aspect of reading, and he sees this sort of work as a possible pathway into media analysis of the denotation and connotation of images.

Case study 4

Fern Faux: multimodal narratives in SEN teaching

▌Background

This involved Fern Faux's work with SEN students of age 12 to 13, undertaken as part of her doctoral research. The research set out to investigate three case studies in one setting, with Fern acting as teacher/researcher. She provided lessons and intervention techniques, working with the students throughout the 2001–2 academic year. Throughout the project, the students were withdrawn from classroom lessons, on an individual basis, to undertake the work.

The idea was that the students, whose writing skills and motivation were low, would create 'multimodal' narratives using a range of techniques. Consideration was given to the interactions between the students and the computer, as well as between the students and the researcher, with a particular focus on the spoken word. The narrative tools used in the outcomes of the project included:

- ➡ electronic text
- ➡ a 'talking word processor' with electronically generated spoken narrative
- ➡ background imagery
- ➡ animated images
- ➡ sound effects
- ➡ sound and image combined
- ➡ video of students talking to camera
- ➡ sound-recorded narration by students.

The students were allowed to produce their own stories or re-tell well-known tales, the latter providing a helpful narrative framework for the initial work, giving them confidence to go on to author their own stories. Fern Faux explains the procedure behind Student B's telling of the Beowulf story:[1]

Beowulf (Student B)

B. was keen to include the video clips that he had made, perhaps because this was novel for him but also because it allowed him to play a central part in his own story. He was also keen to incorporate artwork into his stories and overlay music on the writing but, even so, writing remained an important part of his creation.

B.'s re-telling of the story of Beowulf opens with writing that reads *'Hello Beowulf, this is a spooky story.'*. Reading from left to right, and top to bottom, this writing is followed by an image of a decapitated head attached to which is a sound file which says, 'spooky' and, to the side of the image, 'spooky' is written, thus reinforcing the notion of 'spookiness' for the reader. This multimodality allowed B. to convey the message of 'spookiness' three times, in different ways ... Whether intentional, or otherwise, this had the effect of making the story genre explicit. The next picture shows Beowulf fighting Grendel. B. has attached a sound file which reads, *'I am famous'*. However, the writing to the side of this image reads, *'this is the cave of Grendel.'* Thus, it can be seen that the image conveys one thing, the attached sound another and the accompanying writing a further dimension.

B. ends this story with three video clips of himself acting. These are placed at the bottom of the screen and are to be viewed from left to right. An emphasis on sound dominated this creation and contributed to B.'s ability to tell the story in the first person, sometimes providing dialogue for his characters.

CD-ROM Ch 4/Pied Piper Movie

Another student took on *The Pied Piper* (see the accompanying CD-ROM) using different methods.

The Pied Piper (Student A)

The story opened with A.'s collage of the Pied Piper, to which he had attached a recording of himself saying, *'Hello, my name's the Pied Piper, and how are you?'* By addressing the reader directly, the creation was instantly interactive. The next image, of the Pied Piper, was superimposed onto the image of the cathedral and speech was attached to the piper, who said, *'This is my home and I'm going to tell you the story about how I took the children away from their parents.'* A. had used speech not only to have his character narrate the story but, also, to provide an explanation of the creator's (i.e. A.'s) aims. Although the image of the 'vermin' was superimposed onto the image of the lake, no sound was used. Technically, it had been difficult to produce this image but, as A. had good computing skills, it seemed that he was freed from concentrating on the computing processes and so was better able to focus on design issues. With this exception, every image was attached to a recording of A., who acted the part of the Pied Piper, and narrated the story. In this way, he managed to communicate the story without using any text. This may well have been a deliberate ploy on A.'s part as he disliked writing; however, he did not claim in any overt manner that this was why he had produced a story without words.

What worked in the study

Particularly exciting about the outcomes of this work is the variety of approaches to narrative demonstrated. In a way there are no rules or conventions for how multimodal narratives should be produced, and the students drew on the various possibilities in a 'pick and mix' fashion. For example Student B. combined image and sound effectively, as described above, but there is something very immediate about the 'talking head' videos at the bottom of the page that grasps the attention instantly (see figure 4.17).

Fig 4.17

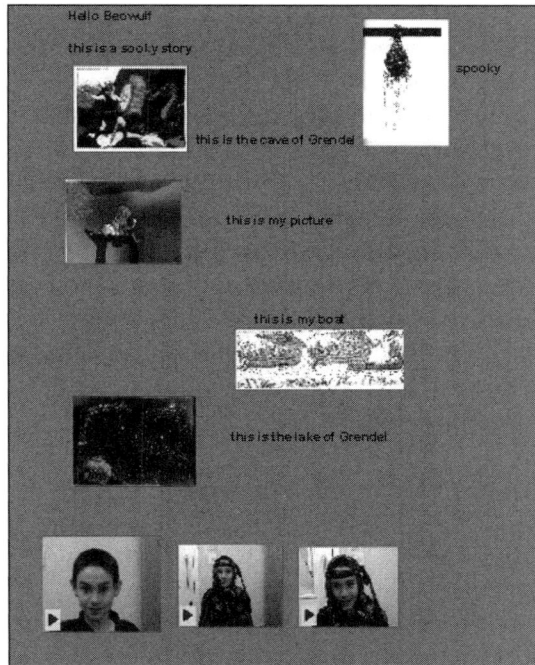

The students had a 'resource bank' where they gathered the constituent parts of the narrative. A simple colour coding of the background makes it clear which is which:

Fig 4.18

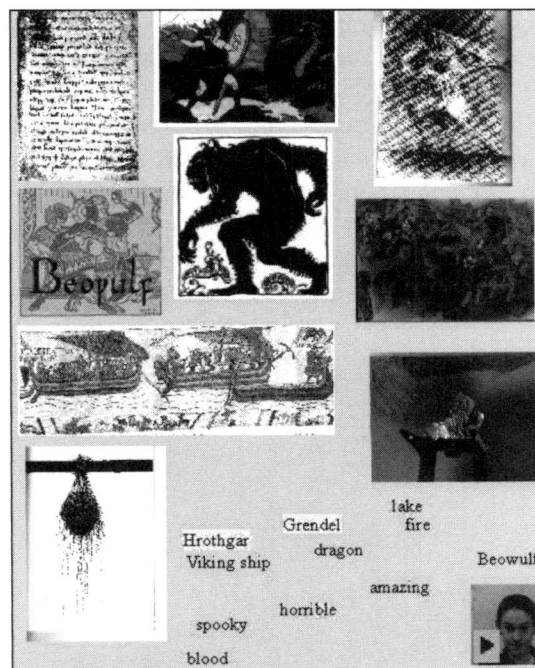

CD-ROM Ch 4/Fairytale Movie

As well as the Pied Piper story, the CD-ROM also features a modern prince and princess fairytale. These examples show that the students had a wide range of possibilities to work with. There is range here in the use of text: while in *Beowulf* there are key words or phrases viewed amidst the imagery, in *The Pied Piper* there is no text at all. In the prince and princess tale there are full sentences of text on the screen which are heard as synthetic speech via a talking word processor. The alienating effect of the speaking word processor is softened towards the end of the narrative by real voices accompanying symbolic imagery, such as a sunset representing a romantic ending.

What is clear from watching the screen recordings of these narratives is that they become, by virtue of their multimodal interactivity, performative in a way which makes them quite different from a 'written' story. They can be performed over and over again and perhaps differently each time. By such repetition students would learn about timing the sound effects, music or voices in the narrative. Another aspect of performance for such stories is the movement required across and down the page to activate audio-visual materials. Some of the movement is automated and some is dependent on the story-teller. In *Beowulf* and *The Pied Piper* all the narrative is contained on a one screen-sized page, while the prince/princess story requires scrolling down the page. These factors are all new and unfamiliar variables in the process of creating a narrative.

Doing this in the classroom

All of the options exemplified in the three case study pieces need to be considered in preparation of any similar work, as well as keeping an open mind to other options as yet untried.

First you need appropriate software. If you don't have Textease, which was used in the case study, or an alternative school-oriented multimedia software such as HyperStudio, then PowerPoint is quite adequate. While these were individual projects, it is likely that this would be best done as collaborative work in mainstream English. The 'talking head' approach would mean that only a low-cost webcam would be needed to create effective video footage to insert as part of a narrative. Students can use image searching for helpful backgrounds or key images, and record their own sound effects.

Creating a 'resource bank' is also recommended, and the students can work in a cross-curricular manner at this stage, generating their own resources in art, music and so on. Video or sound files will need to be stored and edited before being combined in the presentation. In the case of PowerPoint the whole thing could be controlled by mouse clicks, or with a bit more work and rehearsal set up to run as a timed slideshow.

Chapter 5

Audio-visual English

Part 1: Speaking, reading and listening with ICT

In this section you will:

- consider why ICT can be useful to the teaching of reading, speaking and listening;
- consider some general approaches to using ICT in these areas;
- look at examples of good practice and advice in these areas;
- look at practical ways to apply this technology in your teaching.

Part 2: Digital video

In this section you will:

- consider why digital video can be both a useful teaching aid and a medium worthy of study in English;
- consider some general approaches to using digital video in English teaching;
- look at examples of good practice and advice in this area;
- look at practical ways that you can apply this technology in your teaching.

Part 1

Speaking, reading and listening with ICT

Why do it?

There have been attempts recently to investigate 'the grammar of spoken English', which is an interesting but possibly misguided approach to the issue of how we teach Speaking and Listening. Such an approach seems to be about a desire to focus on the measurable aspects of English. For this to be at all feasible it requires a very functional approach to language development and the Holy Grail of 'progression'. This is not a wholly undesirable thing, but the fact that it is an area which excites more interest from teachers of English as a foreign language suggests much about the limitations of such an approach. English is a much broader subject area. Not only does it cover literature as well as language, it encompasses our culture and – the point of this book – all our ways of communicating.

Sometimes it seems that there is less a concern to encourage young people to expand their interest in speaking and listening, than a desire to constrain that interest and have it conform to some standards conceived in ancient Greece and lionized in the debating chambers of universities or on the political stage. In other words, we have not really let go of classical rhetoric as our reference point for quality in this area, because nothing has ever challenged it. And a nice but dubious conflation of Quintilian's and Cicero's views on the topic has left us with the generally accepted view that the 'art of speaking well' is also the art of persuasion. The web has been a boon to those promoting the value of rhetoric, especially in the USA, where its virtues are more explicitly extolled. The huge American Rhetoric website has online clips exemplifying various classical rhetorical figures, which is at once rather stuffy in conception and fascinating in execution.[1] While political speakers, not surprisingly, dominate the examples, there are amusing clips from film and broadcasting such as *Austin Powers* and *The Wizard of Oz* to exemplify alliteration and, bizarrely, Sting demonstrating *scesis onomaton*![2] Whether or not we feel it necessary that

WEBSITE

the full range of Greek terms for techniques of public speaking are known, there is certainly something to be taken from this formal approach to spoken language. UK English teachers will teach as standard a core selection (metaphor, simile, assonance, alliteration) but often treat them as features of written English rather than appreciating them for what they are – figures of *speech*.[3]

In that highly formalized way of treating speaking and listening characterized by rhetoric, there is an emphasis on 'correctness' and an implicit anxiety about informal modes of speaking. But alongside this approach is another which is not about public speaking and not so explicitly about power exchanges: that of oral history and folklore. And this too, if not so obviously, has been boosted by ICT. In a sense the digital age enables us to re-create the age of oral tradition, by facilitating not only the recording of speech, which has been possible now for a century, but also the editing, storage and retrieval of these recordings. The British Library Sound Archive is leading the way by providing online access to some of its immense resources, including some useful sample materials. The oral history resources such as the Opie Collection of Children's Games and Songs are searchable online, and recordings of items can be ordered at special education rates. More readily available are 131 recordings from the Collect Britain archive of local accents and dialects, showing regional variations in speech in the UK.[4] The 'corpus' of 'naturally occurring' speech is a phenomenon arising from academic (usually linguistic or sociological) interests, and has grown enormously in the past 20 years on account of the new recording technology.[5]

WEBSITE

WEBSITE

So, if we have these two models of increasing appreciation of spoken English using ICT, are we doing anything about it in the classroom? The use of recorded sound files in English teaching is not widespread, but is gathering interest as teachers begin to appreciate the ease with which they can be made and managed, and the ways they can supplement and perhaps transform approaches to speaking and listening. The majority of school computers now have sound cards; microphones and headsets are readily available and inexpensive; the necessary software, typically Windows Recorder, is bundled with the operating system, offering limited but adequate functionality. There are few physical barriers to the more widespread use of computer recording and playback techniques. Schools that are exploiting the potential of computerized sound recording make use of easily available software, such as RealPlayer, QuickTime, Windows Media Player, and Audacity (a free recording and file manipulation program). Some have approached their music colleagues for help, and the use of more powerful and sophisticated sound mixing software.

Another area which deserves some attention is the link between listening and reading, where the new technology can address issues of accessibility and inclusiveness. There is considerable activity in the area of electronic 'talking books', which are seen as an aid to early reading development. Listening to stories has traditionally been seen as standard practice for infants, and these books are produced generally for Key Stage 1 or SEN use.[6] Special education is leading the way in exploring the possibilities of this technology, because of the way it makes texts more accessible to those who have difficulty in reading without support. At one level, then, it is being used to help overcome barriers such as difficulties with motor control or visual impairment. One as yet unproven technology emerging is that of speech recognition software which some have suggested might offer benefits to learners who have difficulty writing. If it is intended to overcome learning problems rather than physical barriers, it is not clear even in theory what benefits speech-to-text transmission will bring. In the meantime, the technology itself is clearly not at the stage where it can easily be used by learners, and especially those with learning difficulties.[7]

There is also a completely new concept emerging from digital technology: the 'talking word processor'. In a sense we are being technology-led in this area, and are still waiting to see how its potential will be realized, but the use of 'text-to-speech' technology already shows signs of being beneficial to readers. A talking word processor, in conjunction with carefully structured materials, has been shown to produce dramatic improvements in reading age. Teachers also observed increases in concentration; in time spent on task; in attitude and self-esteem; and transferability of skills to other areas of the curriculum.[8] Furthermore, if the technology is handed over to pupils to serve creative ends, then it can become a multimedia compositional tool, as the case study on multimedia texts (see Chapter 4; Case study 4) showed with SEN pupils.

General teaching approaches

Recording for corpora

The corpus approach seen in the academic field is something which can be imitated at local school level. The kinds of tagging of corpora used academically are of a wide variety according to parts of speech, meanings, 'prosody' and even emotion. Accents and colloquialisms can be examined, and transcription and/or paraphrase of speech into writing can be practised. If we enable pupils to gather a corpus of speech, in a similar methodology to that of our text messaging ideas, then the scope for work with this recorded material is very significant. There are numerous sound archiving software packages; it might be worth consulting with the music department to see if the software they use is suitable, so that students are working with familiar tools.

Text-to-speech

As well as the recording of sound, a new technology offers emerging possibilities. Text-to-speech software presents the same information both visually and aurally, the one reinforcing the other. 'Talking word processors' – Easiteach, PenDown, Clicker – offer immediate feedback of what has been written, enabling pupils to check that what appears on screen is what they intended to write.[9] ReadPlease will render any text in Word as speech, and a 'Reading Bar' added to Internet Explorer will even read web pages.[10]

Talking stories

If listening to stories has not traditionally been deemed appropriate for the age range this book addresses, it is now possible for learners actually to produce talking stories themselves, and this therefore becomes a speaking as well as a listening exercise.

There is already extensive use of sound files to support dyslexics, both as readers and as writers, and as always this specialist use is equally valid in mainstream applications.

WEBSITE

WEBSITE

WEBSITE
WEBSITE

Streaming audio broadcasts

If a school radio station seems to be an extra-curricular indulgence, we are underestimating the very focused speaking and listening work which, by necessity, goes into it. The imperative of broadcast quality material promotes close attention to, and reflection on, speaking performance, whether it be in interview, or reading aloud a prepared piece. This means that the quality of spoken English is being examined by students themselves at three stages:

➡ preparation and rehearsal

➡ performance (repeated 'takes')

➡ editing.

Furthermore there is a real audience, with the opportunity for feedback, developing dialogues within, or even between, schools.

Teaching ideas, examples and advice

1. Using recorded speech for language study and reflection on language

This can be done using what used to be called Dictaphones but are now known as digital voice recorders. Not all enable you to download (via a USB port which would be a requirement) onto a PC, and at present they are a little expensive, but having a few of these available in an English department would create many opportunities. In the longer term I envisage their use becoming more common, as their functionality is increasingly being incorporated into other hand-held items such as mobile phones, MP3 players, and even digital cameras.

I can see three fruitful ways of approaching this, following on from the Tim Shortis approach to text message language seen above, and from the two approaches of formal rhetoric and oral history:

➡ Language study: language change, spoken versus written English, and so on.

➡ Figures of speech – make your own compendium.

➡ Oral history: ask Gran to tell how life used to be and record it for an archive.

2. Spoken stories

Producing a story for younger children is always a good task for older students, making them think about the audience's needs, and this applies just as well to audio stories. Versions of myths or folk tales are an obvious way into this, using the opportunity to incorporate work on reading texts from other cultures and traditions. The objective is to produce a recording suitable for playing to a younger child at bedtime. This will require sustained work, recording in sections, saving and editing and joining together for the final product. Set some objectives for the timing – for example, between three and six minutes in length. Work on pace, fluency of transitions from one part to the next, dramatizing direct speech, adding appropriate intonation to increase tension, and so on. Music fading in and out at the beginning and ends of sections adds dramatic effect, and can be achieved easily using Audacity's multi-tracking options. Sound effects can be inserted later too, recording them as the track plays back in real time.

WEBSITE

The Hounslow Language Service uses sound files on CDs to present multilingual stories, targeting parents and children for whom English is an additional language, simultaneously building bridges between home and school and making texts accessible. There is also, in a simple but wonderful use of the web, a story 'The man, the boy and the donkey' presented online in dual text in eight different languages alongside the English.[11] The text, just two or three sentences per page, is combined with images and audio, so that readers can listen over and over again in both languages to help reinforce the learning (see figure 5.1).

Fig 5.1

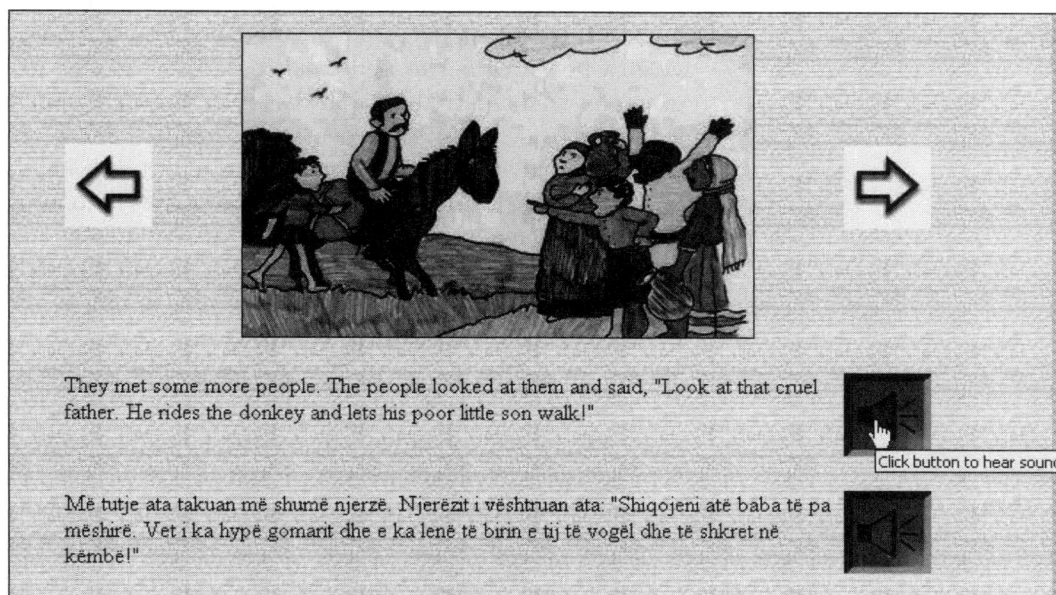

They met some more people. The people looked at them and said, "Look at that cruel father. He rides the donkey and lets his poor little son walk!"

Më tutje ata takuan më shumë njerzë. Njerëzit i vështruan ata: "Shiqojeni atë baba të pa mëshirë. Vet i ka hypë gomarit dhe e ka lenë të birin e tij të vogël dhe të shkret në këmbë!"

Click button to hear sound

WEBSITE

There are real possibilities here for inclusiveness, for pupils in households where more than one language is spoken: as the Hounslow site suggests to teachers, 'why not enlist the help of some of your bilingual parents to record some?'.[12] Using the same methods (for example PowerPoint) suggested for audio-visual books in Chapter 4, this could be a project that combined reading with artwork and appreciation of other cultures, while crossing the home-school divide.

WEBSITE

In a similar vein, the Ganton Special School has some fascinating multilingual examples of poetry presented with the aid of recorded sound, in English and in Norwegian.[13] Dr Isobel Fleming, a primary adviser specializing in the use of ICT to support children with special needs, has also reported extensive use of sound files to support dyslexics, both as readers and as writers. This evidence suggests that the approach of visual and auditory reinforcement of reading using ICT is certainly worth pursuing.

3. Streaming radio

This is an exciting innovation, enabling large audio files to be played as they download, rather than having to wait for the whole file to be downloaded before it is heard (the same principle that is making online video more feasible). Streaming radio seems to be an easily manageable technology, sufficiently transparent and easy to use to make it very accessible to pupils as a medium. It has clear social benefits, and offers pupils a forum to address questions and issues that stretch them beyond their immediate experience, or invite them to explore and reflect on what they feel they already know. Writing and talking for a real purpose, aimed at a real audience, involves pupils in speaking and listening – with quality assurance determined by audience feedback – and in real editorial skills.

WEBSITE

WEBSITE

A web-based software application which has cleverly adapted 'streaming radio' technology to schools use is the BECTA award-winning Radiowaves.[14] Pupils log in to access and publish material in an attractive environment which can incorporate text and images. The Radiowaves site offers advice on sound editing, recommending the use of the free software Audacity already cited in this book.[15] This is a very accessible medium and less daunting, perhaps, than digital video when it comes to performance. It also has clear social benefits, as the examples featured on the Radiowaves site illustrate. Pupils are offered a forum to address questions and issues that stretch them beyond their immediate experience, inviting them to explore and reflect on what they feel they already know. An online radio system like Radiowaves is only one option, and this could be effected internally on a school's own network. There is opportunity too for language-study work derived from the outcomes of radio recordings.

4. Text-to-speech helping reading

WEBSITE
WEBSITE

Studies into pedagogy and ICT, conducted by the University of Newcastle for the Teacher Training Agency, found that the use of 'speech support' software made a big impact on progress in reading comprehension of children up to Year 5.[16] The use of Intellitalk and iansyst software with Year 2 children produced 'a five-month increase in reading age over a three-month period'.[17] Texthelp, which applies 'assistive technology' to both word processing and browsing, was used in another study with Year 4 children and contributed to gains in reading comprehension of 14 months during an eight week term. As a result of this success the policy of using speech support was continued into Year 5. The reports on these studies, which date back to 1997/98, suggest that this technology is likely to have a significant impact on reading progress with an average ability group, though one study suggested that where children already have a high reading age the perceived effect will be less dramatic.[18] One of the Newcastle studies also found that the use of speech support assisted in the writing process as well as in reading comprehension:

WEBSITE

> When speech was used to support writing, [teachers] noted that some of the pupils preferred to use this facility to check at the end when their work was completed, whereas others relied upon it more heavily to reassure them that what they were writing made sense.[19]

WEBSITE

Part 2

Digital video

Why do it?

Digital video (or DV) is one of those examples of a new technology whose educational value is both cross-curricular and also specific to English. DV is video recorded as digital data that can be stored, edited and broadcast on a computer. It only started happening in schools in 1998 when Apple Computer began incorporating FireWire ports into their desktop computers, to which you could connect camcorders. Before long Sony and Canon had built a compatible port into their camcorders so that computers and cameras could be linked via a new connection protocol. Since then most laptop manufacturers have built FireWire ports into their machines, and more recent computers come with video editing software supplied as part of the basic operating system. In the past, video editing was based on time points and counters linked to large reel-to-reel machines. Now a range of software is available which turns editing into a 'point-and-click' activity on the computer screen. Thumbnails and timelines show the contents and position of each video clip which has been 'grabbed' from the camera, so that the parts and their relation to the whole can be seen all on one screen. Once edited the final movie can be sent back to the camera as a finished version on tape, or turned into a digital file for publishing on a network or the internet.

One pragmatic issue for work in schools is that there are a range of file formats for saving and distributing digital video clips. The international standard file format for digital video is known as MPEG (Moving Picture Experts Group), but there are other options and this can cause compatibility issues. If a movie is made and saved on the Apple using iMovie the export option is as a QuickTime file – a format developed by Apple but available as a player for Windows-based PCs. If the file is transferred to the Windows platform it will not play unless the QuickTime player is installed. The Digital Movie player on the PC Windows Media Player does not recognize that file type, and similarly files produced on Windows-based machines will not play in the QuickTime player on the Mac unless extra translator files (known as codecs) are installed. If there is one limiting factor in the potential of digital video as a speaking and listening resource it is probably this lack of compatibility between different systems.

WEBSITE

But if the hardware and software is generally available in schools, what use is being or can be made of it in English teaching? DV is almost a cross-curricular subject unto itself at the moment, being associated with a general notion of creativity as well as being a tool for presentation and recording of work.[20] It is also often seen as an ideal tool for special needs, and for involving students in marginal curriculum subjects like PSHE and citizenship.[21]

WEBSITE

The annual BECTA Digital Video Awards for the most creative use of digital video in schools have helped raise the profile of the medium as well as providing a good reference point for work schools have done.[22] In addition, the motivational aspect was seen in that 'using DV as part of learning tasks improves behaviour and on-task concentration'. It also appears that English teachers are exploring this new medium, whether as a tool in drama teaching or in filming and broadcasting digital video news across their school networks.[23] DV has made the process of video editing much easier, and so more likely to happen, if it is an option within the crammed curriculum.[24] Even so, digital video editing is a specialized set of skills which really requires some training, and there is a significant technical skills gap to be filled before we even get to the question of how to use it effectively within English teaching.[25]

A quite different rationale for English teachers embracing digital video is that it can (and perhaps should) also become a medium for study in itself, a means to the proper study of the moving image at school level for the first time. In media studies, where it is optional at GCSE but necessary at Advanced level, DV editing is an extension of the study of the medium itself. There is a second skills gap here then for the conventional English teacher, as David Parker of the BFI (British Film Institute) found when attempting to use DV animation as a tool for narrative. In the Key Stage 3 media and literacy Animating English project, he found that partly because of the lack of a teaching vocabulary for moving image, 'the animation work became a technologically mediated task, rather

WEBSITE

than a linguistic or narrative one'.[26] Likewise, the BFI report into a pilot scheme using DV in 50 schools concluded that 'in working with DV, teachers and

WEBSITE

pupils need to recognize the distinctiveness of the moving image as a unique mode of expression and communication'.[27] This is certainly true if we include media studies in our definition of English, but it is not clear that there is room in the English curriculum for such emphasis on the language of the moving image. In the national curriculum statutory order for English 'moving image texts' get included as a sub-section of reading, shared with 'media texts', for the 11 to 16 age range, but as far as national tests in English at age 14 are concerned, there is no reference at all to such things.

WEBSITE

In March 2004 the Northern Ireland Film and Television Commission launched *A Wider Literacy*, a substantial document making the case for moving image media education.[28] It gives examples of work that has been done in schools from Key Stage 1 to AS level, and in the chapter on Moving Image Literacy and the Curriculum it focuses on the relevance to Language and Literacy. It cites the revised primary curriculum to support its applicability there, and gives some example tasks using moving image sources for GCSE English. Most interesting perhaps in relation to our concerns was the reference to research done at the University of Minnesota which showed that

> … children's reading comprehension at age eight can be better predicted by looking at 6-year-olds' understanding of stories in non-print media than by looking at 6-year-olds' basic skills like word recognition and

WEBSITE

vocabulary ... In other words, reading comprehension shares many cognitive processes with comprehension of other kinds of media. Understanding how stories work – how characters and settings are established, how narratives are structured – is to a large extent a generic skill rather than a media-specific one.[29]

This goes to the core of the question of relevance to English: if understanding film and understanding written text are cognate skills, then the argument is already made. The question that remains is how we use the new technology to make the most of that connection.

If we are looking at applications of DV rather than the investigation of the medium itself, the speaking and listening aspect is the obvious (though not necessarily the only) place to start, utilizing this new ability to edit and revisit the spoken word. The opportunity to draft, redraft and perform spoken texts as digital video recordings, and then to be able to return to them and assess them critically, opens up clear routes to improvements in speaking. There are many opportunities for motivating and framing the development of speaking and listening skills, in tasks such as composing and presenting a voiceover, creating an accurate transcript as a text track subtitle, or summarizing a video in text.

It is clear also that, as with new audio-recording and editing capacities, ICT could have a role in assessment as well as teaching of Speaking and Listening. At present we lack even a methodology for assessing progress in these modes of communication, perhaps because we have never had the practical means. It will be interesting to see if now that we have the technology, more attention will be paid to this, but in the meantime we can certainly put into practice some DV-based English teaching ideas.

General teaching approaches

The video editing software most widely used in schools in the early days seems to have been iMovie on the Apple Mac, although Apple only claims to have 13 per cent of the school computer market. A number of schools seem to have bought a single Apple computer specifically for digital video use. Apple has been actively promoting digital video as an important tool for education for some time, and with the release of Windows Movie Maker for all new Windows-based PCs, most schools now have some software available. Nowadays, if a school has a £300 digital camcorder (with digital out/FireWire), a PC or Mac with a FireWire port and free software, it has a basic digital video-editing suite. While Windows software produces files for the Windows Media Player, Apple's QuickTime format is the main competitor. QuickTime Pro (which is available for Mac and PC) allows the cutting and pasting of sections of video, as well as marking up sequences with text under the video screen. Within a school it's a matter of deciding on your chosen format and being consistent: while Windows Media Player is very common (BBC News uses it for example) it doesn't allow the cut-and-paste editing, tagging or easy download afforded by QuickTime video files as used for example on the National Curriculum in Action site.[30]

WEBSITE

As a way of enabling VAK learning, the usefulness of this tool can hardly be doubted; look, for example, at the prize-winning videos on the BECTA site. Leasowes Community College, which is renowned for its progressive whole-school policy on ICT, ran a digital video project with Year 11 students which had unexpected general impact, as Neil Shaw described later:

> The 'buzz' created by the arrival of our first iMac was quite remarkable. Students clustered around the new iMac equipment, intrigued by its aesthetic at first but fascinated by its possibilities and the 'sexy' DV software. We are an ICT-rich school but the arrival of the new digital video equipment certainly aroused great curiosity and launched the DV work with no teacher effort at all.
>
> Although a lot of the work carried out on DV was completed during Flexible days where time is generously allocated, the 'Write Now' lunchtime writers group (predominantly Year 8 girls) instantly decided to become a video club for the duration of the project. We had a full house for all of its meetings and students happily devoted time after school, at home (on planning) and even during break to develop ideas and edit movies.
>
> Interestingly, the equipment, although initially of special interest to upper school 'tecky' boys, soon captured the lower school girls' imagination and perhaps as the project has developed it might be true to say that the equipment has been used by a more representative group of students than other software that has been used in school. The ease of operation and friendly help systems has really attracted reluctant ICT users of both genders to the project, along with the lure of stardom and Hollywood money.[31]

Although Neil Shaw is indeed an English teacher, this use of digital video was a cross-curricular project. What then of its specific relevance to English teaching? Should the skills of filming and editing be within the remit of English teaching? This would involve a broadening of what is normally considered the English curriculum, at least in schools. It is not yet clear where it belongs. Although at university level, the broader category of 'English studies' will often now include film studies, this is usually in terms of critical reading of films rather than film-making. Even in the discrete but overlapping area of media studies it is not generally practised below A level. The British Film Institute has mourned the minor role that the study of moving images has been assigned within the discipline of media studies, suggesting that it is mere laziness to prefer the study of brochures over film and video and bemoaning their relegation to the bottom of a ragbag of media forms that are referred to together in the national curriculum English document.

Teaching ideas, examples and advice

1. Making movies make sense

WEBSITE

A starting point might be to use the excellent resource, *Making movies make sense,* which is sampled on the Media Education Wales website.[32] This is a ground-breaking attempt to introduce the language of moving images in a way that makes it generally accessible, even to primary level students. This innovative approach is itself only made possible by DV, since it is now possible to show and name examples of film-making techniques, such as camera shots, editing, lighting and sound (see figure 5.2, opposite).

Fig 5.2

The five main areas illustrated with images or video are:

➡ framing

➡ shot names

➡ lens and focus

➡ camera angles and position

➡ movement.

The last of these areas, movement, is illustrated with brilliant simplicity by the use of two adjacent screens showing simultaneous video of both the camera shot and the person taking the shot, along with textual commentary. Using actual students in a classroom, the CD-ROM shows how high quality filming can be achieved without access to a studio, special lighting or other equipment (except perhaps for a shopping trolley, which is used imaginatively for tracking shots!). As well as illustrating and educating about the language of film, it provides a model for activities which students themselves could do. They could create their own guides, using the same headings as those on the CD-ROM, and in the case of the still images this could be done using one of a range of multimedia software applications.

2. Marking up video

For hands-on work with video, a new opportunity offered by QuickTime Pro is that you can 'mark up' video clips with text buttons – so that users can label or annotate parts of the video (see figure 5.3). For text to appear inserted before or between clips the procedure is very simple:

1. Copy the text or graphic to the clipboard.
2. Move the playback head to the point at which you want to insert the copied item.
3. Choose Edit > Paste.

A number of different ways of editing video with text are available with the Pro version, each explained in the online help. In the example below a text file has been imported and converted to video format before being added into the video frame: this is called 'overlaying'. The QuickTime movies on *Making movies make sense* provide useful material to work with.

Fig 5.3

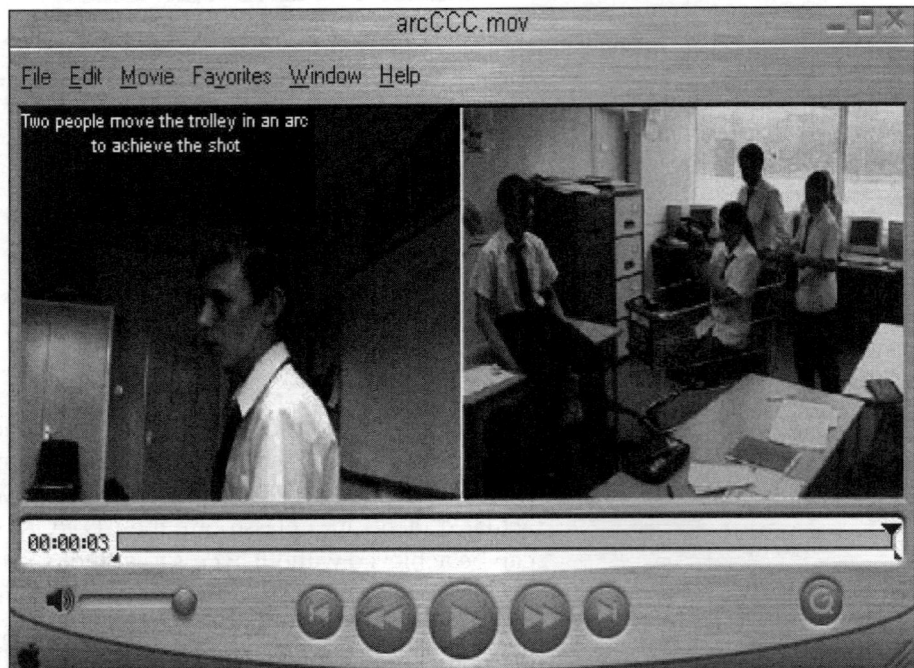

There are two ways in which this integration of text and video might be effective in the teaching of Speaking and Listening:

a) Studying public or other speakers

You could take digitized video footage of interviews, speeches or even less formal situations, and mark it up, identifying figures of speech or other significant features such as changes in tone of voice, or non-verbal communication.

Use the *Making movies make sense* vocabulary if you have this available, for example, 'rhetorical question', 'interjection' and 'irony' could be made available from a drop-down menu.

Other ideas:

➡ In the style of American Rhetoric's 'Audio Figures' (rhetorical figures as sound files) construct a video compilation of figures of speech.

➡ Use online searches (see Chapter 3) for video files of famous people speaking and look for distinctive, describable features.

b) Reflection on your own behaviour as a speaker

WEBSITE

Among the key findings of the BECTA DV Pilot Project was that 'DV enables pupils to reflect on themselves, their behaviour and their performance'.[33] The ability to observe yourself and others immediately in a speaking and listening situation, and to discuss such issues as their contribution to group talk, collaborative skills, precision of language usage and non-verbal communication, would be enhanced by the use of digital video. An extension of this is to adopt a similar methodology in drama, using DV not to create a final product but to let students watch their performance.

Modelling

The ideal way to model the process of reflecting on performance would be to show unedited video using a projector or interactive whiteboard: the ability to rewind and repeat means that you can emphasize a teaching point.

Applying what is learned

Devise a set of key questions or headings as prompts for the students when subsequently evaluating their own performances, whether in drama or other speaking and listening contexts. For example, in the case of speaking to camera a list of possible forms of non-verbal communication:

➡ eye-contact

➡ body-language

➡ hand gestures

➡ movement in relation to the viewer.

For these visual features you could capture stills and label them electronically, and even print them out.

3. Voice-overs and commentary

You can exploit students' pre-existing tacit knowledge gained from watching TV, articulating it through not only performance but also by imitating the conventions of the 'voice-over' commentary. Voice-overs provide opportunities for pupils to adapt their normal speaking to a more formal situation within time constraints. To provide topical material for this sort of exercise download trailers for the latest movies, or video news items.

In this area, the 'director's cut' concept (a convention emerging from the commercial DVD market) is particularly useful and likely to be both familiar and attractive to students. This is one approach used successfully by primary teachers Paul Turner and David Cook in their award-winning work at Round Diamond School, Stevenage. They make a second audio overdub to their initial performance saying what they identified as strengths and what they wanted to improve. Part of the power of the director's cut approach is that it is predicated on careful listening, and attention to details of their own performance.

4. Animation using DV

Using the DV camera to take still shots then combine them in series to produce animations is an extension of the usefulness of the medium. Using collages, puppets or plasticine figures you can produce simple classroom animation sets to re-tell stories from literature or invent new narratives. One of the 2004 BECTA DV Competition prize winners, 'Speccy 4 eyes', shows how this can be done to great effect even with Key Stage 1 children.[34] After an introduction spoken to camera (and including some choral speaking) animation is combined with voice-over acting and narration from different children to produce a collaborative final result.

Figure 5.4 shows models and sets created for the DV animation 'Speccy 4 eyes'.

WEBSITE

Fig 5.4

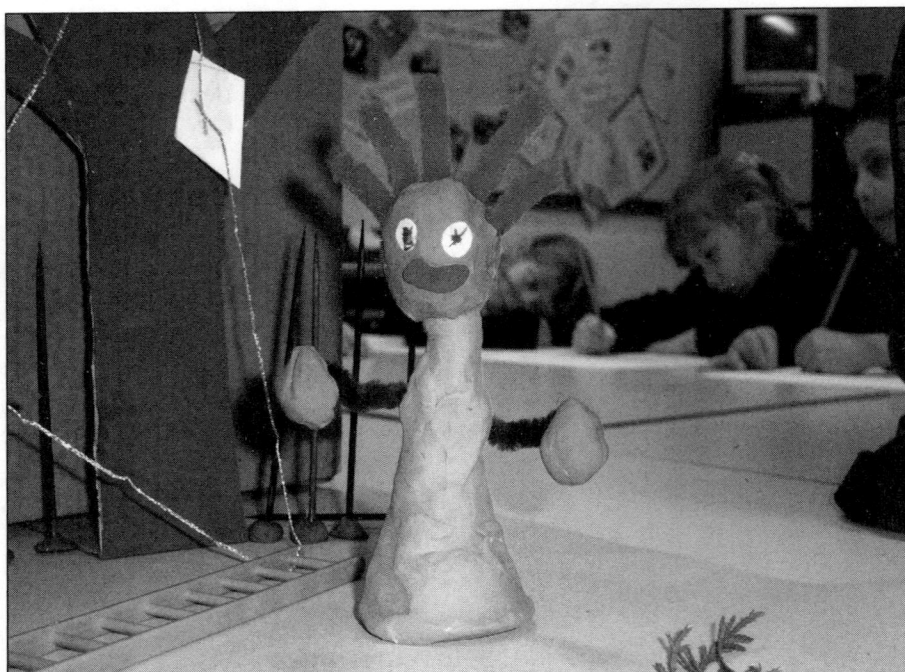

5. Video poems

A great example of a video poem can be found on the BECTA Digital Video Awards website, 'City Life Poems' created by the children at St Stephens C of E Primary School, Lambeth, London.[35] This winner in the 8 to 11 year age range (from 2003) provides an interesting model for integration of poetry and video. Both the poems and video were produced by the Year 6 children, whose readings of the poems are interspersed with images (some still, some hand-held video) of places and people in the city. Both the process and the end-product were collaborative: different pupils read out their lines during the video. This is effectively a new text type, the video poem, where words and images have the same lyrical effect, suggesting feelings and meanings rather than simply stating. Obviously, some of the effectiveness is derived from the video editing, which might need substantial teacher input, but producing the component parts of video footage and verses, and storyboarding the video, can all be done by pupils working in groups.

WEBSITE

Fig 5.5   Students film a video poem

This sort of collaborative work – done in a new medium, inventing new modes of presentation – is evidence of the potential digital video has to put new vigour into standard English teaching practice. The case study for this chapter, looking at digital video and Shakespeare, is equally impressive evidence of its potential for literary study.

Case study 5

Vivi Lachs: digital video and Shakespeare

Background

These two Year 9 projects involved pupils selecting key scenes from a Shakespeare play and using video to consider and then perform different interpretations of that scene. The English class looking at *Twelfth Night* videoed three different interpretations of the same scene and then used them to create an interactive web page giving the user a choice of which version they wanted to view. For Vivi Lachs it was important that the performance itself became the object of study rather than the written text. This was made feasible by the ability to view alternative performances and compare them easily. The drama class studying *Macbeth* looked at character motivation and used video to explore the different motivations that characters might have, then published these videos onto a web page. Key to the success of these projects was the availability of resources and expertise at Highwire City Learning Centre where the video was edited and put into web pages. Vivi Lachs, who led the projects, is creative director of Highwire, which runs regular projects with local schools in the Hackney area of inner-city London.

Teaching and learning objectives

➡ To use video authoring to explore different interpretations of key scenes from a Shakespeare play.

➡ To explore how video can be used to convey different meanings to any audience.

➡ To explore the text as performance.

➡ To use editing tools to develop their critical and analytical skills.

How it was done

Trippingly on the Tongue was a project involving two Year 9 classes from different schools: an English class studying *Twelfth Night* for their Key Stage 3 national tests, and a drama class studying *Macbeth*. In each class they were asked to select key scenes from the play. Working in groups, they considered one of these scenes – thinking about what happened in that scene and how it related to the rest of the play. They then had to think about how the text could be interpreted through performance in different ways. They were asked to do this by considering character intention; what characters might be thinking at the beginning of the scene, and letting the other characters respond. For example, Olivia feeling anxious about meeting Sebastian, or feeling excited, or in love. The groups filmed their three interpretations of extracts of the scene – also considering how to perform for a video camera and how the use of video techniques might add layers of interpretation and meaning, for example, by using a close-up to emphasize a point.

Pupils brought in costumes and props and filmed the first version of their scene in the school playground on a sunny day. At Highwire they filmed further versions and edited them using iMovie. Each group then created two web pages to contain their videos. Instead of filming three different versions of the same scene, some groups chose to make only one video of the scene itself, but added extra video pieces of the characters speaking their thoughts before and after the scene directly to camera. The videos were then put into a web page offering the audience different choices of how they wanted to view the scene. Each of the scenes were then linked together with supporting text explaining what had happened in the play in the intervening scenes, producing an online version of the play using performance as well as plain text.

Outcomes
The combined use of DV and web pages meant students could go beyond actual performance in their creative interpretations of the play.

As Vivi Lachs put it,

> Through performing, filming and editing scenes from the play collaboratively the pupils were interacting with the text, with each other and with the technology. Although they could have performed the play without the technology, the technology added another level of interactivity. The final web pages also involved pupils thinking about audience and how the audience for their work would interact with their pages – through the choices they would make about which version of the scene to select.[1]

WEBSITE

The web pages combined both text and video, so the final outcome was a multimodal presentation of ideas. The web pages also used scanned collages and images that pupils produced and used as backgrounds, conveying atmosphere and contributing to the overall quality of the work. Examples can be seen on the Highwire website.[2]

WEBSITE

Doing this in the classroom
The lesson plans used on the Trippingly on the Tongue project (available on the Highwire website) are a useful guide to how similar work can be achieved. There are obstacles with this sort of work, such as availability of hardware, software and expertise, not only for producing the videos but also for mounting them in an interactive way on the web pages. It should be pointed out, though, that these do not have to be published on the internet – they could be published locally on a school network for viewing. It might be an occasion for cross-curricular work, with ICT and of course with drama where it is a discrete subject. Both the *Twelfth Night* and *Macbeth* work involved substantial

preparation and rehearsal before the filming and editing, so it might constitute a half-term or even full term's work.

With *Twelfth Night* the students were first grouped and then chose a favourite scene from the play. They were then asked to consider what the characters were feeling when they began that scene, and suggest different possibilities. This established the basis for the alternative interpretations which would be presented.

The groups were allowed an early view and practice with the cameras but most of the preparation was done away from the camera. The second session looked at perspectives, using these prompts:

➡ Taking an everyday situation, what are the characters feeling?

➡ Give a different motivation, and how does the scene play differently?

➡ Introduce the word 'motivation' and make what they have done explicit.

➡ Re-play the scene with students speaking the thoughts.

➡ Try it on the scene from Shakespeare.

The third session involved storyboarding the scenes, and listing properties and costumes that would be needed. In the last two sessions at the Highwire Centre itself the performances were filmed and edited, then transferred to web pages. This is the part of the process which in a normal school context might take longer and involve some co-ordination with ICT.

With *Macbeth* there was whole-class work on the story of the play first, then the idea of character motivations was introduced. Teachers in role acted out a scene in two different ways, to model what the students then went on to practise, using a script rather than improvising. You could try this different ways, as a whole class watching pairs, or in groups watching pairs, then end with feedback and discussion.

To ensure that the students were clear about the concept of the 'inner monologue', they role-played a playground situation with students acting words and others speaking thoughts. Try this in groups and show to the whole class. Groups were next given scenes from the play to read through, then were divided into those who would act the scene as per the script and those who would say the 'thoughts' straight to camera.

In the next session groups were asked to look at what comes just before, and what comes just after, the scene, to help establish character motivation. They then tried acting/thinking alternative motivations, and as with the previous session, they ended with feedback and discussion. Then there was rehearsal, interspersed with consideration of video presentation and the possibilities of using multiple videos on the web. As with *Twelfth Night*, listing of props and costumes followed by storyboarding preceded the final filming and editing.

An alternative and interesting use of the video editing stage would be to transcribe the spoken thoughts of the actors and add them as 'subtitles' to the video. As seen in Chapter 5 (figure 5.3) this could be done even with simple editing software like QuickTime Pro, but it can also be done with iMovie or Ulead. Woody Allen's use of the technique for comic effect in *Annie Hall* would be an amusing introduction to this for older students.

Chapter 6

New ways of reading

Part 1: E-texts online

In this section you will:

- consider the value of using electronic versions of texts for study;
- look at some online sites that provide access to electronic texts;
- look at some practical approaches and ideas for study of these.

Part 2: Electronic poetry

In this section you will:

- consider why ICT can be useful in teaching poetry;
- look at some general approaches to electronic poetry;
- look at practical ways to use ICT to enhance the study of poetry and make it more exciting.

Part 1

E-texts online

Why do it?

One of the most exciting things about the internet for teachers of literature is the increasing number of literary texts available online.[1] Is this a good thing? Well undoubtedly it is very useful to have electronic versions of texts, for a variety of reasons:

➡ you can navigate around them rapidly;

➡ you can search for occurrences of key words;

➡ you can copy and paste quotations from them and annotate them easily.

WEBSITE

What are the 'downsides' then? Well not everything is free. Sites giving free access to electronic text are often of 'classic' literature taken from editions which are out of copyright, so as far as English literature is concerned you're going to be able to find plenty of Austen but sadly not much Auden, and more Brontës than Betjeman.[2] Even pay-to-view sites like the renowned Chadwyck-Healey poetry archives relied heavily on editions of poetry without any copyright issues, so they are sometimes only as good as the editions they drew from.

There is also the issue of accuracy. In some cases texts will have been typed in by hand, so there is always room for human error. Chadwyck-Healey's method for English Poetry was for it to be typed in by hand twice by two different operators, and then a comparison program highlighted any discrepancies for review.[3] In other cases there has been the application of text recognition technology (technically referred to as OCR, or Optical Character Recognition), which involves scanning and then conversion to digital text. This technology is imperfect, being vulnerable to factors such as unusual assortments of letters or punctuation, or the distortion when scanning caused by the curve of the page towards the spine of an open book. OCR quality will also depend on the print quality of the original: where a letter or two are badly printed, or where there is a blemish on the page, it will go for the best match. At the very least, careful and thorough checking of the text by proof-readers is required.

Finally, there is the issue of readability. Is screen reading a good thing when it comes to literature? I think there is little doubt that if electronic books were going to become popular they would have done so by now, and the obvious truth is that most people prefer books to screens. People find reading text on a screen less easy than on pages of a book for a number of reasons, one of which may well be to do with the glare of the white on-screen page. A resourceful approach has been taken by the Classic Bookshelf site, which allows you to customize font and background colour, font size and type to your own preferences.[4] This is indeed addressing some of the issues (I found indigo Times New Roman against a mustard yellow background quite easy on the eye) but there is also the scrolling factor to be taken into consideration. Some find the experience of scrolling down a long on-screen page more difficult than moving from page to page in a book. It is also worth remarking, from the English teacher's point of view, that quoting from or citing episodes in a novel is rather awkward when you have no pages to reference!

WEBSITE

General teaching approaches

If you want 'classics', especially pre-twentieth-century, then you can find an astounding range of material online, including medieval and early modern texts, and you can therefore bring these to the attention of pupils much more easily. If we feel that providing some sort of historical context for the English literature we teach is essential to understanding its value and significance, then the resources online are enormously helpful. We can pull off the web all kinds of texts from the last thousand years or more of English literature, and often show them as they actually were, in facsimile.

Major authors like Shakespeare have numerous sites containing the complete works, and the work of many other poets, playwrights and even novelists can be found online. I am certainly not going to try to give an exhaustive list of sites you might use, but will describe some of the different kinds of site available:[5]

CD-ROM Additional Weblinks – Literature

➡ Concordances such as the collection of Victorian literature from Nagoya University, Japan;

➡ Full text, for example, the University of Virginia's collections or the online publisher Bartelby;

➡ Facsimiles, for example, on the University of Pennsylvania Library site;

WEBSITE

➡ Portal sites, such as Links to Literature.[6]

Shakespeare is useful to exemplify the range of materials available. The availability of his work is not, however, representative of all writers, and material on some authors will prove difficult to find. The web boasts numerous versions of the complete works, and portal sites too.[7] There are also some extraordinary sites that exploit the potential of electronic publishing more fully. The Internet Shakespeare Editions offer transcriptions of both folio and quarto versions of the plays in original spellings, along with the option to view them with either their original pagination or in the Act and Scene divisions of later editors.[8] There is a searchable collection of facsimile works of illustrated Shakespeare from the University of Wisconsin-Madison, which offers an unusual and stimulating historical perspective on Shakespeare's plays.[9] And there are the University of Virginia's extraordinary facsimile presentations of Shakespearian prompt-books from the seventeenth century.[10] Here you can view at once facsimile pages, full-page and close-up, and notes on the player's annotations to the text. This enables you to show how Shakespeare's plays were

WEBSITE

WEBSITE

WEBSITE

WEBSITE

WEBSITE

actually being performed only a few years after his death. In the section shown in figure 6.1 we can see the severe cuts made to Hamlet's long soliloquy 'O what a rogue and peasant slave am I!'

Fig 6.1

The ability to view facsimiles, whether of medieval manuscripts, early modern printed books or more recent works, can be a real boon in teaching the history of English.

▌Teaching ideas, examples and advice

Below are some possible approaches to using either poetry or prose found online for literary study. As always, I am not trying to prescribe how anything should be done, but rather showing how you can use the internet to make your own interests more interesting to learners, by involving them actively in some research and bringing their own knowledge in too.

1. Novels and stories online

a) Traditional tales

WEBSITE

Online collections of short stories or traditional tales are often good teaching resources. A particularly stimulating set of collections can be found in the University of Southern Mississippi's online archive of fairytales.[11] These include both facsimiles and transcriptions of three well-known tales: *Cinderella, Jack the Giant Killer* and *Little Red Riding Hood* (referred to in Chapter 1). You can view either the texts with facsimile images interspersed, or just the images. Comparative work on the versions of the stories encourages critical reading, and the ability to show the story in images as well makes for greater engagement. The *Cinderella* story is a good one for discussions of traditional attitudes to women, and the *Red Riding Hood* story, seen as an allegory of growing up, is a good starting point for discussions on adolescence. *Jack the Giant Killer* (or *Jack and the Beanstalk*) seems to be concerned with individual enterprise and the acquisition of wealth, which is another interesting discussion point. Decoding these stories simply using the images available is a way of increasing visual literacy as well as reflecting on our cultural heritage.

Using software such as PowerPoint or HyperStudio, ask pupils to write commentaries on the various graphic versions of the tales, highlighting the differences, as in figure 6.2.

Fig 6.2

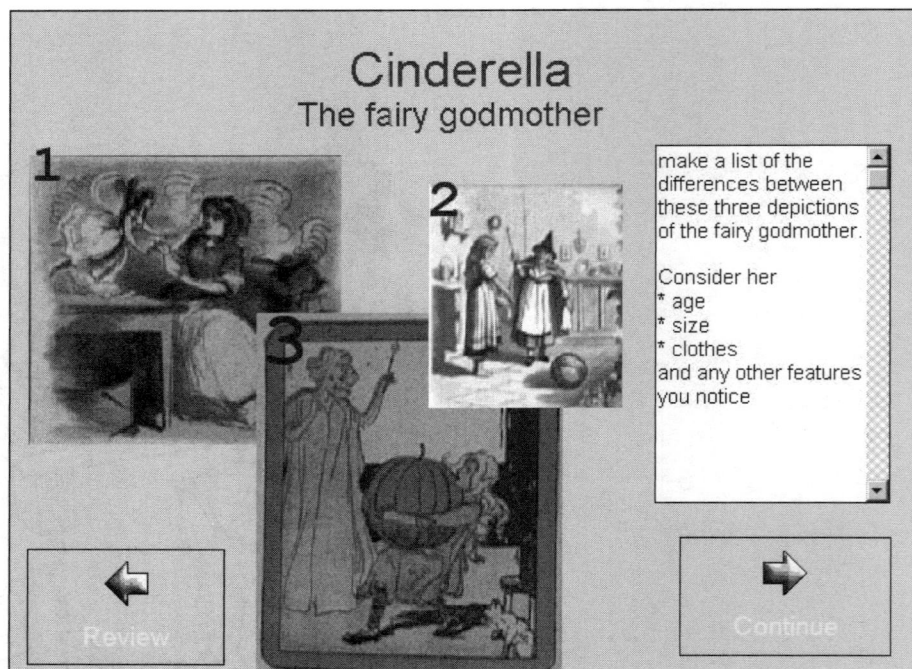

b) Novels

Having the full text of a novel in electronic form might not be the best way to read the whole story, but it has all kinds of benefits for study and analysis. The word-search option might seem a little mundane but with novels it can enable readers to range through a text rapidly looking for patterns.

WEBSITE

Take the electronic text of *Great Expectations.* I tried versions at Bibiliomania and Literature.org.[12] The latter version is in a more readable font and has only one, scroll-down web page per chapter, which makes searching easier. However, the textual accuracy is higher in the Bibiliomania version. The Literature.org version shows rather too much evidence that it was derived from a printed text using OCR software: misspellings and inappropriate hyphenations are not uncommon.

Do a word-search in each chapter for 'fire'. Working in a group of two or three is ideal, so that the chapters can be divided up for this labour-intensive but not unsatisfying research task. If the story is being studied via a film version, with only selective use of the text, this is an easy and unthreatening way into the text.

1. Copy and paste a paragraph or so of surrounding text under the chapter headings.
2. Highlight the word 'fire' in each excerpt.
3. Establish what the context is (the point in the story, the time and place, and who is there).
4. Consider what the associations of fire are in each of these.
5. Can these associations be grouped together under thematic headings? For example:

   ➡ domestic warmth
   ➡ brightness and excitement
   ➡ danger and fear
   ➡ destruction/death
   ➡ purification (for older students).

With younger or less able readers simply ask them to place the uses into either of two columns: positive or negative connotations (and perhaps a third for neutral or uncertain).

CD-ROM Ch 6/Great Expectations Word doc

Using a template of boxes or columns for each of these, cut and paste the excerpts into the chosen category, as in figure 6.3 (see the example on the accompanying CD-ROM, with quotations taken from the first 20 chapters).

Fig 6.3

Chapter	domestic warmth & safety	Calm reflection	brightness and excitement	danger and fear	destruction / death
		Fire associations in *Great Expectations*			
2		My thoughts strayed from that question as I looked disconsolately at the fire. Joe, slowly clearing the fire between the lower bars with the poker, and looking at it: he [Joe] sat slowly munching and meditating before the fire		I twisted the only button on my waistcoat round and round, and looked in great depression at the fire. the marsh winds made the fire glow and flare	
5	the weather was cold and threatening, the way dreary, the footing bad, darkness coming on, and the people had good fires in-doors		the bellows seemed to roar for the fugitives, the fire to flare for them, the smoke to hurry away in pursuit of them	The torches we carried, dropped great blotches of fire upon the track, and I could see those, too, lying smoking and flaring. I could see nothing else but black darkness.	
6	his coat was taken off to be dried at the kitchen fire				
7	Give me,' said Joe, `a good book, or a good news- paper, and sit me down afore a good fire, and I ask no better.' We got a chair out, ready for Mrs Joe's alighting, and stirred up the fire that they might see a bright window	'Well, Pip,' said Joe, taking up the poker, and settling himself to his usual occupation when he was thoughtful, of slowly raking the fire between the lower bars you see, Pip,' said Joe, pausing in his meditative raking of the fire, I could not help looking at the fire, in an obvious state of doubt			Well?' said my sister, in her snappish way. `What are you staring at? Is the house a-fire?'
8			When I first went into it, and, rather oppressed by its gloom, stood near the door looking about me, I saw her pass among the extinguished fires, and ascend some light iron		

Compare the findings of each pair or group regarding the symbolism of fire in the novel. This can lead into discussion of the thematic structure of the book – the fires at the cottage and at the forge, Estella's candle, Miss Havisham's demise, and so on.

Why is Joe always looking at the fire, or tending to it or raking the embers? What does this tell us about him?

Compare descriptions of the constantly tended kitchen fire at the cottage and the fire at Miss Havisham's (Chapter 11).

Obviously the quality of the work you are likely to get from using electronic text in this way will depend on the quality of the teaching, the teacher's knowledge of the novels and their own imaginative input. But the speed with which searches can now be done through texts means than even very large novels become less daunting, both to learn and to teach. Given a number of carefully thought through searching tasks, students can be led to understand narrative patterns and structures through a process of exploration and discovery, but without the arduous page-turning and scanning that has been the traditional way to study a novel.

2. Poetry online

I recently heard of a school production of *Twelfth Night* which set the words of Feste's songs to Beatles' tunes, which was a reminder that the simple medieval ballad form, with its 4:4 time, has also been a standard form for pop songs. If you want children to understand the relationship between medieval song and twenty-first century pop lyrics, then you can show them the original manuscripts along with transcriptions and modern translations at the click of a mouse. Bella Millet at the University of Southampton has made this possible with the late medieval 'Harley Lyrics' in an ongoing project, the Wessex Parallel WebTexts.[13]

WEBSITE

By looking at these examples you can see that it is our modern editing which arranges the song's text in lines, because here only a forward slash indicates a rhythmic break:

Fig 6.4

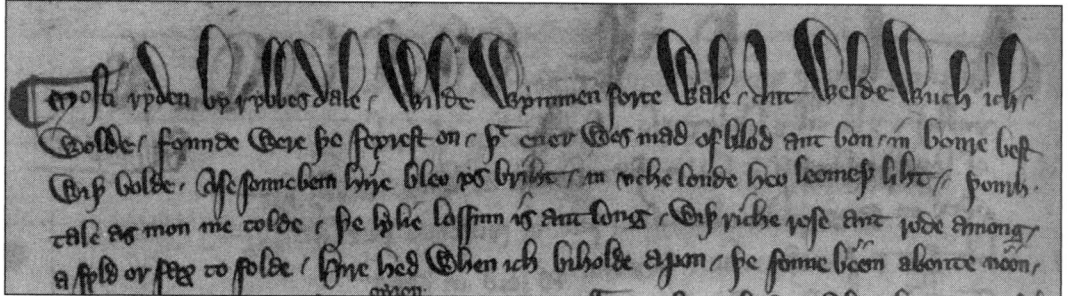

This example is 'Mosti ryden by Rybbesdale', a love song describing a woman's beauty from her head downwards. While this form is a traditional one, its theme is familiar enough in the context of today's popular music. The slightly risqué ending (coy perhaps by today's standards) should strike a chord with teenaged readers too. Make it clear that while these lyrics might have been heard sung by minstrels, they were not intended for reading, any more than the pop lyrics of today. Instruct pupils to find a modern love song and compare its lyrics with those of a 700-year-old song from the Harley manuscript. There are numerous sites where they can search for song lyrics[14], both from 'classics' and current songs that pupils will be listening to now. There is even a site dedicated entirely to love songs, though some of that site's areas such as 'Flirting tips' and 'Types of kiss' might prove a distraction in the classroom.[15]

WEBSITES

WEBSITE

Extension work with older students

With older pupils you might compare 'Mosti ryden by Rybbesdale' (sometimes referred to as 'The Fair Maid of Ribblesdale') with Shakespeare's sonnet 'My mistress' eyes are nothing like the sun'. These are quite adult in content, but fun too. Shakespeare appears to be parodying the style of poem seen most notably in Petrarch's Italian sonnets from the fifteenth century. In this 'blazon' style, the elements of a woman's beauty were described in detail from the head down. As the Harley lyrics show, he might also have been drawing on a much older, oral tradition.

Ask pupils to consider:

➡ Would the sonnet work as a song?

➡ In what ways is the sonnet unlike the Harley lyric?

➡ What sort of rhythm do you think the Harley lyric would have had?

➡ Why has the sonnet got 'metre' while the song has 'rhythm'?

In the final section we will look further at the arguments for focusing on the aural aspects of poetry, and employing a range of ICT approaches.

Part 2

Electronic poetry

▌ Why do it?

Reading poetry using ICT merits its own section because of a number of factors:

1. Poetry is more web-friendly than prose.

2. A significant degree of written poetry's meaning derives from 'formatting'.

3. Poetry is, both in its origins and predominantly today, an aural experience.

4. The annotation of poems for study purposes lends itself to ICT.

The number of poetry websites online has already been mentioned, and these sites often combine two functions in one, allowing people to read examples of work by renowned poets as well as encouraging them to submit their own verses. The reason for the popularity of these sites is in the nature of poetry, or at least lyric poetry: it is usually relatively short. It is a well-established principle of web publishing that where text is concerned the optimum size of a page is a single screenful, and certainly the less scrolling required the easier it is on the reader. Even a long poem like Whitman's *Leaves of Grass* will segment **WEBSITE** conveniently into screen-sized passages of text that can be consumed in one.[16] Poetry.com acknowledges this principle by specifying that its competition submissions are no more than 20 lines, so that they are always framed nicely **WEBSITE** by the page.[17] The similarity of text message poetry to haiku has already been noted, and of course haiku is especially suitable for web page presentation, as the Children's Haiku Garden website beautifully demonstrates, with its haiku **WEBSITE** presented simply, alongside illustrations by children.[18]

The fact that written poetry is about form means that the formatting and editing possibilities of electronic text can be employed to help students look afresh at poems, as we will see below. Perhaps most exciting, though, is the way we can use audio-visual presentation of poems. Poetry has its historical origins in song and recitation, but with the exception of the Harley manuscript referred to above there is almost no recorded lyric poetry in English before the sixteenth century. In the Middle Ages, and still as late as the sixteenth century, lyric poetry was generally heard by the public, not read by them. With live performance by a minstrel, quite possibly accompanied by dancing, songs would have been a complete VAK experience! In spite of the 'textualization' of English poetry during the past 450 years (perhaps since the first English sonnets by Wyatt) we still assume that most poetry should be read aloud to be appreciated fully. People have sung songs for millennia, but only relatively recently has lyric poetry been thought worthy of committing to print. So impressing upon children that poetry is not a dull text-bound activity – either historically or, necessarily, today – is perhaps a useful approach to a notoriously difficult part of English teaching.

Teaching ideas, examples and advice

1. Focusing on sounds

A notable example of using ICT to focus on sounds in poems is what ICT author Chris Warren calls 'text collapsing', the most interesting function of which is the alphabetical ordering of words in poems. With a bit of fiddling one can achieve this in Word, but he has produced a special tool for doing this which is accessible on the English Online website even to non-members.[19]

WEBSITE

The example here (see figure 6.5) is a familiar poem sorted alphabetically, with upper case initial letters (that is, the first words of each line) being sorted separately. The fact that the words can also be sorted by their final letter means that this can be used not only as an introduction to alliteration in a poem, but also to highlight rhymes and internal rhymes. Get pupils to read aloud the words in this order to appreciate the repeated sounds within the poem.

Fig 6.5

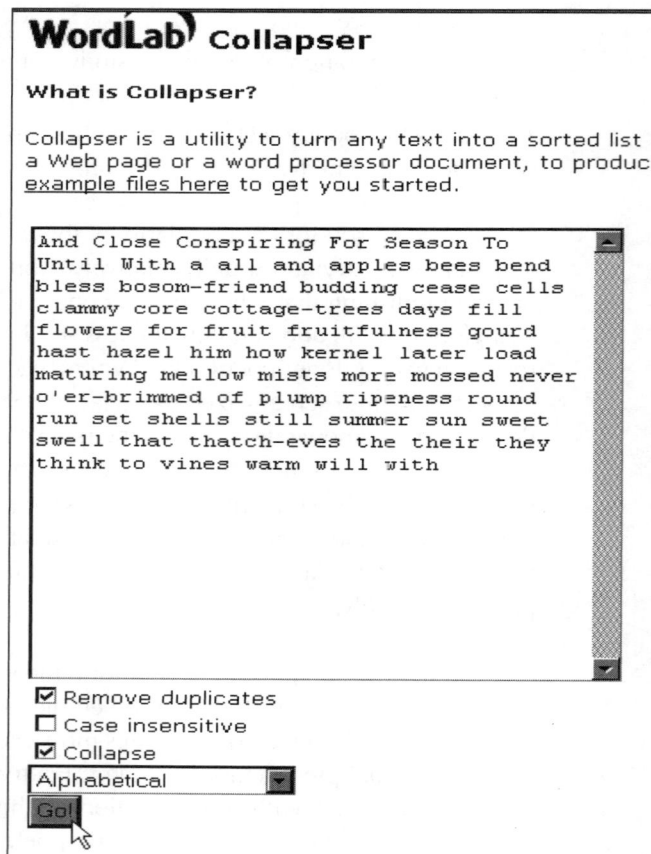

2. Focusing on visual aspects

ICT can help pupils to appreciate the visual/spatial aspects of a poem. Take a poem, in this case Betjeman's 'Slough'.[20] Remove some of the formatting and punctuation depending on the level of pupil ability. In this example I have removed the line-breaks, the exclamation marks, most of the commas and all capitals that begin lines:

> Come friendly bombs and fall on Slough. It isn't fit for humans now, there isn't grass to graze a cow. Swarm over Death. Come bombs and blow to smithereens those air-conditioned bright canteens tinned fruit tinned meat tinned milk tinned beans tinned minds tinned breath.

Ask the pupils to work out where the line ends are and format it appropriately. The decisions they make will test their understanding of rhythm and rhyme. In the case of this poem it is not an entirely expected rhyme scheme:

> Come friendly bombs and fall on Slough!
> It isn't fit for humans now,
> There isn't grass to graze a cow.
> Swarm over, Death!
>
> Come, bombs and blow to smithereens
> Those air-conditioned, bright canteens,
> Tinned fruit, tinned meat, tinned milk, tinned beans,
> Tinned minds, tinned breath.

What is demonstrable from this experiment is how the visual arrangement is very helpful in enabling us to see the rhyming link, which in turn would help us to read this aloud. After reading the first verse you are expecting, and somewhat disappointed by the lack of, a rhyme on the fourth line. This is because, until then, it seems to be using a classic 'ballad' format of four beats per line, but in fact we get only two stresses at the end of each quatrain, leaving an uncomfortable feel right to the end of the poem.

The punctuation's contribution to meaning can also be examined: without the comma and exclamation mark you wouldn't understand the fourth line at all, and without the line break after tinned beans, the last line would seem simply to be part of a list, rather than in apposition to the previous line.

3. Reading poetry as a VAK experience

Poetry can be experienced in a number of ways. It can be an auditory experience; both a left and right brain experience; indeed sometimes almost a kinesthetic one, since the rhythms of poetry, like music, can be experienced as movement. This is where we appreciate poetry's origins in song, and gain that original pleasure which some might feel is being lost as poetry becomes increasingly textual.

In the case of the first Betjeman poem it was helpful to see two verses at a time in order to understand its structure and rhythm. But with many poems you need only see, or hear, one line at a time, to appreciate its effect, as in 'Upper Lambourne' by the same poet:

> Up the ash tree climbs the ivy,
> Up the ivy climbs the sun,
> With a twenty-thousand pattering,

Has a valley breeze begun,
Feathery ash, neglected elder,
Shift the shade and make it run.[21]

Each line could be taken in succession, with the first two quite understandable on their own, the next four being grasped in pairs of lines, so that the wait for meaning is only brief. The effects of this kind of poem can be accentuated, and therefore better appreciated, with the use of a PowerPoint presentation, in which each line is inserted into a separate slide in sequence. Showing each line successively slows down the reading, but makes you focus on structure too: the way we are eased in with two very simple lines, then the meaning of the third is suspended until we see/hear the fourth, then a final pair of lines that complete the visual impression by a kind of reinforcement of the previous two.

The creation of the text template is quick and easy. Simply paste the verse into the first slide:

Fig 6.6

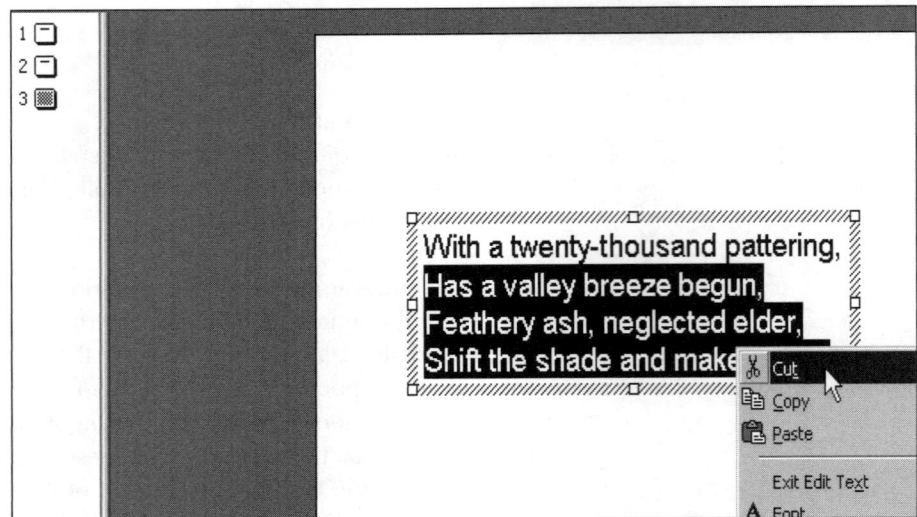

Then cut and paste all but the top line into successive slides until you have finished:

Fig 6.7

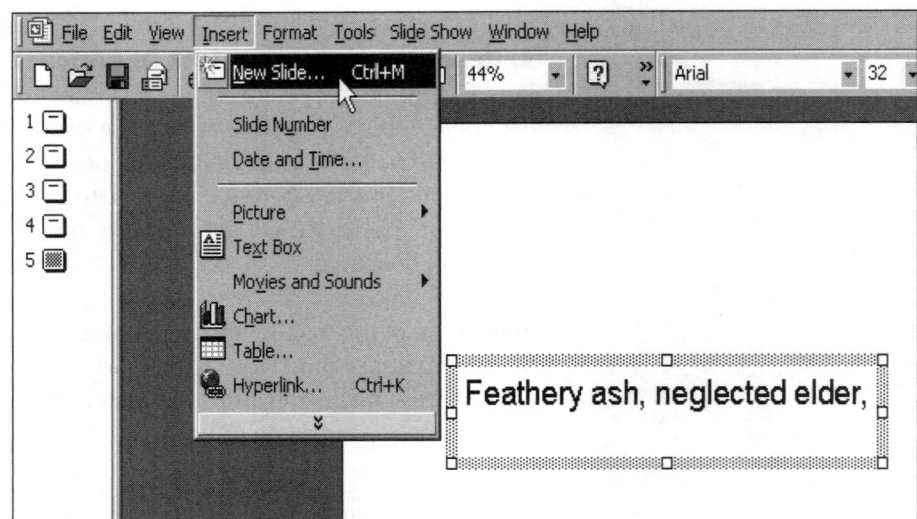

There is plenty of scope for self-differentiated activity here, using a range of VAK effects.

Try unusual fonts (WordArt) such as this one which implies the movement described.

Fig 6.8

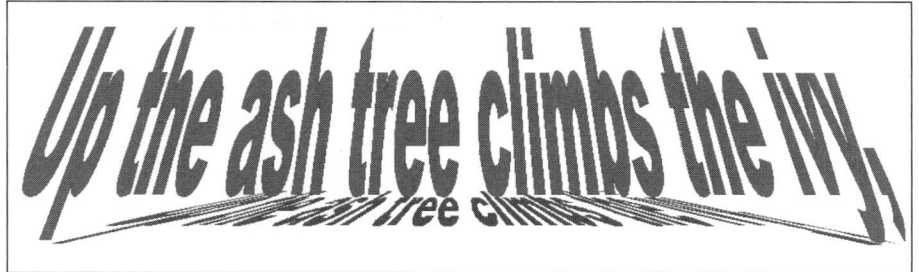

Try adding additional graphics and movement to the text, using the Custom Animation function:

Fig 6.9

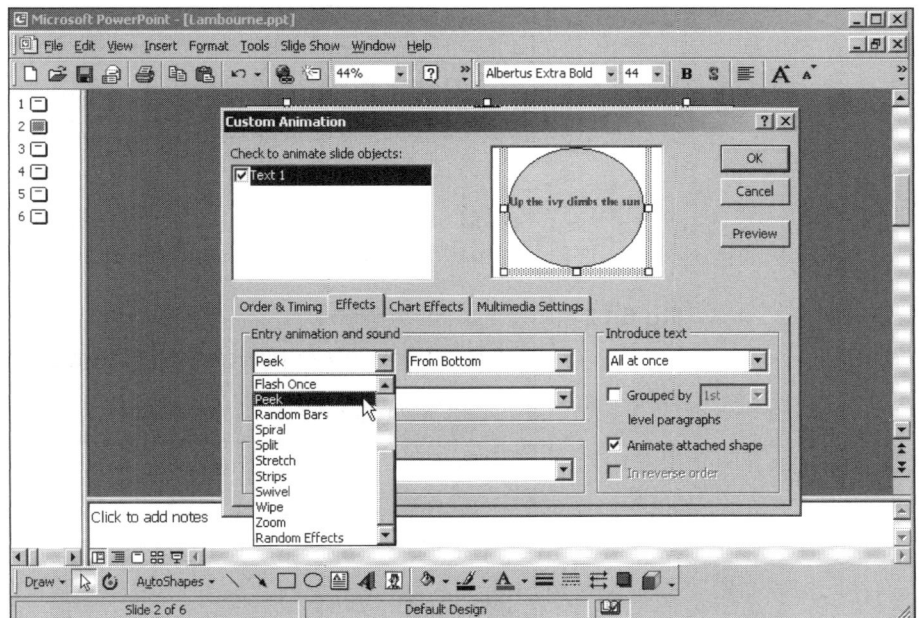

In this example, the text is made to rise from the bottom of the slide slowly, imitating the rising of the sun – either 'peek' or 'crawl' would work here (see an example of this on the accompanying CD-ROM).

CD-ROM Ch 6/Upper Lambourne PowerPoint presentation

Fig 6.10

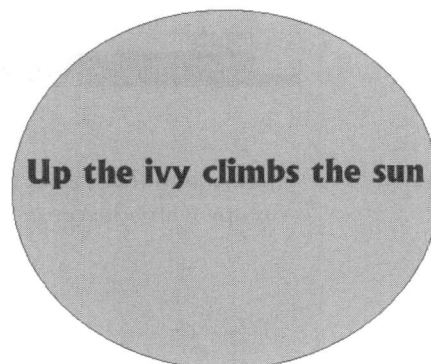

And here the pattering leaves are imitated by animating the individual letters, making them skip in one by one from the left to make up the line:

Fig 6.11

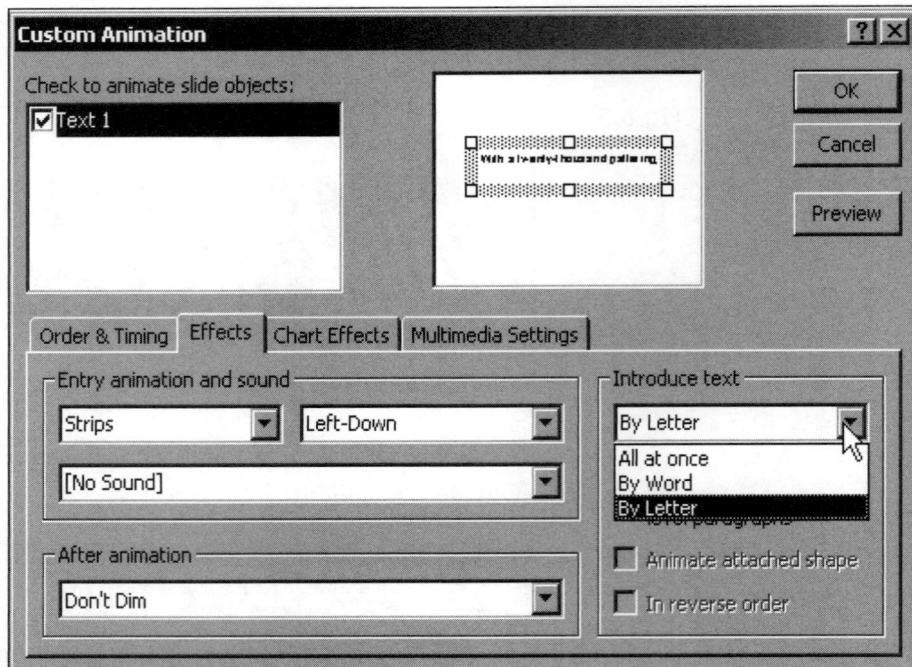

Sound of course is the final element, and this can also be added in the Custom Animation, with a single sound file for each slide:

Fig 6.12

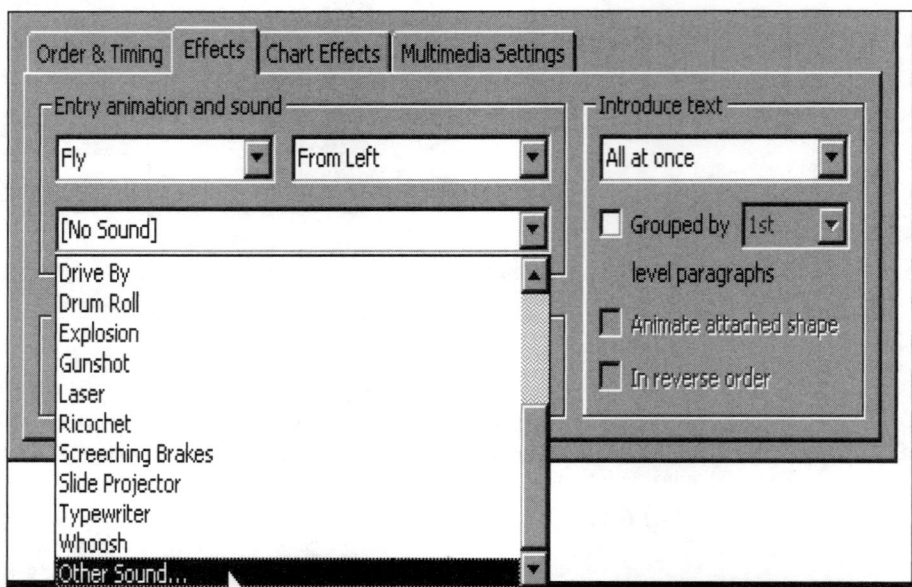

These sound files could be recordings of one or more voices reciting the lines, perhaps with added sound effects for the breeze.

4. Annotating poetry

Electronic annotation might be a very useful way of approaching difficult words or lines in Shakespeare which need glossing. Ask pairs of students to mark up a key speech or passage with explanations or paraphrases. Not only does this focus attention closely on the text, involving the delivery of the words as well as literal understanding, but also the page can be stored for revision purposes. With Shakespeare study statutory for most 13 to 14 year olds in the UK, and specific scenes being set for close examination, this seems to be an ideal way of approaching the difficult language.

CD-ROM Ch 6/Twelfth Night Word doc

In one of the plays deemed appropriate for study at this age, *Twelfth Night*, the racing comedy is often lost through lack of understanding of the text. Take as an example this speech from Viola, who while dressed as a boy has inadvertently attracted the amorous attention of the Lady Olivia. The text is marked up with explanatory glosses on difficult words or phrases. Figure 6.13 (see also an electronic version on the CD-ROM) shows how you might mark up the text in Word. Students might also include a sound file with themselves saying the lines, or paraphrasing them to show their understanding.

Fig 6.13

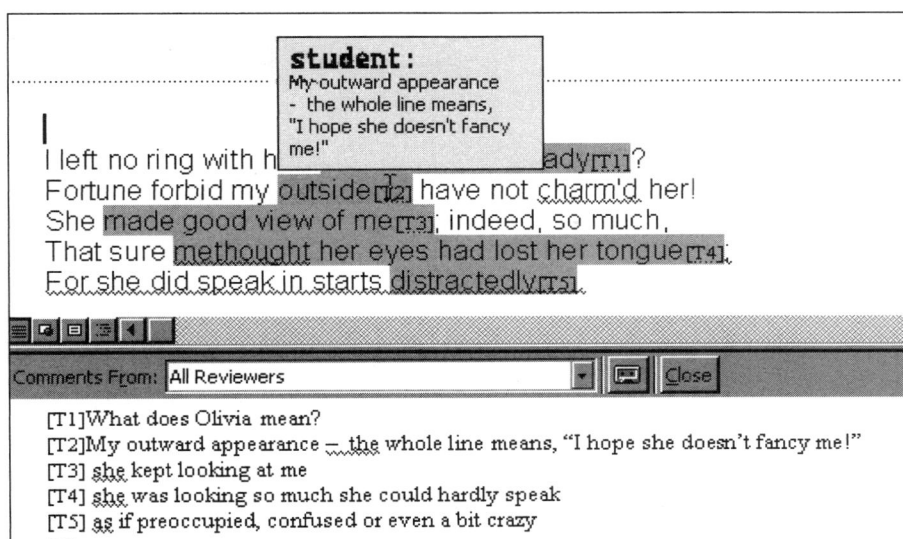

5. Video interpretations of poems

WEBSITE

Taking up the idea of the 'video poem' from Chapter 5, where BECTA award-winners wrote poems and conjoined these with video-montage, we can use the same methodology for reading and understanding poetry.[22] After watching this video, ask pupils to produce their own videos which will convey the ideas, emotions or images suggested to them by a poem they have studied. Integrate a reading of the poem into the video, so that you have both text and interpretation within the final product. Possibilities include conveying emotions by videoing facial expressions, videoing action or scenery, and creating animations. Choosing the right poem here is obviously vital, but thereafter the options are limited only by the imagination of the pupils.

Case study 6

Magic Book: augmented reality books

WEBSITE

WEBSITE

CD-ROM Ch 6/eyeMagic
Book Movie

▌ Background

The 'Magic Book' project from HITlab (Human Interface Technology Laboratory) is an innovative approach to reading, with implications too for our ideas about writing.[1] It applies 'augmented reality' technology to children's literature, which means combining the real and the virtual in a 'seamless' way. Virtual reality (or an 'immersive' environment) currently requires use of a headpiece; augmented reality requires a head-mounted display which adds 3D models to the real environment, with a marker triggering the display. Applications in education are only just starting to be explored. At a BECTA Expert Technology Seminar in May 2004 Adrian Woolard described a trial with 10 and 11 year olds which suggested that using augmented reality favoured kinesthetic learners.[2] That trial was in geography, using 3D representations of the solar system; the Magic Book project suggests that there are also implications for readers and for literacy. The case study described below was part of the project, designed in order to get feedback from both students and teachers about the processes involved.

A story by Gavin Bishop entitled *Giant Jimmy Jones* (see the movie on the accompanying CD-ROM) was written specifically for the purpose of being transformed from the physical reality of a picture book to an augmented reality (AR) artefact mediated by computer technology. This technology allows tableaux and animated sequences incorporating sound tracks to appear 'magically' in three dimensions during the reading/viewing process. In September, 2003, during the development of the Magic Book, seven girls and three boys, aged 10 to 14, attended a five-day workshop. They were introduced to AR technology, shown Gavin Bishop's work in progress, given lessons on picture book art (including paper engineering) and finally led through a process of 3D computer modelling to construct scenes for their own version of *Giant Jimmy Jones* to be incorporated into an AR environment.

WEBSITE

Teaching and learning objectives

The learning objectives were not predefined inasmuch as there were no clear expectations about outcomes, but there was an intention to explore the 'educative opportunities that the technology might bring' and the implications for literacy of pursuing this kind of story-telling.[3] The active participation of the students in constructing their own 3D elements made this a kind of writing exercise too, but only in the broadest sense of writing. In this sense, the objectives – to do with appreciation of virtuality and three-dimensionality as functions of narrative – are not catered for by the English curriculum as it stands. Other objectives related to investigating the 'added value' that AR brought to reading stories.

How it was done

Pairs of children from three primary and two secondary schools in the Christchurch area, New Zealand, attended a five-day workshop where they used Anim8or, a 3D drawing program chosen for its ease of operation and its suitability for the construction of objects to enhance the story.[4] The Anim8or training was conducted by Claudia Nelles of Hitlab (University of Canterbury), and the activities to introduce the regular picture book and the pop-up picture book were conducted by John McKenzie. Each day, a teacher from one of the contributing schools was available to make observations of individual students and to comment on their own perceptions of the group's reactions to the workshop. A second College of Education researcher acted as recorder/observer throughout the workshop.

On Day One it was necessary for students to share available computers in groups of three or four, by Day Two they were working in pairs with one group of three, and by Day Three they had individual access to computers. Animations in the program were produced by combining and shaping 'primitives' (basic building blocks of squares and cubes). Students were shown how to select a shape, show faces (in three dimensions), select a point, extend a point and apply a mesh (to modify the shape), then to apply surface shading to make the object appear solid. By the end of Day One students were able to produce and rotate a basic house shape (including roof and windows) with a solid appearance.

Days Two and Three covered the skills needed to construct other objects. In constructing a fish, under Claudia's direction, students decided which primitives to select, applied a mesh, highlighted the intersections, and extruded points to modify the shape of the object. They used the line tool to construct a fin which they were then able to scale, click, and drag towards the body shape. Copy and rotate functions were used to create a second tail fin, which could then be dragged into position. To construct a hand, students were shown how to access and modify a suitable shape for the palm, then how to select a face and extrude a thumb and fingers. They were shown how to choose and apply a suitable skin colour from the colour palette, and then how to apply the colour to selected faces.

Finally, working in pairs on Days Three and Four, students planned the page they would illustrate in the story. Each pair undertook to create the objects needed for their scene, and between them, they began busily creating mountains, lakes, the sun, Giant Jimmy, houses, hands, feet, a globe, trees, flowers, a picnic blanket, clouds, fish, flowers and people.

When the construction of objects was well under way, students were shown how to construct the base landscape for their animation and also how to add textures to create more realistic 3D objects. They were shown how to take objects and textures created in 'object mode' and place them into a 'folder' to be transferred into 'scene' mode for the creation of the planned picture.

When the final scenes were completed they were collected from the individual computers and combined by the technical expert ready for the final presentation as page illustrations. The workshop concluded on Day Five with the presentation of the students' own interpretations of the story.

Outcomes

Certainly the Magic Book overturns traditional notions of the reader as passively receptive, offering as it does the high degree of interactivity involved in this type of 'reading'. It is almost certainly the most 'futuristic' of ideas for ICT in English, and perhaps the least adaptable to either the classroom or the curriculum of today. It is also difficult to imagine many English teachers being able to invest the time required to acquire the knowledge and skills necessary to explore the possibilities of VR and AR elements in story-telling. Even so, the detailed breakdown of the five-day process described above makes it clear that children aged between 10 and 14 were able to pick up the skills necessary to produce appropriate 3D elements for the story (although it is not clear how much extra work was required from the 'technical expert' in order to achieve the end product). And it is clear too from the report that in some ways it is a lack of visual literacy which inhibited the children and led to rather literalistic interpretations. If AR is to become an interpretative reading tool rather than just a way of re-versioning a story, it will require new ways of thinking, as well as new ways of reading.

Fig 6.14   **Images from *Giant Jimmy Jones***

Feedback from teachers was revealing. Apart from worries about practicability, the fear was expressed that this new technology might 'raise expectations' of children, causing them to devalue the traditional stories found in the stock-cupboard. The idea that raising expectations is something to be avoided is a telling indictment of the confused thinking with regard to ICT in English. Perhaps the teachers wanted to transfer to this project their anxieties about the lack of social interaction associated with computer games, in spite of the fact that the work was clearly highly collaborative throughout.

The main issue for the English teacher would be the one which this book has repeatedly highlighted – the difference between using AR as a tool and investigating it as a medium. Adrian Woolard of the BBC was interested in AR as an educational tool, seeing pupils as users rather than makers. In contrast, John McKenzie, as mentioned in Chapter 4, has been interested in the impact this technology has for the way we, and children, think of stories, or 'Story' considered in the abstract. He sees AR story-telling as playing an almost intermediary role in the putative opposition between the book and digital technology. But it is a potentially disruptive force too, since its interactive possibilities seem to supplant the conventions of a linear plot:

> Does AR have the potential to redefine the construction of the reader/viewer/listener/gamer in the story event? There is the future possibility for the reader to be more actively engaged in object manipulation, making choices, interacting with characters that consequently influence plot sequence. As interactivity becomes more technologically seamless (using voice recognition technology for example), multiple viewpoints could be used to tell the story as different characters give different takes on the action, depending on the commands of the reader/gamer. This allows for a greater complexity of story and interpretation. Clearly, postmodern emphases on the metafictive, the pastiche, the parodic and the playful could be used to great effect using AR approaches.[5]

English teachers will necessarily be concerned about these associated issues of what constitutes the telling of a story. We have seen several times in the course of this book that new media are forcing us to re-think narrative form, whether it be multi-stranded, open-ended, multimodal or interactive in a virtual way. New technologies help us to stand back a little from our veneration of the written word, and value the story itself, for what it offers, because it is clear that stories do have value as stories, and are not dependent on a particular medium to be interesting, engaging and valuable.

Doing this in the classroom

From a practical point of view, the Anim8or program is available free as a download, therefore any teacher wishing to explore its potential can do so. The only cost will be in time spent familiarizing yourself with the sophisticated processes involved in 3D modelling. There are various tutorials on the website (and many more by enthusiasts on linked sites and online communities), and some ready-made downloadable 3D objects to help get you started. Adrian Woolard had used the open source software AR Toolkit which is a parallel project from HITlab and also downloadable free of charge.[6] While the Magic Book worked with animation software, the AR Toolkit allows you to manipulate video taken from a simple webcam in real time.

WEBSITE

We might need to wait a few years before we have the kind of software that will be easily adapted for classroom use, but the possibilities demonstrated by the existing tools suggest that it will be worth the wait. The 3D animation software Kahootz[7] from Australia might be the first big step towards virtual reality story-telling in the classroom.

WEBSITE

Chapter 7

The way forward for ICT in English

We have seen a range of ways in which ICT can both enhance what has traditionally been known as 'English teaching' and also extend and enrich that tradition. The two sections of Chapter 1 presented a microcosm of this larger effect that ICT can have on English: electronic visual aids can assist the writer with the customary modes of paragraphed extended writing, while new types of text are moving us beyond paragraphs as the structural frame for writing. Something is worth saying here about the status of these two features of ICT in English. While electronic visual aids seem an attractive option, engagement with hypertext seems to be essential. This leads to an important distinction – the use of ICT as a tool as opposed to the consideration of new media as objects of study. The distinction is not always easy to keep a hold on. For example when considering digital video, some practitioners see its value as moving image text, while many users will see it primarily as an easy means of recording performance. What proponents of the study of the language of the moving image are trying to get across is that DV makes possible, for the first time within the context of schools, a radical re-think of the way we teach drama, speaking and listening, and story-telling itself. The medium is now manipulable, an object of study rather than merely a means to an end. Sometimes it seems that the focus is so much on the end product, as with the BECTA awards cited earlier, that the process and its methodology are taken for granted. This is why innovations like the *Making movies make sense* CD-ROM (see Chapter 5) are so important at this stage in showing the way forward.

If we think of electronic text and digital video as two ends of the spectrum of ICT in English, there is a range of text and image combinations in between. In addition, database technology and the internet offer us not only tools, but also new areas of English study. The basic principles of website structure and content management are already well enough established for us to start teaching them with some confidence. Asking pupils to understand web publishing is not the equivalent of asking them to understand the book publishing process. As with DV editing, there is a revolution going on in publishing which means we can all do it and all understand it, and in the future it is likely that we will need that understanding and skill in order to call ourselves fully literate. As for databases, perhaps English teaching would benefit from a less defensive attitude when it comes to the 'information' dimension of ICT. We have already become data handlers by using online search engines, and data managers by using email address books. Recent software has made data at once more sophisticated and more manageable than ever, not only for specialist uses but increasingly for everyday accounting and household management. As such usage becomes commonplace, it is important that English teaching is both aware of it and is able to contribute in this new area of literacy. By considering ICT as a medium we will at last move beyond the perception of ICT in English as being about 'drag and drop' exercises, games and gimmicks.

Creativity, ICT and English

Some lip-service has been paid to creativity in the classroom in the past few years, in order to offset the decidedly anti-creative ambitions of state educationalists hoping to reach 'targets' and achieve 'value added' results in tests. It is strange, and rather dispiriting, to see that ICT has been very much undersold as a way of encouraging creativity across all subjects. In 2003 the UK government published online some 'case studies' on creativity in English and drama, as part of the creativity across the curriculum project which had run for a year in a number of schools. If the outcomes of this were rather unimpressive as far as English teaching was concerned, they also suggested, misleadingly, that ICT was pretty much irrelevant in encouraging creativity. When we look at the criteria for 'creative thinking and behaviour' which teachers had been asked to look for and promote, then we can easily see where ICT could and should be playing a part:

- ➡ making connections and seeing relationships;
- ➡ envisaging what might be;
- ➡ playing with ideas;
- ➡ representing ideas in a variety of ways.[1]

These are four of the six key criteria, and the applications of ICT with regard to these could not be more obvious. Indeed, if the 'variety of ways' in which things are represented did not include ICT then they would be very limited in scope. And yet the published results of the creativity project did not show effective or creative use of ICT. There seemed to be a feeling that we should be looking for creativity within traditional modes of English teaching rather than doing the obvious and drawing on exactly the new media which excite young people and are likely to encourage creativity.[2] Instead it fell to ICT curriculum leaders to see the potential of new technologies for creativity across different subjects, not least English and drama. They saw the creativity project as an opportunity to show how far ICT has come since it was thought of as simply a set of technical skills.

It is helpful for English teachers to take note of the findings of the ICT team from QCA. In looking at the criteria for creative thinking and behaviour developed by the project, they suggested a number of ways that ICT was of necessity going to encourage such creativity. Some of the key terms which they devised for describing ICT's contributions to creativity may well be relevant to us as we develop a vocabulary for ICT in English:

➡ The non-linear nature of mixed media information from the web, CD-ROMs, multimedia databases and spreadsheets, allows a variety of pathways to be taken through content.

➡ Multimodality provides opportunities for different learning styles.

➡ The interactivity of computers allows manipulation, modelling, trialling, making comparisons, and asking 'what if...?'.

➡ Provisionality enables revision, modification, storage of versions, presentation of alternatives. ICT enables speed of production, reproduction, transformation and dissemination of different outcomes or products.[3]

WEBSITE

More English teachers would perhaps be inclined to engage with ICT if they were able to see it in such terms, rather than just as a matter of operating hardware and software. There is also a strong case for saying that English teachers ought to engage with the notions of non-linearity and interactivity in particular, because they identify new forms of communication that have emerged as a result of ICT. The same can be said of the moving image. The BFI report on the BECTA Digital Video Pilot Project pointed out that 'high-quality work showed a greater attention to the uniqueness of the "language" of the moving image. Understanding and control of this language, rather than simply of the technology, gives pupils access to expression through DV'.[4] This is to some extent a problem common to all ICTs: when it comes to pedagogic issues, the deficiency of a teaching vocabulary precedes the technical skills deficit. It is here that we are in need of a positive lead from the centre to help in establishing people's terms of reference.

Strategies for change

The new media provide new ways of connecting people, ideas, images and information, thereby offering new possibilities for learning. So perhaps at last we have moved beyond the drag and drop mentality and ICT is no longer dismissed as a flashy but non-essential tool. But we still lack a sufficiently developed teaching vocabulary to exploit these new ways for learners to make connections. There is a slow seepage of new terminology, but nothing systematic. Those preparing the national curriculum for English in 2000 did not feel ready to make any firm commitments about the role of ICT, and so it was relegated to the grey, non-statutory marginalia. The reticence was understandable because we do not even have a set of terms available, for example, to describe the way text is ordered and structured online, or in an email, or in a text message. The more important challenge is seen to be the measurement of progression in traditional English skills which we already know how to describe. Given a current institutional obsession with the analytical and diagnostic breakdown of the components of 'English', new media indeed seems threatening. Ideas of non-linearity or multimodality, for example, are unhelpful distractions to a literacy strategy grounded at text level in the notion of 'writing frames', and at word level by spelling rules and patterns.

WEBSITE

One progressive thing to emerge in the area of ICT and English in recent years was the BECTA guidance document on *Teaching and Learning with ICT in English* mentioned in the introduction to this book.[5] This introduced a very useful binary opposition to describe the role of ICT in English teaching, opening with the words, 'As both a medium and a tool, ICT...' In that phrase it has already done something which was much needed. For all teachers, ICT can be a useful tool, but in English especially it is a medium which should be studied, considered and examined in itself. As a new medium for communication, it is automatically within the remit of an English teacher to take it on board and explore its potential. The BECTA document mapped out the range of ICT activities that might add value to English teaching, listing six areas of English activity that could be enhanced by ICT. Those six areas formed the basis for Trevor Millum's resource book for the 7 to 11 age range, *ICT and Literacy*,[6] and more recently have been the basis for exemplification work by NATE on 'ICT supporting English' funded by the DfES.[7] These quite generic categories are applicable to ICT in almost any subject, but the more specific coverage of the document is actually quite impressive, including as it does a range of imaginative applications of ICT in English, including:

WEBSITE

➡ The use of hypertext to explore relationships between and within texts;

➡ The use of databases to explore language;

➡ The use of multimedia presentations to juxtapose words with images or recorded voices;

➡ Recording speech for transcription and analysis;

➡ Designing web pages;

➡ Using online environments for surveys, discussion and debate.

Initially, this document looked like the first step on a path towards creating a vocabulary for English teachers using ICT. Now, however, it seems that even the basic principles of that document have been misunderstood, or ignored, with a focus instead on ICT as merely a tool to support English. Since the publication of this document, BECTA has co-opted NATE to lead on ICT in English. The first online newsletter from the NATE/BECTA collaboration in 2003 asked the question 'Why bother?' but did little to answer that beyond blandishments about raising standards. In fact it only highlighted the lack of any coherence about our approaches to ICT in English, by quoting BECTA's ImpaCT2 report:

> especially in English at secondary level, there is no ... correspondence between the content of the ICT used and the content of the examination. The skills that pupils are learning in becoming more expert at presenting their work effectively on the computer are not tested in Key Stage 3 national tests, or at GCSE.[8]

WEBSITE

There are positive signs from some of the organizations that dictate policy. The ICT subject association NAACE has made some significant contributions in the area of ICT and literacy in recent years, and was represented on the working party that produced the entitlement document in 2002. But that group was dissolved in the same year and nothing of substance has replaced it. Recent BECTA research found that one of the three key needs for English teachers was that both teachers and pupils 'should understand visual literacy', and yet this is not reflected in the statutory demands of the English curriculum.[9] A co-ordinated approach still seems to be lacking, and there is, in truth, little clarity of thought on the issue at any level, except in terms of the most mechanical understanding of ICT as a performance-enhancer. So where is the impetus going to come from for English teachers and practitioners to embrace ICT as a new medium rather than just as a tool? We might yet see some advances in addressing ICT in English in the next iteration of the UK national curriculum,

WEBSITE

but the 'statutory order' is understandably always a cautious one, responding to change once it is clearly established rather than trying to blaze a trail. The likely truth is that initiatives here will need to be from 'ground up' rather than 'top down'. In a sense this is quite liberating, since most areas of the curriculum are now minutely prescribed, but here teachers can exercise some creative freedom to explore the possibilities of the new media.

ICT and the assessment of English

Assessment using ICT has not been a focus for this book. There are ways in which ICT is going to impact upon the assessment of English and literacy, and indeed it is already doing so in some contexts. In terms of the assessment of written English there does not seem to be a great deal of scope beyond quite unexciting ideas such as multiple-choice questions. If electronic assessment of English does indeed become common in the future, then the curriculum would need to be shaped (or shrunk) to those aspects of English which can be assessed without the need for the subjective judgements of assessors. There are signs that this is indeed the direction in which we are heading, but it seems only to be possible with a rather functional approach to language study, and is perhaps a destination we will never reach.

One area of English assessment which certainly could be affected by ICT – and for the better – is Speaking and Listening. Digitally recorded sound and audio offers the opportunity to start exemplifying standards of linguistic ability in order to bring a degree of precision about this area of assessment which has hitherto been impossible. Best practice in assessment of Speaking and Listening has often come from EFL/ESOL teaching, and the various awarding bodies which make up this huge industry. The QCA-led 2003 ESOL Core Curriculum has begun to standardize at least 'descriptors' for levels, and the reliable exemplification of these levels is another, very challenging issue.[10] The implications may in time be substantial both for native English speakers and for EFL learners, but progression in Speaking and Listening is still largely an uncharted territory where ICT may provide the mapping tools. QCA has recently taken a significant step in this direction with its exemplification of Speaking and Listening. This is presented as digital video examples on a CD-ROM, with linked online commentaries that include indications of the attainment level of which they provide evidence.[11]

WEBSITE

The role of the teacher

Back in 1960, when the television was becoming culturally entrenched, Jerome Bruner saw it as an age of increasing spectatorship, leading him to the judgement that 'motives for learning must be kept from going passive ... they must be based as much as possible upon the arousal of interest in what there is be learned, and they must be kept broad and diverse in expression'.[12] Of course it is exactly those dangers of passivity which we can avoid with the new media; the only sensible way to treat the possibilities of the web and other forms of digital communication is to exploit their potential for interactivity and involvement. People who think of the web as an information store analogous to a library are rather missing the point. It is the fact that it is constantly in flux, and the fact that we can, if we have just a few skills and tools, affect and change it, be part of it, that makes the web a worthwhile and increasingly valuable medium. There is therefore something intrinsically interesting in the medium itself, and we need to take this on board when we evaluate its pedagogic usefulness, and in the context of English teaching, when we teach how to use it.

One of the consequences of the redefinition of the subject area for English is that the dividing lines between disciplines are blurred. As we have seen repeatedly in this book, cross-curricular teaching often seems the most appropriate approach where integration of ICT and English is happening. Projects that bring together art, design, ICT, music, citizenship, PSHE can all be envisaged. Of course this takes more than unilateral action by a keen teacher: it requires a flexible system within schools which might seem fanciful (at secondary level in particular). Yet it can and does happen, as evidenced by schools like Leasowes Community College, Birmingham, which set aside all of its five-hour Friday for different subject areas to use digital video, or Thistley Hough School that has the same arrangement on Fridays, when cross-curricular work is made possible.

The timetabling issue brings in the larger, and perhaps primary, role which needs mention, and which is presupposed by everything in this book: the role of the English teacher in creating and managing access to the hardware and software which is required. It is clear that at secondary level in particular there is still a gulf between English teachers who use ICT well and often, and those who use it little and/or badly. Teachers, heads of department, team leaders all need to make the case for ICT in English in order to make sure they have the resources available to do exciting or useful things in their teaching. It is hoped that the foregoing chapters have provided some arguments for making that case for ICT in English. It is clear from the many examples and ideas described in this book that where there is the will there are many ways to take advantage of the richness of ICT.

Appendix 1

Text messaging database option

Text messaging data is ideal material for constructing a database, linked to work done on text message language (see Chapter 2). Given the fact that text messages, like data in database fields, are unformatted, there is even scope for storing messages themselves.

Suggested fields (see figure A1.1):

➡ name
➡ sex
➡ friend or family
➡ number of contacts
➡ approximate number of messages per day (ranges in drop-down menu)
➡ favourite opening
➡ favourite close
➡ type of smiley face used.

Fig A1.1

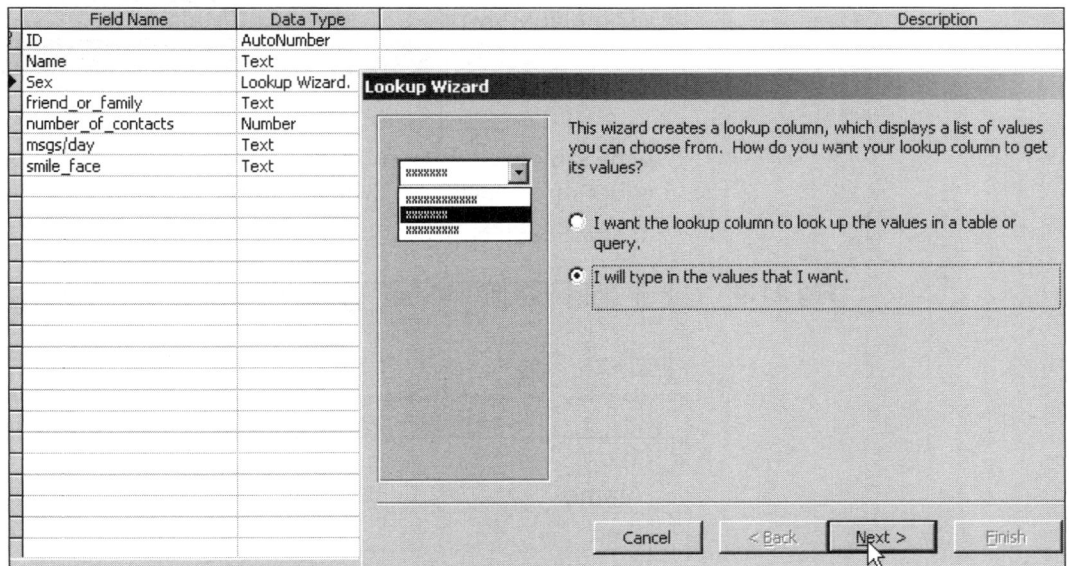

Fig A1.2

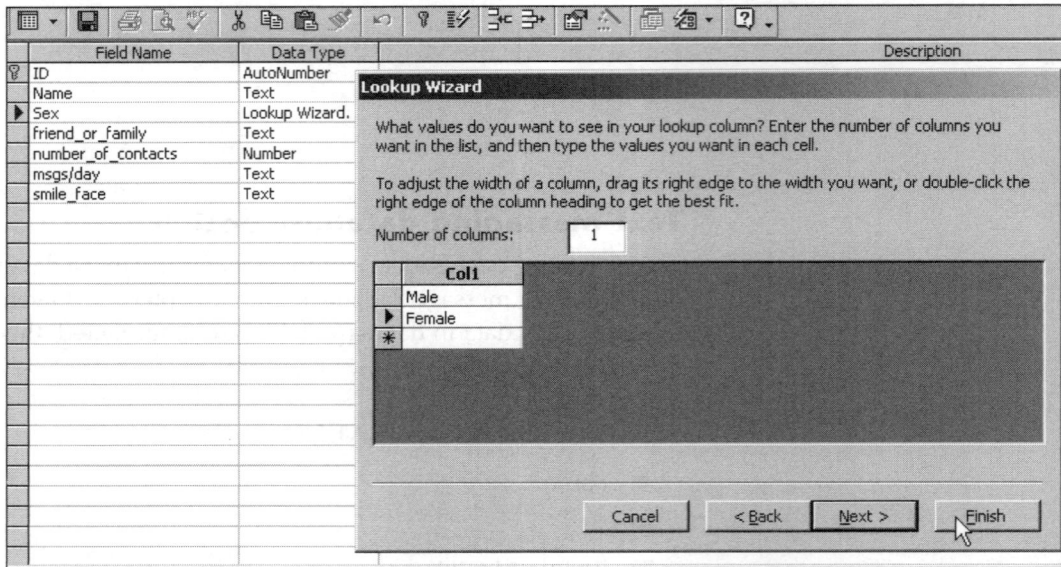

Fig A1.3

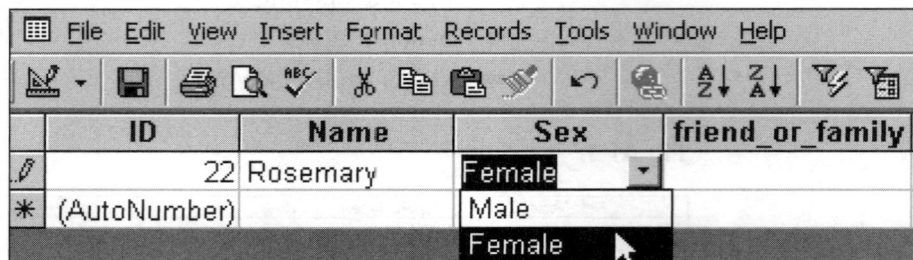

Use the same method to produce drop-downs for other options, except for the 'number of contacts', for which you set the field to 'Number' in the Design view of the table:

Fig A1.4

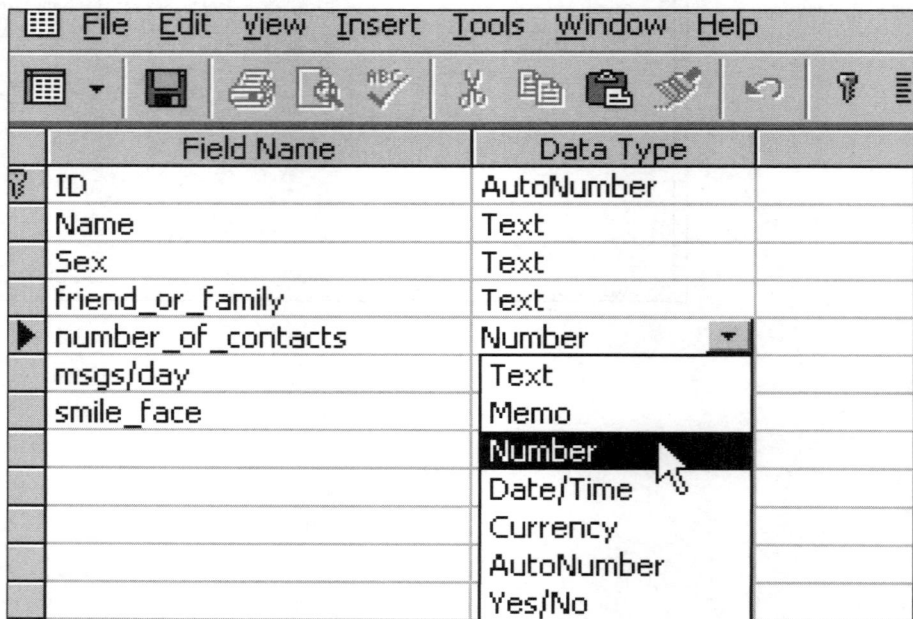

For 'messages per day', it's probably best to use ranges, for example 1–5, 6–10, and so on, which can be typed in as options in a text field.

Of course, not all fields need to be look-up fields, and there is no reason why actual text messages should not be stored. If you wanted to put a whole collection in one field, then use 'memo'.

A single message will easily fit in the 'Text' data type in Access (maximum size 255 characters).

Exciting ICT in English

References to National Curriculum English Programme of Study, KS2–3

Three modes for English: En1=Speaking & Listening; En2=Reading; En3=Writing

Key Stage	Key Stage 2			Key Stages 3/4		
Mode	En1	En2	En3	En1	En2	En3
Chapter 1: The excitement of electronic text						
1. Visual aids to structured writing			1a; 2a-f; 7d			1; 2; 7c,d
2. New types of text	6a,c	2c; 5e	1; 6; 7d	6d,f	1a,c,e; 6	1; 7c,d
Case study 1: g8way project (SMS poetry)		4f	1a,c,d; 6	1		1a-d; 9a; 11
Chapter 2: Beyond words						
1. VAK approaches to language study	1a-f; 2d; 5; 6	1; 5a-c,f; 6	3; 4	1c,d; 5; 6	5a,b; 6	3; 4a-c; 6
2. Text messaging and language study		1; 6	3; 4j		1a,e; 5a,b; 6	3; 6
Case study 2: VAK teaching of spelling	1a,b	1; 5a-c,f	3; 4	6		4a-c; 6
Chapter 3: English and information						
1. Information handling with ICT	3; 9b	3d,e,f; 9b			4a,c; 5a,c; 9b	1n
2. Databases, thinking skills and writing		3d,e,f; 5e	1a-c			1e-h; 7c,d
Case study 3: Census at School Project	3; 9b	3d,e,f	1a-c		4a,c; 9b	
Chapter 4: New ways of writing						
1. Writing for the web		5e,f; 6	1a,c-e; 11		4b; 5	1; 2; 7d
2. Whole text work using multimedia	1	5e,f	1a-e		5	1; 2
Case study 4: multimodal narratives	1; 4; 8	4c,d	1; 2		2; 5	1; 2
Chapter 5: Audio-visual English						
1. Speaking, reading and listening	1; 2b,c; 3; 5; 6			1; 2; 5; 8	2; 3	
2. Digital video	1; 6; 4; 8			1; 2; 3; 4; 5	5	
Case study 5: DV and Shakespeare	4; 8	4			1b,f; 5b,d; 2; 8a-i	
Chapter 6: New ways of reading						
1. E-texts online		3a-e; 4; 6			1; 2; 3; 4b; 5; 8; 9	
2. Electronic poetry	1e	3a-e; 4a,f; 6			1a,c,j,k; 2; 8	
Case study 6: Magic Book: augmented reality		2b; 4c,d			1e,g,i; 5	

National Curriculum English coverage

This shows the sections of the book where these aspects of the curriculum are addressed, with teaching ideas, examples or advice.

			Programme of Study reference	Occurrences	No.
Key Stage 2	En1	1	Speaking	2.1; CS2; CS4; 4.2; 5.1; 5.2; 6.2	7
		2	Listening	2.1; 4.2; 5.1; 5.2; 6.2	5
		3	Group discussion	CS1; 3.1; CS3; 4.1; 5.1; CS5	6
		4	Drama	CS4; 5.2; CS5	3
		5	Standard English	2.1; 3.1; 5.1; 5.2	4
		6	Language variation	1.2, 2.1; 5.1; 5.2	4
	En2	1	Reading strategies	2.1; 2.2; CS2; 5.1; 6.1; 6.2	6
		2	Understanding texts	1.2; 5.1; 5.2; CS5; 6.1; 6.2; CS6	7
		3	Reading for information	3.1; 3.2; CS3; 6.1; 6.2	5
		4	Literature	CS1; CS4; 6.1; 6.2; CS6	5
		5	Non-fiction & non-lit texts	1.2; 2.1; CS2; 3.2; 4.1; 4.2	6
		6	Lang structure & variation	2.1; 2.2; 4.1; 6.1; 6.2	5
	En3	1	Composition	1.1, 1.2, CS1; 3.2; CS3; 4.1, 4.2; CS4	8
		2	Planning & drafting	1.1; 4.1; 4.2; CS4	4
		3	Punctuation	2.1; 2.2	2
		4	Spelling	2.1; 2.2; CS2	3
		5	Handwriting		0
		6	Standard English	1.1; 1.2; 2.1; CS2	4
		7	Language structure	1.1; 1.2; 2.1; 2.2; 6.1; 6.2	6
Key Stages 3/4	En1	1	Speaking	2.1; CS2; CS4; 4.2; 5.1; 5.2; 6.2	7
		2	Listening	2.1; 4.2; 5.1; 5.2; 6.2	5
		3	Group discussion	CS1; 3.1; CS3; 4.1; 5.1; CS5	6
		4	Drama	CS4; 5.2; CS5	3
		5	Standard English	2.1; 3.1; 5.1; 5.2	4
		6	Language variation	1.2; 2.1; 5.1	3
	En2	1	Understanding texts	1.2; CS1; 2.2; CS5; 6.1; 6.2; CS6	7
		2	English Literary Heritage	CS5; 5.1; 6.1; 6.2	4
		3	Texts of diff cultures/tradns	5.1; 6.1	2
		4	ICT-based information texts	3.1; CS3; 4.1; 6.1	4
		5	Media & moving image texts	2.1; 2.2; 3.1; 4.1; 5.2; CS5; 6.1; CS6	8
		6	Lang structure & variation	1.1; 1.2; 2.1; 2.2; 6.1; 6.2	6
	En3	1	Composition	1.1; 1.2; CS1; 3.1; 3.2; 4.1; 4.2; CS4	8
		2	Planning & drafting	1.1; 4.1; 4.2; CS4	4
		3	Punctuation	2.1; 2.2	2
		4	Spelling	2.1; 2.2; CS2	3
		5	Handwriting		0
		6	Standard English	1.2; 2.1; 2.2; CS2	4
		7	Language structure	1.1; 1.2; 3.2; 4.1; 6.1; 6.2	6

References

Introduction

1   BECTA (www.becta.org.uk), *Teaching and Learning with ICT in English* (2002), downloadable from http://www.vtc.ngfl.gov.uk/ictenglish.

Chapter 1 The excitement of electronic text

1   For a useful summary of the various 'graphic organizer' methods used in Australian schools, see Helen Dobson, 'The Australian Way' in *Secondary English Magazine,* Vol 6, No 5 (June 2003), pages 19–23.
2   Vivi Lachs, *Making Multimedia in the Classroom* (London: Routledge, 2000), pages 76–91.
3   http://www.mind-mapping.co.uk/mind-mapping-definition.htm. A site about mind mapping run by *illumine training* (www.illumine.co.uk). See also http://news.bbc.co.uk/1/hi/education/1926739.stm.
4   For mind-mapping software see http://www.mind-mappingsoftware.co.uk/mindgenius.htm (http://www.mind-mapping.com; http://www.mindgenius.com).
5   *Planning for Writing* (QCA, November 2003), page 4.
6   Kearlsey's summary of Bruner's ideas in *The Process of Education* (Harvard University Press, 1960); see Kearsley, G. (1994), The Theory Into Practice Database: http://tip.psychology.org/bruner.html.
7   For interesting investigations at the University of Texas into the application of new technologies to constructivism see http://www.edb.utexas.edu/mmresearch/Students97/Rutledge/home.html.
8   NAACE, *ICT and Literacy (2000)*, pages 42–5. The document is downloadable as a PDF at http://www.naace.org/searchView.asp?menuItemId=2&resourceId=190.
9   http://office.microsoft.com.
10 Trevor Millum, *ICT and Literacy*, (NATE, 2003).
11 http://www.newi.ac.uk/englishresources/neab.html.
12 http://www.kented.org.uk/ngfl/subjects/literacy/Writing-frames/frames3.html.
13 This case study was written up as exemplification of ICT in English for the UK National Curriculum in Action website: see http://www.ncaction.org.uk/search/entry.htm?id=1367.
14 http://www.poetryzone.co.uk.
15 http://www.mind-mapping.com; http://www.mindgenius.com.
16 http://www.inspiration.com/productinfo/inspiration/index.cfm; http://www.inspiration.com/productinfo/kidspiration/index.cfm
17 http://curriculum.becta.org.uk/docserver.php?docid=1523. A BECTA (www.becta.org.uk) website.
18 http://www.northcanton.sparcc.org/~elem/kidspiration/collection.html.
19 See 'Favorite poem' from the Canby School District collection at http://www.canby.k12.or.us/Technology/Integration/kidspiration/kidspiration.html.
20 Vivi Lachs (see reference 2), pages 86–87.
21 All taken from the Canby School District collection at http://www.canby.k12.or.us/Technology/Integration/kidspiration/kidspiration.html.
22 http://www.mind-mapping.co.uk/make-mind-map.htm.
23 Interestingly, this hierarchical approach is exactly what is required in mapping the structure of websites (as we will see in Chapter 5), therefore there is perhaps complementarity here too.
24 http://curriculum.becta.org.uk/docserver.php?docid=1523. A BECTA (www.becta.org.uk) website.
25 NAACE, *ICT and Literacy* (2000) (see reference 8).
26 http://www.usm.edu/english/fairytales/lrrh/lrrhhome.htm.
27 William Trochim reflected on this dichotomy in his report on research into the scientific reliability of mind mapping in 'Concept Mapping: Soft Science or Hard Art?', at http://www.socialresearchmethods.net/research/epp2/epp2.htm.
28 http://www.cchsonline.co.uk.
29 http://ted.hyperland.com.
30 Landow, G.P., 'Hypertext in literary education, criticism, and scholarship', *Computers and the Humanities*, 23 (1989), page 174.

31   Foltz, P.W., 'Comprehension, Coherence and Strategies in Hypertext and Linear text', http://www-psych.nmsu.edu/~pfoltz/reprints/Ht-Cognition.html, also published in Rouet, J.F., Levonen, J.J., Dillon, A.P. & Spiro, R.J. (eds) *Hypertext and Cognition* (Hillsdale: NJ: Lawrence Erlbaum Associates, 1996).

32   http://www.cultos.org.

33   http://www.visualthesaurus.com.

34   Foltz (see reference 31), 'Where can Hypertext succeed?'

35   http://www.standards.dfes.gov.uk/literacy; see also http://www.ictadvice.org.uk for advice on how to set up an email project.

36   http://www.rm.com/Primary/Articles/ArticleDetail.asp?cref=IICTA3814.

37   Tim Shortis, *The Language of ICT* (London: Routledge, 2001) pages 80–91.

38   NAACE, *ICT and Literacy* (2000), page 68.

39   Vivi Lachs (see reference 2), pages 149–153.

40   http://www.mape.org.uk/activities/index.htm; see also ClozePro from Crick software: http://www.cricksoft.com/uk/products/clozepro/default.asp.

41   This was written up as an ICT in English case study for the Curriculum in Action website (http://www.ncaction.org.uk/search/entry.htm?id=1368).

42   For a warm-up exercise, see the British Council education site at http://www.learnenglish.org.uk/words/activities/ms01b.html.

43   Tim Shortis (see reference 37), page 86.

Case study 1 g8way project: SMS poetry

1   Andrew Wilson was behind the Leeds *Citypoems* project – see http://www.citypoems.co.uk and *The Guardian* Text Message Poetry competition, http://www.guardian.co.uk/mobilepoems.

2   For information about Peter and Ann Sansom, see http://www.poetrybusiness.co.uk.

3   http://www.g8way.org.uk.

4   http://www.smsbug.com.

5   http://www.poetryzone.ndirect.co.uk.

6   Andrew Wilson, *Text Messages* (Smith/Doorstop Books, 2003).

7   http://www.centrifugalforces.co.uk/web/pages/mob_sms.html.

8   http://www.gigglepoetry.com.

Chapter 2 Beyond words

1   http://www.amblesideprimary.com/ambleweb/lookcover/lookcover.html.

2   http://www.wordroot.co.uk.

3   Tim Shortis, *The Language of ICT* (London: Routledge, 2001).

4   http://www.macromedia.com/shockwave/download/download.cgi?P1_Prod_Version=ShockwaveFlash

5   http://www.hyperstudio.com/

6   http://www.softease.com/

7   Tino Ferri, of NAS/UWT, quoted by BBC News, 3 March 2003.

8   http://www.m-learning.org/index.shtml. One of the findings of the survey associated with the project was that 49 per cent of young adults expressed an interest in using a mobile phone for learning English.

9   In one example of young people's SMS corpus research supervised by Tim Shortis, only four obviously 'sloppy' spelling errors were found in a total of 1,776 words in the sample.

10   'Texts and literacies of the Shi Jinrui', *British Journal of Sociology of Education*, Vol 25, No 2, April 2004.

11   Andrew Wilson of g8way/Centrifugal Forces reported that in the Community Arts project in Leeds around 250 people submitted poems, and there were approximately 2,500 requests for the location-specific poems.

12   Lucy Neville and Peter Bryant, *Cn U rEd dis? The Causes and Consequences of a 'Text Message Language' in Young Teenagers*, unpublished dissertation, 2004, page 32.

13   Carrington, V. (forthcoming) 'Txting: The end of civilization (again)?' Cambridge Journal of Education, Vol 35, No 2 (Summer 2005), page 19. Carrington's essay deals with the example from March 2003 of a 13-year-old Scottish schoolgirl's essay in text message-style which was widely reported in the media.

14   NATE, *Secondary English Magazine*, (June 2003), pages 7–9.

15   http://ist-socrates.berkeley.edu/~nalinik/mobile.html; http://www.m-learning.org/index.shtml

16   Work on text message language can be seen as an extension to the UK national curriculum of En3 6: study of 'variations in written standard English and how they differ from spoken language'.

17   See En2 1e, g and j.

18   Crispin Thurlow, *Generation Txt? The sociolinguistics of young people's text-messaging*, in DAOL (Discourse Analysis Online) 2003, http://www.shu.ac.uk/daol/articles/v1/n1/a3/thurlow2002003.html.

19   http://www.netting-it.com.

20   NATE, *Secondary English Magazine*, (June 2003), page 7.

21   For more information on PaintShop Pro and Animation Shop, visit http://www.jasc.com/en/products/default.asp?locid=4096

22   There are a number of colloquial phrases which are typically abbreviated but would not be suitable for classroom use. So that pupils aren't able to exploit their superior knowledge of the medium, it is worth being aware of common usages listed on the reference site Webopedia at http://www.webopedia.com/quick_ref/textmessageabbreviations.asp.

23   http://www.lingo2word.com.

24   http://www-2.cs.cmu.edu/~sef/. Click on the 'Smiley Lore :-)' link.

25   http://www.smileyworld.com/emoticons; http://www.smileydictionary.com; http://www.emoticons4u.com.

Case study 2 VAK teaching of spelling

1   http://www.wordroot.co.uk.

2   Reprinted by permission of the publisher, from *The Culture of Education* by Jerome Bruner, page 14, Cambridge, Mass.: Harvard University Press, Copyright © 1996 by the President and Fellows of Harvard College.

3   Jerome Bruner (see reference 2), page 84.

Chapter 3 Information and English

1   http://en.wikipedia.org; Columbia is one of several online encyclopedias accessible via the portal site at http://www.bartleby.com/reference.

2   http://www.big6.com.

3   http://www.hinchbk.cambs.sch.uk/resources/resources.html.

4   http://www.virtuallrc.com.

5   http://www.google.com; http://www.altavista.com; http://www.hotbot.com; http://www.ask.com.

6   http://www.metacrawler.com; http://mamma.com.

7   http://www.w3.org/WAI/References/Browsing.

8   A handy online tutorial in the basics of Boolean expressions can be found at http://library.albany.edu/internet/boolean.html.

9   http://www.standards.dfes.gov.uk/keystage3/respub/en_ict.

10   http://www.googlewhack.com.

11   For example, http://www.giga-usa.com/index.html.

12   'Nelson Mandela' screen shot and movie reproduced by kind permission of the director, Karl Owens (http://www.karlowens.com).

13   http://www.putlearningfirst.com/infohand/index.html.

14   In the *NC in Action* collection of exemplar work for ICT, I found some examples which appear to have used MS Access. See http://www.ncaction.org.uk/search/entry.htm?id=216; and http://www.ncaction.org.uk/search/entry.htm?id=208.

15 http://www.flexible.co.uk/FlexiDATA3.html

16 There is in fact a graphic view of the table relationships in Access but it is not particularly user-friendly or visually attractive.

Case study 3 Census at School Project

1 http://www.censusatschool.ntu.ac.uk.

2 http://www.standards.dfes.gov.uk/keystage3/respub/ict_csy9.

3 http://www.flexible.co.uk/FlexiDATA3.html.

Chapter 4 New ways of writing

1 As of April 2004, Livejournal featured 2,500 journals in Antarctica, 92,000 in the UK and 123,000 in the state of New York alone; Faceparty contained 2.5 million personal profiles worldwide; and http://www.poetry.com boasts over 5 million online poets.

2 This is a finding from a recent study of progression in writing at Key Stage 3, to be published by QCA as *Moving on: Progression in Writing at Key Stage 3*.

3 One of the most popular in the UK is http://www.poetryzone.co.uk which is used by many schools.

4 The National Curriculum for England: English, Key Stage 2, En3, 11.

5 A useful reference site for the new science, or art, of 'information architecture' can be found at http://www.aifia.org – home of the Asilomar Institute for Information Architecture.

6 http://www.nc.uk.net; http://www.standards.dfes.gov.uk.

7 http://www.bbc.co.uk/schools/ks3bitesize.

8 http://www.becta.org.uk/page_documents/research/wtrs_english.pdf.

9 NIFTC/BFI Education Policy Working Group, *A Wider Literacy* (2004), page 17. See also Chapter 6, Section 2. See also *The Role of Early Narrative Understanding in Predicting Future Reading Comprehension* by Kathleen E. Kremer, Julia S. Lynch, Panayiota Kendeou, Jason Butler and Paul van den Broek, University of Minnesota, and Elizabeth Pugzles Lorch, University of Kentucky, paper presented at AERA Conference 2002, and available online at: http://www.ciera.org/library/presos/2002/2002aera/02aerapb.pdf.

10 John McKenzie, *Subjectivity, agency and new genres of Story: lessons from Middle Earth*; a paper presented to the Australasian Children's Literature Association for Research, Sydney 2004.

11 http://www.standards.dfes.gov.uk/schemes2/secondary_ICT/ict01/?view=get.

12 Vivi Lachs, *Making Multimedia in the Classroom* (Routledge, 2000), page 59.

13 http://www.ictadvice.org.uk. A BECTA (www.becta.org.uk) website.

14 http://www.mape.org.uk/activities/BookMaker/bookmaker.htm; http://www.mape.org.uk/activities/VideoBookMaker/bookmaker.htm.

15 http://www.highwire.org.uk.

16 'Rabbit and Fox' animated GIF reproduced with permission of John Davitt at WordRoutes Ltd. http://www.wordroot.co.uk

17 http://www.becta.org.uk/corporate/display.cfm?section=21&id=3207.

18 http://www.kar2ouche.com.

19 http://vpb.concord.org.

20 http://www.artchive.com.

Case study 4 Multimodal narrative in SEN teaching

1 Faux, F. (2004) *Literacy, Special Needs and the Use of Information Technology*. Doctoral thesis. University of Bristol, pages 253, 256.

Chapter 5 Audio-visual English

1 http://www.americanrhetoric.com/rhetoricaldevicesinsound.htm.

2 For those, like me, who had never heard of this before, *scesis onomaton* denotes a series of successive, synonymous, descriptive expressions reinforcing the same point.

3 English teachers in the UK might feel it is helpful to teach a few more terms such as oxymoron, paradox, personification, sententia. However, these are more often taught in the context of appreciating literature than in speaking.

4 http://www.bl.uk/collections/sound-archive/holdings.html; http://www.collectbritain.co.uk/collections/dialects. The British Library is also in the first stages of developing another major initiative, 'Sound Thinking', due to launch in 2006. Initial projects will include the transmission of songs and myths between cultures, and narrative performance and music inspired by fairytales in different cultures.

5 In the UK, the University of Lancaster's Centre for Computer Corpus Research on Language is a good reference point for academic study: http://www.comp.lancs.ac.uk/computing/research/ucrel/.

6 There has, of course, been a good market in narrated books for adults for many years, thanks mainly to the personal stereo. Recently, there has been a move away from analogue cassette recording to digital recording formats such as CDs and increasingly to downloadable sound files.

7 A three-year project in a UK primary school to assess the educational use of speech-recognition software produced disappointing results; see http://www.becta.org.uk/page_documents/teaching/kirkhallam.pdf.

8 See the Somerset Talking Computer Project at http://www.cesi.ie/pcjan97/tog.html.

9 You can find the Easiteach software at http://www.easiteach.com and Pendown at Logotron, http://www.logo.com. Clicker, a writing and multimedia tool aimed at younger learners, is from Crick Software (http://www.cricksoft.com).

10 http://www.readplease.com.

11 http://www.hvec.org.uk/HvecMain/index.asp Not an easily navigated site: go to *Parents and Visitors*, then *Hounslow Language Service*, then *Resources*.

12 http://www.hvec.org.uk/HvecMain/index.asp (multilingual resources page).

13 http://www.universalteacher.org.uk/contents.htm#specialpoetry.

14 http://www.radiowaves.co.uk; http://www.becta.org.uk/corporate/display.cfm?section=21&id=3123.

15 http://audacity.sourceforge.net.

16 http://www.tta.gov.uk/php/read.php?sectionid=47&articleid=696: *Reading challenging text with speech and dictionary support in Year 4.*

17 http://www.tta.gov.uk/php/read.php?sectionid=47&articleid=696: *Improving reading and spelling with speech feedback in Year 2*, page 3.

18 http://www.tta.gov.uk/php/read.php?sectionid=47&articleid=696: *Reading challenging text with speech and dictionary support in Year 4.*

19 http://www.tta.gov.uk/php/read.php?sectionid=47&articleid=696: *Using short rhymes and other texts to enhance reading comprehension in Year 4.*

20 Jack Kenny, *The Guardian*, Nov 19, 2002: http://education.guardian.co.uk/digitalvideo/story/0,12641,842724,00.html.

21 The BECTA guidance on 'Using Digital Video in Teaching and Learning' points to creativity, thinking skills and participation in group-work as the chief benefits.

22 http://www.becta.org.uk/corporate/display.cfm?section=21&id=2663.

23 Sharnbrook High School, Bedfordshire send 'TV crews', consisting of students, to video school sports fixtures at the weekends. The DV is then edited and broadcast to classrooms as a multimedia assembly.

24 QCA is planning to conduct further research exploring the possibilities for using digital video in English teaching.

25 The BFI has led the way in promoting the educational use of DV, with teacher training courses and now an MA module in Digital Video Production in conjunction with the Institute of Education.

26 http://www.bfi.org.uk/education/research/teachlearn/eaz/animatedenglish.php.

27 *Evaluation Report on the Becta Digital Video Pilot Project*, October 2002, page 4. See http://www.becta.org.uk/page_documents/research/dvreport_241002.pdf.

28 http://www.niftc.co.uk/doc/download/a_wider_literacy.pdf.

29   http://www.niftc.co.uk/doc/download/a_wider_literacy.pdf. page 19. See also: *The Role of Early Narrative Understanding in Predicting Future Reading page Comprehension* by Kathleen E. Kremer, Julia S. Lynch, Panayiota Kendeou, Jason Butler and Paul van den Broek, University of Minnesota, and Elizabeth Pugzles Lorch, University of Kentucky, paper presented at AERA Conference 2002, and available online at: http://www.ciera.org/library/presos/2002/2002aera/02aerapb.pdf.

30   http://www.ncaction.org.uk; http://news.bbc.co.uk.

31   Neil Shaw, Report on Leasowes Community College's work for BECTA Digital Video Pilot – Capturing Creativity, 2002.

32   http://www.mediaedwales.org.uk/publicity/mmms.htm.

33   http://www.becta.org.uk/page_documents/research/dvreport_241002.pdf, page 6.

34   http://www.becta.org.uk/corporate/display.cfm?section=21&id=3207.

35   http://www.becta.org.uk/corporate/display.cfm?section=21&id=2669.

Case study 5 Digital video and shakespeare

1   Vivi Lachs, curriculum director – Highwire CLC. See *Trippingly on the Tongue* project report in the Teacher Resources section at http://www.highwire.org.uk.

2   http://www.highwire.org.uk/offer/projects/tripping/index.html.

Chapter 6 New ways of reading

1   I have not looked at the myriad sites providing commentary on literature, whether in essays, on teaching sites or in online literary encyclopedias. These are generally as good as the material in them, and that is as much as one can safely say.

2   Further texts can be found online with payment, most notably via the Chadwyck-Healey databases, once on CD-ROMs and now online at http://www.il.proquest.com/chadwyck/.

3   This work was completed, famously in the case of the immense Patrologia Latina, by cheap, off-shore data-entry workers.

4   http://www.classicbookshelf.com/. A similar and very effective approach is taken with the MAPE Big Books for early learners, which are downloadable at http://www.mape.org.uk/activities/bigbooks/index.htm.

5   A more extended list is available on the CD-ROM (see Additional Weblinks – Literature).

6   http://victorian.lang.nagoya-u.ac.jp/concordance; http://etext.lib.virginia.edu/modeng/modeng0.browse.html; http://www.bartleby.com/index.html; http://dewey.library.upenn.edu/sceti; http://www.linkstoliterature.com.

7   For example http://shakespeare.com; http://efts.lib.uchicago.edu/efts/OTA-SHK; http://www.sourcetext.com/sourcebook/e-texts-shake.htm.

8   http://ise.uvic.ca/Annex/DraftTxt/index.html.

9   http://libtext.library.wisc.edu/IllusShake.

10   http://etext.virginia.edu/bsuva/promptbook/index.html.

11   http://www.usm.edu/english/activities.html.

12   http://www.bibliomania.com/ and http://www.literature.org. You can also find a customizable text version at http://www.classicbookshelf.com/.

13   http://www.soton.ac.uk/~wpwt/harl2253/harley.htm.

14   These are just a few web sites where you can search for song lyrics: http://www.thesonglyrics.com; http://www.lyrics.com/; http://lyrics.astraweb.com/; http://www.letssingit.com/; http://www.sing365.com/; http://www.azlyrics.com/; http://www.lyricsfreak.com/; http://www.lyricsworld.com/; http://www.songlyrics.com/; http://www.getlyrics.com/; http://lyricsearch.net/.

15   http://www.romantic-lyrics.com

16   http://www.whitmanarchive.org/archive1/works/leaves.

17   http://www.poetry.com.

18   http://homepage2.nifty.com/haiku-eg/.

19   http://www.englishonline.co.uk/englishnon/sf/wordlab/collapser.html.
20   John Betjeman, *Collected Poems* (London: John Murray, 1958), page 21.
21   Betjeman (see reference 20), page 48.
22   http://www.becta.org.uk/corporate/display.cfm?section=21&id=2669.

Case study 6 Magic Book: augmented reality books

1   http://www.hitl.washington.edu/magicbook.
2   http://www.becta.org.uk/etseminars; for a general discussion see Mark Billinghurst, *Augmented Reality in Education*, New Horizons for Learning, Dec 2002:
     http://www.newhorizons.org/strategies/technology/billinghurst.htm.
3   John McKenzie and Doreen Darnell, *The eyeMagic Book: A Report into Augmented Reality Storytelling in the Context of a Children's Workshop*, 2003, page 3.
4   Anim8or is the work of software engineer Steven Glanville. See http://www.anim8or.com.
5   John McKenzie 'Surprising moments: the interface between the book and technology', a paper presented to IBBY World Congress, Cape Town, South Africa 2004, page 6. See also McKenzie, 'Subjectivity, agency and new genres of Story: lessons from Middle Earth', a paper presented to the Australasian Children's Literature Association for Research, Sydney 2004.
6   http://www.hitl.washington.edu/research/shared_space.
7   http://www.kahootz.com.

Chapter 7 The way forward for ICT in English

1   See *Creativity: find it, promote it* (QCA, 2002). They started from the basis of the four characteristics of creativity proposed in the NAACE findings published as *All our futures* (DfEE, 1999).
2   There was some irony in the choice of the 'Napster' project carried out by a group of Year 9 girls, as an exemplar of creativity. In this they prepared materials relating to the closure of the online music site Napster, using VHS video recording and an A2 sized poster which was a paper collage. When it came to preparing these for the web, there was, as with most of the case studies, little in the way of digitally recorded material to use.
3   http://www.ncaction.org.uk/creativity.
4   Evaluation Report of the BECTA Digital Video Pilot Project, October 2002, page 3.
5   *Teaching and Learning with ICT in English* (BECTA, 2002), downloadable from http://www.vtc.ngfl.gov.uk/ictenglish.
6   Trevor Millum, *ICT and Literacy*, (NATE, 2003).
7   http://www.standards.dfes.gov.uk/keystage3/respub/en_ict.
8   English in ICT newsletter, October 2003, http://www.ictadvice.org.uk/index.php?section=il&catcode=nwslttr_ictsub_english#research. A BECTA (www.becta.org.uk) website.
9   http://www.becta.org.uk/page_documents/research/wtrs_english.pdf.
10   The ESOL Core Curriculum (QCA, 2003) pooled knowledge from EFL/ESOL awarding bodies about English Speaking and Listening progression, and brought it within a framework that could be used to compare different qualifications in the discipline.
11   http://www.ncaction.org.uk/.
12   Reprinted by permission of the publisher from *The Process of Education* by Jerome Bruner, page 80, Cambridge, Mass.: Harvard University Press, Copyright © 1960, 1977 by the President and Fellows of Harvard College, Copyright © renewed 1998 Jerome Seymour Bruner.

Index

Other publications from Network Educational Press

ACCELERATED LEARNING SERIES
Accelerated Learning: A User's Guide by Alistair Smith, Mark Lovatt & Derek Wise
Accelerated Learning in the Classroom by Alistair Smith
Accelerated Learning in Practice by Alistair Smith
The ALPS Approach: Accelerated Learning in Primary Schools by Alistair Smith & Nicola Call
The ALPS Approach Resource Book by Alistair Smith & Nicola Call
ALPS StoryMaker by Stephen Bowkett
MapWise by Oliver Caviglioli & Ian Harris
Creating an Accelerated Learning School by Mark Lovatt & Derek Wise
Thinking for Learning by Mel Rockett & Simon Percival
Reaching out to all learners by Cheshire LEA
Move It: Physical movement and learning by Alistair Smith
Coaching Solutions by Will Thomas & Alistair Smith

ABLE AND TALENTED CHILDREN COLLECTION
Effective Provision for Able and Talented Children by Barry Teare
Effective Resources for Able and Talented Children by Barry Teare
More Effective Resources for Able and Talented Children by Barry Teare
Challenging Resources for Able and Talented Children by Barry Teare
Enrichment Activities for Able and Talented Children by Barry Teare
Parents' and Carers' Guide for Able and Talented Children by Barry Teare

LEARNING TO LEARN
Let's Learn How to Learn: Workshops for Key Stage 2 by UFA National Team
Brain Friendly Revision by UFA National Team
Creating a Learning to Learn School by Toby Greany & Jill Rodd
Teaching Pupils How to Learn by Bill Lucas, Toby Greany, Jill Rodd & Ray Wicks

PRIMARY RESOURCES
Promoting Children's Well-Being in the Primary Years: The Right from the Start Handbook
    edited by Andrew Burrell and Jeni Riley
But Why? Developing philosophical thinking in the classroom by Sara Stanley with Steve Bowkett
Foundations of Literacy by Sue Palmer & Ros Bayley
Help Your Child To Succeed by Bill Lucas & Alistair Smith
Help Your Child To Succeed – Toolkit by Bill Lucas & Alistair Smith
That's English! by Tim Harding
That's Maths! by Tim Harding
That's Science! by Tim Harding
The Thinking Child by Nicola Call with Sally Featherstone
The Thinking Child Resource Book by Nicola Call with Sally Featherstone
Numeracy Activities Key Stage 2 by Afzal Ahmed & Honor Williams
Numeracy Activities Key Stage 3 by Afzal Ahmed, Honor Williams & George Wickham

EXCITING ICT

New Tools for Learning: Accelerated learning meets ICT by John Davitt
Exciting ICT in Maths by Alison Clark-Jeavons
Exciting ICT in History by Ben Walsh

CREATIVE THINKING

Think it–Map it! by Ian Harris & Oliver Caviglioli
Thinking Skills & Eye Q by Oliver Caviglioli, Ian Harris & Bill Tindall
Reaching out to all thinkers by Ian Harris & Oliver Caviglioli
With Drama in Mind by Patrice Baldwin
Imagine That... by Stephen Bowkett
Self-Intelligence by Stephen Bowkett
StoryMaker Catch Pack by Stephen Bowkett

EFFECTIVE LEARNING & LEADERSHIP

Effective Heads of Department by Phil Jones & Nick Sparks
Leading the Learning School by Colin Weatherley
Closing the Learning Gap by Mike Hughes
Strategies for Closing the Learning Gap by Mike Hughes with Andy Vass
Transforming Teaching & Learning by Colin Weatherley with Bruce Bonney, John Kerr & Jo Morrison
Effective Learning Activities by Chris Dickinson
Tweak to Transform by Mike Hughes
Making Pupil Data Powerful by Maggie Pringle & Tony Cobb
Raising Boys' Achievement by Jon Pickering
Effective Teachers by Tony Swainston
Effective Teachers in Primary Schools by Tony Swainston
Effective Leadership in Schools by Tony Swainston

EFFECTIVE PERSONNEL MANAGEMENT

The Well Teacher – management strategies for beating stress, promoting staff health & reducing absence
   by Maureen Cooper
Managing Challenging People – dealing with staff conduct by Maureen Cooper & Bev Curtis
Managing Poor Performance – handling staff capability issues by Maureen Cooper & Bev Curtis
Managing Recruitment and Selection – appointing the best staff by Maureen Cooper & Bev Curtis
Managing Allegations Against Staff – personnel and child protection issues in schools
   by Maureen Cooper & Bev Curtis
Managing Redundancies – dealing with reduction and reorganisation of staff
   by Maureen Cooper & Bev Curtis
Paying Staff in Schools – performance management and pay in schools by Bev Curtis

VISIONS OF EDUCATION SERIES

Discover Your Hidden Talents: The essential guide to lifelong learning by Bill Lucas
The Power of Diversity by Barbara Prashnig
The Brain's Behind It by Alistair Smith
Wise Up by Guy Claxton
The Unfinished Revolution by John Abbott & Terry Ryan
The Learning Revolution by Gordon Dryden & Jeannette Vos

EMOTIONAL INTELLIGENCE
Becoming Emotionally Intelligent by Catherine Corrie
Lend Us Your Ears by Rosemary Sage
Class Talk by Rosemary Sage
A World of Difference by Rosemary Sage
Best behaviour and Best behaviour FIRST AID by Peter Relf, Rod Hirst, Jan Richardson & Georgina Youdell
    Best behaviour FIRST AID also available separately

DISPLAY MATERIAL
Move It posters: Physical movement and learning by Alistair Smith
Bright Sparks by Alistair Smith
More Bright Sparks by Alistair Smith
Leading Learning by Alistair Smith

NEWLY QUALIFIED TEACHERS
Lessons are for Learning by Mike Hughes
Classroom Management by Philip Waterhouse & Chris Dickinson
Getting Started by Henry Liebling

SCHOOL GOVERNORS
Questions School Governors Ask by Joan Sallis
Basics for School Governors by Joan Sallis
The Effective School Governor by David Marriott (including audio tape)

For more information and ordering details, please consult our website www.networkpress.co.uk

Network Educational Press – much more than publishing...

NEP Conferences – Invigorate your teaching

Each term NEP runs a wide range of conferences on cutting edge issues in teaching and learning at venues around the UK. The emphasis is always highly practical. Regular presenters include some of our top-selling authors such as Sue Palmer, Barry Teare and Steve Bowkett. Dates and venues for our current programme of conferences can be found on our website www.networkpress.co.uk.

NEP online Learning Style Analysis – Find out how your students prefer to learn

Discovering what makes your students tick is the key to personalizing learning. NEP's Learning Style Analysis is a 50-question online evaluation that can give an immediate and thorough learning profile for every student in your class. It reveals how, when and where they learn best, whether they are right brain or left brain dominant, analytic or holistic, whether they are strongly auditory, visual, kinaesthetic or tactile ... and a great deal more. And for teachers who'd like to take the next step, LSA enables you to create a whole-class profile for precision lesson planning.

Developed by The Creative Learning Company in New Zealand and based on the work of Learning Styles expert Barbara Prashnig, this powerful tool allows you to analyse your own and your students' learning preferences in a more detailed way than any other product we have ever seen. To find out more about Learning Style Analysis or to order profiles visit www.networkpress.co.uk/lsa.

Also available: *Teaching Style Analysis* and *Working Style Analysis.*

NEP's Critical Skills Programme – Teach your students skills for lifelong learning

The Critical Skills Programme puts pupils at the heart of learning, by providing the skills required to be successful in school and life. Classrooms are developed into effective learning environments, where pupils work collaboratively and feel safe enough to take 'learning risks'. Pupils have more ownership of their learning across the whole curriculum and are encouraged to develop not only subject knowledge but the fundamental skills of:

- problem solving
- creative thinking
- decision making
- communication
- management
- organization

- leadership
- self-direction
- quality working
- collaboration
- enterprise
- community involvement

"The Critical Skills Programme... energizes students to think in an enterprising way. CSP gets students to think for themselves, solve problems in teams, think outside the box, to work in a structured manner. CSP is the ideal way to forge an enterprising student culture."

Rick Lee, Deputy Director, Barrow Community Learning Partnership

To find out more about CSP training visit the Critical Skills Programme website at www.criticalskills.co.uk